Praise for
A Brave and Cunning Prince

"Few individuals, European or Native American, had as much impact on early America as the Pamunkey leader Opechancanough. In *A Brave and Cunning Prince*, the renowned historian of early Virginia, James Horn, offers a masterclass on historical reconstruction and narrative style, deeply informed by an unparalleled mastery of evidence and sensitivity to the nuances of lived experience. Horn takes us across a century and the entire Atlantic basin, enlightening at every unexpected twist and turn. Opechancanough, a monumental figure, comes to prominence again in this true-life page-turner of narrative history."

—PETER C. MANCALL,
author of *The Trials of Thomas Morton*

"Like most Native people in early American history, Opechancanough generally plays a brief part as a violent and tragic figure. In contrast, James Horn constructs a remarkable life story that spanned a century. At a time when America is digging more deeply into its origins, this eye-opening narrative challenges well-worn tales of Pocahontas and congenial first encounters with a grim record of kidnapping, starvation, and total war."

—COLIN G. CALLOWAY, author of
The Indian World of George Washington

"This book tells the story of one of the most fascinating figures in American history—the older brother of the more famous man we know as Powhatan. Most Americans probably have never heard of Opechancanough, but *A Brave and Cunning Prince* makes it clear that his name ought to ring in our mythology with the tragic names of Chief Joseph of the Nez Perce, Sitting Bull and Crazy Horse of the Sioux, the Apache's Geronimo, and the Comanche's Quanah Parker. Opechancanough's experiences and travels rival those of John Smith, and his leadership was demonstrably more effective. Though eclipsed in the records by both Smith and his own brother, Opechancanough might have been the most important of the three. Opechancanough's story is long overdue, and who better to tell the tale than our generation's foremost authority."

—JOSEPH KELLY, author of *Marooned: Jamestown, Shipwreck, and a New History of America's Origin*

"*A Brave and Cunning Prince* is brilliant, stunning, original, and un-put-downable. Horn's gripping prose and remarkable detective skills transport the reader to the Chesapeake Bay, Madrid, Mexico City, Havana, and London and into the mind of the talented, indefatigable Powhatan chief, Opechancanough. Upending the traditional Jamestown colonization narrative, Horn centers the Powhatan people, uncovering their priorities and their perceptions of the invaders who tried to colonize their land. Horn has crafted a magnificent, important biography, essential reading for anyone who seeks to understand early America."

—LORRI GLOVER, Saint Louis University

"James Horn combines cutting-edge scholarship with vivid, accessible prose in this sweeping narrative of Opechancanough's eventful and eye-opening life story."

—JAMES RICE, author of *Tales from a Revolution: Bacon's Rebellion and the Transformation of Early America*

"James Horn has produced the first full biography of Paquinquineo/ Opechancanough, making a compelling case that these two important figures in the Indigenous history of Virginia were one and the same. This transatlantic biography will be of great value to anyone interested in the vast history of what in Horn's hands becomes an Algonquian Atlantic."

—MICHAEL LEROY OBERG, SUNY-Geneseo

A Brave and
Cunning Prince

ALSO BY JAMES HORN:

1619: Jamestown and the Forging of American Democracy

*A Kingdom Strange: The Brief and Tragic History
of the Lost Colony of Roanoke*

*Capt. John Smith:
Writings, with Other Narratives of Roanoke,
Jamestown, and the First English Settlement of America*

*A Land As God Made It:
Jamestown and the Birth of America*

*Adapting to a New World:
English Society in the Seventeenth-Century Chesapeake*

A Brave and Cunning Prince

*The Great Chief Opechancanough
and the War for America*

❖

JAMES HORN

BASIC BOOKS

New York

Basic Books
Hachette Book Group
1290 Avenue of the Americas, New York, NY 10104
www.basicbooks.com

Printed in the United States of America

First Edition: November 2021

Published by Basic Books, an imprint of Perseus Books, LLC, a subsidiary of Hachette Book
Group, Inc. The Basic Books name and logo is a trademark of the Hachette Book Group.

The Hachette Speakers Bureau provides a wide range of authors for speaking events.
To find out more, go to www.hachettespeakersbureau.com or call (866) 376-6591.

The publisher is not responsible for websites (or their content) that are not owned
by the publisher.

Print book interior design by Jeff Williams.

Library of Congress Cataloging-in-Publication Data

Names: Horn, James P. P., author.
Title: A brave and cunning prince : the great chief Opechancanough and the war for America /
    James Horn.
Description: First edition. | New York : Basic Books, 2021. | Includes bibliographical references
    and index.
Identifiers: LCCN 2021009603 | ISBN 9780465038909 (hardcover) | ISBN 9781541600034
    (ebook)
Subjects: LCSH: Opechancanough, –1646. | Powhatan Indians—Virginia—Jamestown—
    Biography. | Powhatan Indians—Virginia—Jamestown—History. | Jamestown (Va.)—
    History. | Powhatan, approximately 1550–1618. | Pocahontas, –1617.
Classification: LCC E99.P85 H67 2021 | DDC 975.5004/973470092 [B]—dc23

LC record available at https://lccn.loc.gov/2021009603

ISBNs: 9780465038909 (hardcover), 9781541600034 (ebook)

LSC-C

Printing 1, 2021

For Sally, Liz, Ben, and Alice, with love

... before the end of two Moones
there should not be an Englishman
in all their Countries.

CONTENTS

Contents

PART THREE: PROPHECY FULFILLED

AUTHOR'S NOTE

For the convenience of the reader, I have altered the spelling and punctuation of historical passages to conform to modern conventions and converted dates to the modern calendar. Throughout the book, I have sought as far as possible to present Indian perspectives on the events that shaped their lives during these formative years. However, it is important to keep in mind that while the peoples who made up the Powhatan chiefdom held strong views about their identity and culture, unlike Europeans they did not possess a written language and therefore were unable to record their histories and beliefs in writing. Instead, they passed their collective knowledge of the past from generation to generation by word of mouth. Necessarily, therefore, descriptions of Paquiquineo, Powhatan, and Opechancanough, as with other Indians, are based on Spanish and English accounts of the period. Sadly, we rarely hear the voices of Indian peoples and hence are forced to speculate about what motivated them by studying their actions. The nearest we come to the authentic words of the people themselves are those rare occasions when Europeans reported their words verbatim or in summary, such as when Captain John Smith met Powhatan and Opechancanough in a number of remarkable face-to-face negotiations.

Dramatis Personae

The Indians

Aguirre, Alonso de, Indian name unknown, was an interpreter brought to Madrid from New Spain by Captain Velázquez. He accompanied Paquiquineo from Spain to Mexico City in 1562 and subsequently lived with him at the Dominican convent of Santo Domingo in Mexico City.

Amocis the Paspaheghan (of the Paspahegh people) was described as a spy for Powhatan by the English in 1608.

Esmy Shichans was chief of the Accomac people of the Eastern Shore.

Iopassus was a Patawomeck headman who was on good terms with Captain Samuel Argall and participated in the abduction of Pocahontas.

Kekataugh was a brother or half brother of Powhatan and Opechancanough and a Pamunkey chief, one of the "triumvirate," as William Strachey described them.

Mattachanna was a daughter of Powhatan and accompanied her sister, Pocahontas, to London in 1616–1617.

Namontack was a young Powhatan man who served as an envoy for Powhatan and traveled to England with Captain Newport on two occasions.

Necotowance succeeded Opechancanough in 1646 and signed the treaty of the same year that formally ended the third war.

Nemattanew (d. 1621/22) was a charismatic Powhatan warrior who fought in the first war against the English. He was killed by the English shortly before the attack of 1622.

Opechancanough, also known as Paquiquineo (c. 1547–1646), was the powerful brother of Chief Powhatan. He was war chief of the Powhatans and one of three Pamunkey chiefs. He became *mamanatowick* (paramount chief) in c. 1629–1630, after the death of his brother, Itoyatin.

Opitchapam, also known as Itoyatin, (c. 1550s–1629/30) was another brother or half brother of Powhatan and the third Pamunkey chief of the triumvirate. He took the name Itoyatin when he became paramount chief in 1618 following the death of Powhatan. The English described him as a weak ruler.

Opossunoquonuske (d. 1610) was the female chief of the Appamattocs. She took part in the first war against the English.

Parahunt, known as *tanx* or little Powhatan, was a son of Powhatan who ruled over the Powhatan tribe.

Paquiquineo, also known as Don Luís de Velasco and Opechancanough (c. 1547–1646), was an *indio principal,* the brother or son of a chief from the Bahía de Santa María, later called the Chesapeake Bay. He was abducted when a youth by Spanish mariners and became a Catholic convert who promised to help the Spanish convert the peoples of his homeland.

Pocahontas, also known as Matoaka or Amonute and Rebecca, (c. 1595/96–1617) was reputedly one of Powhatan's favorite daughters. She served as the chief's envoy to the English and visited the fort on several occasions in 1608. Kidnapped by Captain Samuel Argall in 1613, she was held at Jamestown until her marriage to John Rolfe, April 5, 1614, when she took the name Rebecca. Her conversion to Protestantism gave the English hope of eventually converting the entire Powhatan people to the Church of England.

Powhatan (Wahunsonacock) (c. 1545–1618) was the paramount chief of the Powhatan Indians from c. 1570s until his death in 1618. He created the paramount chiefdom, Tsenacommacah, with the help of Opechancanough.

Tackonekintaco, the elderly chief of the Warraskoyacks, fought against the English in the first war. He and Tangoit, his son, were captured and ransomed for corn.

Uttamatomakkin (Tomakin) was sent by Opechancanough to London with his wife, Mattachanna, to learn as much as possible about the English.

Weyhohomo was a chief of the powerful Nansemond people who fought against the English in the first Powhatan war.

Wowinchopunck (d. 1610/11) was chief of the Paspaheghs and enemy of the English.

The Spanish

Acuña, Juan de, a Dominican, accompanied Fray San Pedro on the expedition to the Chesapeake Bay of 1566.

Borgia, Francisco de (1510–1572), was elected superior general of the Society of Jesus (Jesuits) in 1565.

Casas, Bartolomé de las (1484–1566), was a Dominican friar who wrote extensively about the terrible sufferings of American Indians during the Spanish conquest of the West Indies and mainland America. His An Account, Much Abbreviated, of the Destruction of the Indies was highly influential in persuading Charles V to enact the New Laws that abolished Indian slavery.

Charles V, emperor (1500–1558), was king of Spain from 1515 to 1556 and Holy Roman emperor from 1519 to 1556. A deeply religious man, he was a dedicated supporter of efforts to protect the Indians from abuses by conquistadors and, influenced by the arguments of Bartolomé Las Casas, oversaw the passage of the New Laws in 1542 that offered legal protections.

Coronas, Pedro de, was the captain of the vessel La Trinidad, which transported the Dominicans and Paquiquineo/Don Luís in 1566.

Feria, Father Pedro de la (1524–1588), was the provincial of the Dominican convent of Santo Domingo in Mexico City where Paquiquineo/Don Luís and an Indian named Alonso de Aguirre lived.

Gonzales, Captain Vicente, was an experienced mariner who made several voyages to the Chesapeake Bay in the 1570s and after. He was captain of the frigate that took the Jesuits to the Chesapeake in 1570.

Jesuits of 1570: Father Juan Bautista de Segura, Father Luís de Quirós, Brothers Gabriel Gomez, Sancho Cevallos, Juan Bautista Mendez, Pedro de Limares, Gabriel de Solis (a relative of Menéndez), and Cristobal Redondo and a novice, Alonso de Olmos, went to the Chesapeake in 1570 and established a mission among the Powhatans.

Menéndez de Avilés, Don Pedro (1519–1574), was appointed adelantado (military governor) of Florida in 1565 and in the same year led the destruction of Fort Caroline, a French settlement. He was a leading proponent of Spanish settlement in North America and established a string of garrisons and religious missions along the Florida coast, including St. Augustine.

Molina, Don Diego de, was a Spanish captain who was captured by the English in 1611. He spent nearly five years at Jamestown and sent letters back to Spain about the terrible conditions in the colony.

Montúfar y Bravo de Lagunas, Archbishop Alonso de (1489–1572), was a Dominican friar and the second Archbishop of Mexico from 1551 to 1572.

Philip II, king of Spain (1527–1598), son of Charles V, was the most powerful monarch in sixteenth-century Europe and by 1580 ruled over a global empire. He was committed to advancing the conversion of American Indians and to defending Catholicism from the growing influence of Protestantism in Europe and America.

Rogel, Father Juan, and Brother Juan de la Carrera, were among the first Jesuits to arrive in Florida and resided at Santa Elena in 1570, the northernmost Jesuit mission prior to the founding of the mission in the Chesapeake.

San Pedro, Fray Pablo de, a Dominican, was appointed the spiritual leader and governor of a colony planned for the Chesapeake Bay in 1566. Paquiquineo/Don Luís was their interpreter and guide.

Solís de Merás, Gonzalo, was Menéndez's brother-in-law and one of his first biographers. He accompanied the governor in the conquest of Fort Caroline.

Velasco, Don Luís de (1511–1564), was appointed by Charles V as the second viceroy of New Spain (Mexico) in 1550 and governed the province until his death. He supported efforts to improve conditions for Indian peoples and met Paquiquineo/Don Luís when he arrived in Mexico City in 1562.

Velázquez, Captain Antonio, a mariner in the service of Angel de Villafañe, rediscovered the Chesapeake Bay for the Spanish in 1561. He captured Paquiquineo and an unnamed Indian who accompanied him.

Villafañe, Angel de (c. 1504–?), formerly a conquistador in Mexico and Guatemala, led an effort in 1560–1561 to establish a settlement at present-day Pensacola, Florida, as a base for the future colonization of coastal northeast America.

The English

Argall, Captain Samuel (1580–1626), was a master mariner who made numerous voyages to the Atlantic coast of North America. In 1613, he kidnapped Pocahontas while trading along the Potomac River. He was deputy governor from 1617 to 1619.

Berkeley, Sir William (1605–1677), was one of the most important royal governors of the seventeenth century and oversaw the colony from 1642 to 1652 and 1660 to 1677. He led the English in the third Powhatan war.

Beverley, Robert (c. 1667–1722), was a wealthy planter-merchant and historian. He drew upon oral history from the Indians as well as documentary sources to write his influential History and Present State of Virginia, published in 1705.

Brewster, Captain Edward (1582–?), was an important commander in the first Powhatan war.

Charles I, King of England (1600–1649), succeeded his father, James I, in late March 1625 and oversaw the translation of the Virginia Company into the royal colony of Virginia. His reign was a disaster, a complete breakdown in relations with Parliament culminating in civil war and his execution in January 1649.

Claiborne, William (c. 1600–1677), arrived in Virginia in 1621 and served as a land surveyor. He subsequently became engaged in the fur trade and established a settlement on Kent Island in the Chesapeake Bay, which was later claimed by Maryland. He played an important role in the third Powhatan war.

Dale, Sir Thomas (d. 1619), served as high marshal and deputy governor of Virginia from 1611 to 1616. He expanded martial law in the colony and was one of the most important commanders during the first war against the Powhatans.

Ferrar, John (1588–1657), was deputy treasurer of the Virginia Company. Although he never lived in Virginia, he was extremely knowledgeable about the colony and in 1649 wrote important pamphlets describing the colony's affairs.

Gates, Sir Thomas (d. 1622), served as governor in 1610 and as lieutenant governor 1611–1616. He was shipwrecked on Bermuda along with Sir George Somers and Captain Christopher Newport in 1609 before reaching Jamestown in May 1610. Gates introduced martial law into the colony and was a leading commander in the first war against the Powhatans.

Hamor, Ralph (1589–1626), was an early tobacco planter and promoter of Virginia. He took part in the first and second Powhatan wars. His *A True Discourse of the Present State of Virginia* was published in London in 1615.

Harvey, Sir John, was governor of Virginia from 1630 to 1635 and 1637 to 1639, a decade that witnessed a rapid expansion of the English population and settlement, pushing Powhatan peoples off their lands.

James I, king of England and VI of Scotland (1566–1625), succeeded to the English throne in 1603 following the death of Elizabeth I. Although he wished to placate the Spanish, who claimed the whole of the Americas as their own, and maintain the peace he had brokered with the Spanish king, Philip III, he issued the letters patent (charter) that permitted the founding of the colony of Virginia on April 10, 1606.

Kemp, Richard, served as acting governor while Sir William Berkeley was in England in 1644–1645.

Newport, Captain Christopher (1561–1617), was a privateer and master mariner in Atlantic waters. He led the first Jamestown expedition to the Chesapeake of 1607 and with Captain Smith was influential in early discussions with Powhatan and Opechancanough.

Percy, George (1580–1632/33), was with the first expedition that established Jamestown in 1607. He served as president of the colony in 1609–1610 and took part in the opening years of the first Powhatan war before leaving Virginia in 1612. Years later he wrote an account of his experiences, A True Relation.

Ralegh, Sir Walter (1554–1618), was a favorite of Queen Elizabeth and an enormously wealthy courtier who sponsored attempts to establish a colony on Roanoke Island, North Carolina, and in the Chesapeake Bay.

Ratcliffe, Captain John, alias Sicklemore (d. 1610), was with the first expedition of 1607 and served as president of the colony in 1607–1608. He took part in the opening years of the first Powhatan war.

Rolfe, John (1585–1622), married Pocahontas/Rebecca at Jamestown on April 5, 1614. He played an important role in the development of tobacco husbandry and also served as an emissary on behalf of Sir Thomas Dale (as did Ralph Hamor) in the first Powhatan war.

Sandys, Sir Edwin (1554–1629), was a major political figure in England and a principal officer of the Virginia Company of London. He succeeded Smythe in 1619 and in the same year introduced sweeping reforms to reinvigorate the colony, which involved the transportation of thousands of English settlers and conversion of the Powhatans.

Sandys, George (1578–1644), was brother of Sir Edwin and treasurer of the Virginia Company in the colony, 1621–1625. He fought in the second Powhatan war.

Savage, Thomas (1595–1633), arrived in Virginia in 1608 and was sent to live with Powhatan. He became fluent in Algonquian, the Powhatans' language, and served for many years as an interpreter.

Smith, Captain John (1580–1632), fought as a mercenary in the wars in late sixteenth- and early seventeenth-century Europe before becoming one of the prime movers behind the founding of Jamestown. A prolific writer, Smith penned some of the most detailed descriptions of Indian peoples and chiefs he encountered, including Powhatan and Opechancanough, as well as events that occurred in the two decades following his departure.

Smythe, Sir Thomas (1558–1625), was one of the wealthiest merchants in London and a leading figure in the Virginia Company of London besides other commercial companies. He was the Virginia Company's treasurer (effectively governor) for its first decade and remained closely involved thereafter.

Somers, Sir George (1554–1610), was a privateer and experienced mariner who served as admiral of the fleet on the voyage that was shipwrecked on Bermuda, 1609–1610.

Spelman, Henry (1595–1623), was an interpreter who lived with Powhatan and Iopassus, a Patawomeck headman. He fought in the second Powhatan war.

Strachey, William (1572–1621), was a minor gentleman from Essex, England, who wrote an account of the hurricane that devastated the fleet sent to Virginia in 1609, which was subsequently the basis of William Shakespeare's The Tempest. A perceptive and gifted writer, he wrote one of the first histories of English Virginia.

Thorpe, George (1576–1622), was a well-connected gentleman from Gloucestershire who was involved in the founding of Berkeley Hundred on the Powhatan (James) River. He led the Virginia Company's efforts to build an Indian College and was devoted to the effort to convert the Powhatans to Anglicanism and English ways of life.

West, Captain Francis (1586–1634), was a younger brother of Lord De La Warr. He served in the opening months of the first Powhatan war. Later in 1627–1629, during the latter stages of the second war, he served as governor.

West, Captain William (1585–1610/11), was De La Warr's nephew. He died in fighting at the falls of the Powhatan (James) River.

West, Sir Thomas, 12th Baron De La Warr (1576–1618), was a high-ranking nobleman and veteran who was appointed the first lord governor and captain general of Virginia in 1608. He resided in the colony briefly from 1610 to 1611 before returning to England. He died at sea on his return to Virginia in 1618.

Wyatt, Sir Francis (1588–1644), was governor of Virginia on two occasions, 1621–1626 and 1639–1642. He led English forces during the initial years of the second Powhatan war.

Yeardley, Sir George (1588–1627), was also shipwrecked on Bermuda in 1609–1610. Initially one of Gates's captains, he rose to be deputy governor in 1616–1617, the second lord governor and captain general in 1619–1621, and royal governor in 1626–1627. He played an active part in the first and second Powhatan wars.

Prologue

Two Prophecies

I N THE EARLY SEVENTEENTH CENTURY, WILLIAM STRACHEY,
a gentleman-adventurer who had recently arrived in the small,
struggling colony of Jamestown, recorded two Indian prophecies.
The first, told by Powhatan *quioccosuks* (priests), warned that "from
the Chesapeake Bay a Nation should arise, which would dissolve
and give end" to the Indians' empire. Uncertain of how to interpret
this "devilish Oracle," Strachey reported that the great chief of the
Powhatans responded by commanding the destruction of those who
might be implicated by the prophecy, the hapless Chesapeake people
who lived near the mouth of the bay. The killing of the Chesapeakes
was bloody testimony of how seriously the chief had taken the div-
ination. Not by coincidence, the slaughter took place in the spring
of 1607 at about the same time three English ships appeared off the
coast of Virginia.

A second prophecy began circulating shortly after. It foretold
that on two occasions the Powhatans would "overthrow and dis-
hearten" the strangers who had come to "invade their Territories or
labor to settle a plantation among them," but at the third attempt

"they themselves should fall into their [the invaders] Subjection and under their Conquest." Strachey surmised these "strange whispers" might explain why the English settlement was watched so closely by the Powhatans. But whether the prophecy was proof of Satan's sway over Indian peoples, or whether it would eventually come to pass, neither he nor anyone else could say.[1]

PART ONE

Atlantic Worlds

Indian Prince, Spanish Don

A TALL, STRIKING-LOOKING YOUTH DRESSED IN PLAIN BUT respectable clothes strode through the gates of the royal fortress-palace, the Alcázar, which guarded Spain's new capital of Madrid. He was accompanied by a man, also modestly dressed, whose deep tan and lean physique spoke of a life of action outdoors. This was Captain Antonio Velázquez, an experienced mariner recently returned from American waters where he had been in the service of the governor of La Florida, a general term used by the Spanish for the southeastern region of North America. The youth was an Indian named Paquiquineo, an *indio principal*, the brother or son of a chief from the Bahía de Santa María, later called the Chesapeake Bay. Velázquez had brought the youth from the edge of the known world in the fall of 1561 to meet King Philip II of Spain, a meeting that could not have presented a more dramatic contrast. On the one hand was Paquiquineo, an Indian from a remote part of America who knew little of European civilization or Christian religion; on the other was Philip II, ruler of an immense empire, believed by his subjects to be God's lieutenant on earth and protector of the Catholic

Church, who might in time reunite Christendom under *un monarca, un imperio y una espada*, one monarch, one empire and one sword.

During the months following the initial audience, the king became increasingly intrigued by Paquiquineo and the stories he told of his homeland. Philip decided to return the youth to his birthplace and to put in place a strategy to create settlements along North America's east coast that would eventually lead to the conversion of the millions of "benighted" Indians who lived in ignorance of the true faith. The plan would serve also to keep the northern continent free of marauding pirates and heretics (Protestants) who had no claim to any part of the Americas. Ultimately, Philip's grand plan failed, but the attempt, and the Indian boy's role in it, set in train a series of events that would have profound consequences along the mid-Atlantic littoral for the best part of a century to come. Against the background of Spain's invasion of America and the subsequent devastation of Indian societies, Paquiquineo would learn a great deal about Spanish colonization, knowledge that would later shape his own far-reaching interventions to protect his people from European conquest.[1]

PAQUIQUINEO HAD FIRST met Captain Velázquez that summer. Velázquez was a royal factor, an agent instructed to transport provisions from the Gulf of Mexico to Santa Elena, modern-day Parris Island, South Carolina. The king had ordered the immediate establishment of a garrison on the mainland of La Florida to protect Spanish treasure fleets from French pirates who infested the Caribbean and coastal waters off Florida. Accordingly, the new governor, Ángel de Villafañe, left Havana with four small ships in April 1561 and followed the mainland coast to just beyond 32 degrees north latitude where the garrison was to be located. After a brief reconnaissance, he took ownership of the land in the name of the king but was unimpressed with either the harbor or surrounding area,

which appeared to him infertile and sparsely settled. However, he had learned from official reports that years earlier and approximately four hundred miles farther along the coast, local Indians had traded with French mariners for valuable marten skins, gold, and pearls, which, if true, would make the region a far better prospect for settlement. Having decided to continue his voyage, he sailed north and was somewhere off Cape Hatteras on the Outer Banks of North Carolina when his fleet was overwhelmed by a huge storm. High seas and hurricane-force winds battered his ships for a day and a night, causing the loss of two frigates and many of his men, whose pitiful cries could be heard in the darkness as their ships foundered. With inadequate men or supplies to continue, Villafañe decided to abandon the expedition and sail for the West Indies.[2]

Captain Velázquez, meanwhile, had set out in a caravel, the *Santa Catalina*, from Havana toward the end of June, a couple of months after the governor's fleet departed. She was a small ship, about fifty feet long, and carried a dozen crew as well as two Indians from New Spain (Mexico), who were to serve as interpreters—although as Muskogee speakers they would have been no more capable of understanding Algonquian, the language of peoples of the mid-Atlantic littoral, than the Spanish. Caravels were the workhorses of Spanish and Portuguese explorations in the sixteenth century. They were fast, adaptable, and as capable of navigating rivers and shallow waters as of crossing oceans. Besides her masts, the *Santa Catalina* was equipped with oars for greater maneuverability. Heading northward to rendezvous with Villafañe at Santa Elena, Velázquez later reported that he, too, had been caught in a hurricane and driven far off course to an unknown part of the coast. Once the storm passed, he found himself near the entrance of an enormous bay. Prompted by the urgent need to take on fresh water and make repairs to the battered ship, he decided to explore.

On entering the bay, Velázquez likely followed the southern shore, keeping a respectful distance from shore to avoid shoals, although he probably detoured occasionally to reconnoiter promising-looking rivers along the way. Then, after sailing west or northwest for about fifteen to twenty miles, the caravel entered a large tidal river, either the Powhatan (James) or the Pamunkey (York) River, depending on the Spaniards' course. After their recent escape from a hurricane, the crew must have wondered at their good fortune. "Everywhere are extensive woods, undergrowth and trees," a contemporary wrote a few years later, together with abundant game, fish, and flocks of birds so great that, when rising from the riverbanks and marshes, they darkened the sky. Here it seemed was an earthly paradise, a vast unbroken forest, well watered and bountiful, such as in the beginning.[3]

After surveying for about a week, along one of the rivers the Spaniards met a group of Indians who appeared friendly and eager to trade. From among them, two youths made signs indicating that they wished to come aboard the *Santa Catalina*, which Velázquez was happy to allow. One of the boys was Paquiquineo, and the other, unnamed, may have been a companion or servant. What happened next is unclear. Subsequent Spanish accounts suggest the boys voluntarily boarded the ship with the intention of leaving with the Spanish. Bartolomé Martínez, a minor official who was a resident of Santa Elena in the 1570s, the nearest Spanish settlement in Florida to the Chesapeake Bay, claimed that a chief brought his son to the Spaniards' ship and the captain then asked permission to take the boy with him, pledging his word to "return him with much wealth and many garments," to which the chief consented. Yet this is scarcely credible. The kidnapping of Indian boys by Spanish mariners was commonplace in this period. Once on board, Velázquez would have had little incentive to release the two youths. His exploration of the Chesapeake Bay was an extraordinarily valuable discovery, and the capture of the young Indians might be of great significance in helping the Spanish learn more about the region and the peoples who lived there and of the riches that possibly lay in the interior.[4] The young men were probably between twelve and fifteen years old, the usual age when young Indians were seized to serve as translators and messengers.[5]

Once the boys were aboard, Captain Velázquez made the decision to abandon Villafañe's mission and return to Spain directly. Paquiquineo was a "princely person" from a region of North America that might well prove more promising for settlement than any the Spanish had discovered so far. He had little doubt that the king would be most interested to meet the young Indian and learn about the newly discovered land and reward him accordingly. Taking advantage of prevailing westerlies and the Gulf Stream, the *Santa Catalina* made a speedy crossing of about five weeks. But no matter how quick the voyage was, for Paquiquineo and his companion it must have been by turns terrifying, cramped, and mind-numbingly monotonous. Although born in a land of multiple rivers flowing into a bay, nothing could have prepared them for the trackless expanse of the ocean or the massive waves that in bad weather pounded the small ship relentlessly, causing it to shudder from stem to stern. When the seas were especially rough, the boys would have been kept below deck for their safety, forced to endure the stench of the ship's bilges for hours on end. Long days followed, with little to break the tedium of the daily routine. With every passing week, they surely wondered what would become of them. No one from their people had crossed the Atlantic and returned to tell the tale.

During the voyage, the boys began to learn about their captors and the country they were from on the other side of the ocean. They may have picked up sufficient Spanish to communicate in simple terms with the sailors as well as two Florida Indians who had been brought to serve as interpreters on the original mission to Santa Elena. Velázquez was no doubt keen to gather as much information from Paquiquineo as possible about the Chesapeake and its peoples in preparation for their visit to Philip's court.

Reaching Europe at the end of August, a shortage of supplies forced Velázquez to dock initially at the ancient port of Lagos,

Portugal, for what was intended as a brief respite before moving on to Spain's major Atlantic city, Seville. Owing to adverse winds, however, and because the ship was in very bad condition, they were forced to stay longer than planned. Consequently, Velázquez decided to leave them and go overland alone to Seville (a distance of nearly two hundred miles), where he planned to write a report for the king and work on the finances of the venture while waiting for the ship to join him. He also had to make preparations for the next stage of the journey to Madrid by persuading Spanish authorities to provide him with money for his traveling expenses.[6]

The forced delay gave Paquiquineo and his Indian companions an opportunity to experience European society and form their initial impressions. On the southern coast of Portugal facing the Atlantic, Lagos was a small community of several thousand inhabitants that, like the rest of the Algarve province, had been a meeting point of Christian and Muslim cultures for centuries. This long and tangled history was reflected by the region's architecture, customs, language, and diversity of peoples. Temporarily freed from the squalid confines of the ship, the Indians, accompanied by crew members, stretched their legs on the old port's crowded streets and busy waterfront, where ships from various parts of the Algarve, southern Spain, and North Africa were tied up. Besides many novelties and wonders— the sheer number of people, hundreds of buildings, the massive stone walls that surrounded the town, and the strange sounds and smells— they would have also glimpsed a dark side of European life. Lagos was important for the export of European wares in exchange for valuable African goods: gold, spices, and enslaved workers. Passing by the town's castle would have brought the young Indians to the slave market where men, women, and children, captives from Senegambia, the Upper Guinea coast, and farther south, waited to be sold and sent on to Lisbon, other parts of Portugal, and Seville. These Africans may have been the first that Paquiquineo had seen.[7]

Once the weather improved and sufficient repairs had been made, the *Santa Catalina* sailed along the coast eastward toward the Guadalquivir River and Seville, where she arrived at the end of September. Since the opening years of the century, the city had served as Spain's principal port, regulating commerce with the Americas. Benefiting from the colossal wealth of the Indies, Seville had attracted a continuous stream of merchants, bankers, skilled craftsmen, and workers from all over Europe, doubling its population within fifty years. By the 1560s, the city had more than one hundred thousand inhabitants and was one of the largest, most prosperous, and cosmopolitan cities in Europe. Its inhabitants included hugely wealthy landed aristocrats, merchant princes, and church prelates, as well as hosts of vagabonds, beggars, thieves, and prostitutes working along the dockside. Adding to the diversity was "an infinite number of Negroes from all parts of Ethiopia and Guinea," as well as enslaved "Moors" captured in wars against the Ottoman Turks.[8]

Seville's financial district lay close to the city's magnificent cathedral, completed only fifty years earlier and the largest in the world. Among several important government buildings were the offices of the Casa de Contratación (House of Trade) established in 1503 by the Crown as the official clearinghouse of Atlantic commerce. Officials required all goods and products brought from American colonies to be registered so that government duties and taxes would be collected and records of voyages maintained. It was here that Velázquez had come earlier to make his appeal for funds to support the cost of his journey to attend the king in Madrid. Whether the young Indian also visited the Casa de Contratación with Velázquez is unknown, but the single record of his name, Paquiquineo, was made by a clerk certifying he was to be given clothes. His companion from the Chesapeake, described simply as the *otro indio*, was also to receive clothes but only after Paquiquineo had been taken care of first. Velázquez was provided with fifty ducats to meet his and the Indian's expenses on

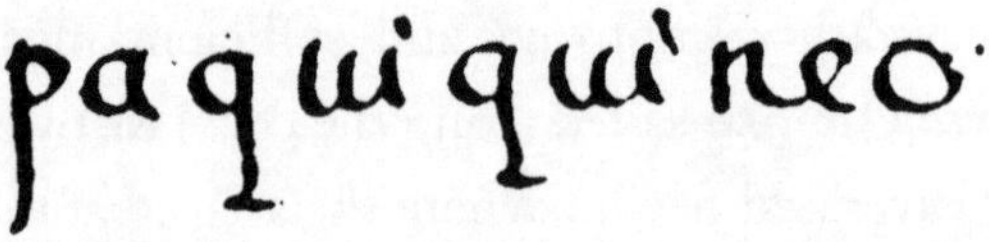

paquiquineo·

FIGURE 1.1. Paquiquineo's name as written by a clerk of the Casa de Contratación, Seville, in September 1561, Archivo General de las Indias, Contaduria 286, No. 1, Datas, fol. 171v., Seville, Spain. It is the only known rendering of his Indian name. *Drawing by Jamie May.*

---

their way to Madrid, an adequate if not generous allowance that did not include Paquiquineo's Indian friend, who was left in Seville.[9]

On the journey, Paquiquineo had ample opportunity to observe the variety of Spain's countryside and landscapes. The beautiful Guadalquivir River Valley that led them to the city of Córdoba, with its ancient mosque, was a vista of orchards, vineyards, and olive trees basking in the early fall sun. Leaving the river valley, they turned north, crossing the dark ranges of the Sierra Morena to the plains of La Mancha, which was given over to vast cornfields and sheep walks. Along the way, they would have stayed with fellow travelers at the many inns that lined the route to Ciudad Real and beyond to the former capital of Spain, Toledo, still a principal spiritual and cultural center of the country.[10]

At the time of Velázquez and Paquiquineo's arrival in the new capital late in October 1561, Madrid was a city of sixteen thousand people and growing quickly. Earlier in the year, Philip II had decided to move his court permanently to Madrid, having no desire to be a peripatetic ruler, traveling from one part of Europe to another, as he and his father, the imperial emperor Charles V, had done over the previous decade. The king and his new wife, Elisabeth of Valois, had been living in the crowded and unwholesome city of Toledo, where he had first established his court, and were keen to leave. Philip's move led immediately to the arrival of thousands of royal officials, courtiers, and churchmen in Madrid, as well as countless retailers catering to the tastes of the rich and scores of skilled craftsmen recruited to repair, rebuild, and refurbish the royal palace, Alcázar, where the king and queen had decided to take up residence.

Philip was determined to transform his new capital into a city worthy of the most powerful monarch in Europe. Following his father's abdication five years before, the vast territories of the Holy Roman Empire had been divided into two parts between Philip and his uncle, Ferdinand. The latter was granted Charles V's lands in Germany, Austria, and Bohemia, while Philip became sole ruler of Spain and its dependencies in the Americas, the Netherlands, Franche-Comté, the duchy of Milan, and the southern half of Italy. From Madrid, he planned to rule his rapidly expanding domains by the establishment of good government, justice, and order at home and overseas alike.[11]

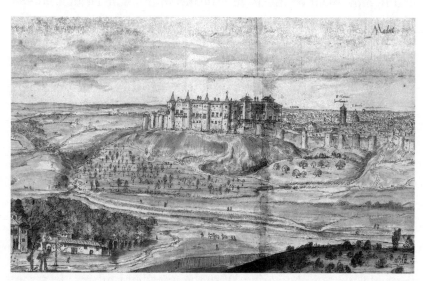

FIGURE 1.2. A detail from a sketch of Madrid by Anton van den Wyngaerde, about 1561, showing the Royal Palace, Alcázar. *Courtesy of the Austrian National Library, Vienna.*

Twenty-eight years old when he became king of Spain in 1556, Philip was described by contemporaries as being of average height, fair-skinned with brown hair and full lips and having the characteristic prominent lower jaw of the Hapsburg dynasty. He was intelligent and consumed by every detail of governing his vast and diverse territories, permitting little official business to escape his attention. He was also a connoisseur of the arts and patronized leading painters, sculptors, cartographers, and architects from all parts of Europe but especially from Renaissance Italy and Flanders. Philip was determined to transform Spain from a cultural backwater to a country where artistic and intellectual life flourished. He oversaw an extensive program of rebuilding and refurbishment of his royal palaces in Castile and personally supervised the construction of the Escorial, a huge complex of buildings that brought together the functions of government offices, palace, monastery, and mausoleum at San Lorenzo near Madrid, which was unquestionably his greatest built legacy. Throughout the kingdom, he encouraged the planting of trees and gardens and improvement of streets and squares to promote cleanliness and reduce the ever-present menace of disease. He paid cartographers to map the country and artists such as the Fleming Anton van den Wyngaerde to render accurate views of major cities so that he could see his kingdom. All of these projects were expressions of Philip's desire to gather as much reliable information about his country as possible, which was vital, he believed, to effective governance.[12]

Besides secular concerns, Philip had no doubt that God had reserved for him the holy task of saving the Catholic Church from the "contagion" of heresy. Yet, as he surveyed the world from his new capital, he saw a Europe fractured by warring sects and doctrinal dissension. Fifty years had passed since the German theologian Martin Luther had initially challenged the Roman Catholic Church on fundamental matters of doctrine. With the spread of Luther's ideas from Germany to other countries, Europe was riven in two, religiously, politically, and culturally, and the unity of Christendom shattered. The forces of international Protestantism were in the ascendant: Protestant schismatics in England and Scotland, Huguenots in France, Lutherans in Germany, and militant Calvinists in Geneva, as well as more ominously, from Philip's point of view, in Spanish Flanders. Writing from Paris in September 1561 about the state of affairs in France, the Venetian ambassador was of the opinion that "unless it otherwise pleases the Almighty, religious affairs will soon be in an evil case, because there is not one single province uncontaminated" by Protestantism. He went on to warn, rightly as it turned out, that a civil war was inevitable and would cause "the ruin both of the kingdom and of religion, because upon a change in religion a change in the State necessarily follows."

The king accepted that Protestantism was too firmly entrenched in many European countries, notably England, to be easily uprooted. Even so, since heresy and rebellion went hand in hand, he feared that if he failed to halt the spread of false doctrine then political and social upheaval would quickly follow. Although he was largely successful at quelling heresy in Spain, his efforts to suppress dissent abroad would in the long run lead directly to the very outcome he dreaded. The revolt of the Dutch provinces, the long sea war with England, and the protracted civil wars in France would tear Western Europe apart in the second half of the sixteenth century, destroying once flourishing cities and provinces and ultimately leaving Spain bankrupt and exhausted.[13]

Philip's fears about the spread of heresy applied as much to the New World as the Old. Following a half century of bloody conquests and invasions from the 1490s, the Castilian crown had come into possession of immense lands and countless peoples in the West Indies and Middle and South America. In his mind, Spain's exclusive title to the Americas was justified by right of first discovery, conquest, and settlement, but above all, Spanish claims were based on the sacred enterprise of extending the Catholic faith to "barbarous" peoples. The New World belonged to Spain by virtue of the duty placed upon the

Spanish monarchy by successive popes to convert American Indians to Christianity. If Philip could not enforce religious unity in Europe, perhaps he would have a better chance of achieving it in America. But other European monarchs, even Catholics, rejected papal authority on such a matter and vigorously contested Spanish claims. The French king, Francis I, allegedly remarked that "I would like to be shown the article in Adam's will that divides the New World between my brothers, Emperor Charles V and the King of Portugal, and excludes me from the succession. The sun shines on me as it does on them." Just as in the Old World, religion became the leaven of conflict in the New.[14]

European monarchs, merchants, and mariners clearly understood the enormous potential value of America and its waters. French, English, Breton, Basque, and Portuguese mariners had been active in the rich fishing grounds of the far northern Atlantic since the late fifteenth century. From the 1550s, French privateers began a rapid escalation of damaging raids on Spanish ships and possessions in the West Indies, South America, and Portuguese Brazil. During the long cycle of wars between the Spanish Habsburg and French Valois kings that punctuated the first half of the sixteenth century, the French regarded Spanish possessions in the Americas as legitimate targets. French ships were so common in the West Indies that a Spanish official commented that "a bird cannot fly without being seen" by a Frenchman. In 1555, the French burned the key port of Cartagena and captured Havana, Cuba, staying for nearly a month before torching the fort and moving on to the rich prize of Santo Domingo. Both were left in ruins. By this point, the Spanish had effectively lost control of the Caribbean, putting at grave risk the enormously valuable treasure fleets that transported great quantities of gold and silver from Mexico and Peru to Spain.[15]

In the early years of Philip's reign, a potent additional threat emerged. The king's ministers had picked up rumors of French plans to locate a privateering base somewhere along the Florida coast from which corsairs (pirate ships) could pillage Spanish fleets. As the system evolved after the king refortified Havana, treasure ships from Panama and Mexico—carrying great quantities of gold, silver, pearls, cochineal, hides, and cacao—sailed to Spain in convoys (*flotas*) protected by heavily armed warships. They assembled first at Havana in late spring then headed northward past the Florida Keys, through the Bahama Channel, which separated the tip of Florida from the Bahamas, and out into the Atlantic where the convoys benefited from prevailing westerlies and the Gulf Stream, which together usually enabled a relatively quick passage to Spain, the Guadalquivir River, and Seville.

Unquestionably, the most perilous part of the voyage was passing through the Bahama Channel. Navigation was difficult owing to reefs and shoals and the risk of hurricanes and because the many islands of the Bahamas offered pirates countless haunts where they could wait for stragglers from the *flotas* to fall into their hands. Any foreign power that successfully established a secure base on the Florida mainland with a harbor for provisioning and repairing ships would be able to wreak havoc on Spain's treasure fleets. Philip noted in December 1559 "that Frenchmen, under the pretext of going to Los Bacallaos [North Atlantic fishing banks], may possibly be desirous of going to that land of La Florida to settle in it and take possession of our lands."

The growing certainty of a French effort to settle somewhere on the mainland provided further impetus to the king's desire to establish a garrison on the eastern seaboard of North America and may have prompted Philip's decision to take advantage of the timely arrival of an Indian of princely bearing and invite him to an audience in Madrid. So far, the northern continent had resisted all attempts by the Spanish to establish permanent settlements despite extensive and costly explorations over the previous fifty years. Perhaps the young Indian would prove the key to unlock the promise of La Florida.[16]

WHAT TRANSPIRED IN the meetings between Paquiquineo and the king in the fall and winter of 1561 is unknown. With Captain Velázquez's account of the voyage in hand, Philip was doubtless keen to learn as much as possible about the new land the Spanish had discovered and the peoples who lived there. Bartolomé Martínez reported that the "King our lord and his Court were very pleased" with Paquiquineo "and other Indians from the land of San Agustín and Santa Elena." Philip "gave them many courtly favors and rich garments," but a very special honor was reserved for Paquiquineo. He was named Don Luís de Velasco after the viceroy of New Spain, a remarkable decree that had important implications. Viceroy Velasco was the most powerful representative of the king in New Spain (the jurisdiction that included Florida) and henceforth would be the Indian's godfather, responsible for the youth's religious education and welfare. Evidently, within a few months of living at court, the young Indian had mastered sufficient Spanish to convince Philip not only of his own princely birth, which merited the title don, but also his eagerness to proselytize the holy word in his own land (from here on I will refer to Paquiquineo as Don Luís).[17]

Don Luís's plea to the king was welcomed. Not only were Spanish attempts to establish colonies in Florida faltering, but Philip and Viceroy Velasco had also become earnest supporters of the ideas of Bartolomé de las Casas, the indefatigable Dominican friar who had called attention to the terrible atrocities inflicted on Indians during the conquest and its aftermath. Velasco, who had been appointed by Philip II in 1550, had made strenuous efforts to protect Indians from the worst abuses of Spanish grandees, such as the hardships suffered by Indian slaves or serfs working on settlers' estates or in mining operations. In his instructions of 1558 for the settlement of Santa Elena, Velasco wrote to the initial leader of the expedition, Don Tristán de Luna y Arellano, "that you should have principally before your eyes . . . the welfare, conversion, and good treatment of the natives, and of the religious [orders] and the Spaniards that go in

your company, keeping them in peace and in justice." The king voiced similar expectations calling for a just government to be established in Florida that would allow Indians "without the light of the faith" to be "illuminated and instructed in it." His view, firmly supported by the church and religious orders, was that settlers should provide as much help as possible to indigenous peoples to achieve salvation and civility and not grossly mistreat them.[18]

A major responsibility of colonial governments, the historian John Elliott remarks, "was the protection of the Indians, and this meant especially protecting them from exploitation by the colonists." On this fundamental point, if not always on the details, Philip and Las Casas were in accord. The king had known Las Casas since his youth, and when the aged priest retired to the Dominican monastery of Atocha in Madrid, Philip ordered that he should be supported financially. In 1561, Philip joined him at the monastery for a public debate on the Indian question, how Indian peoples should be treated by settlers, which had swirled around imperial politics for decades. For his part, Las Casas attended Philip's court and may well have been present at some of the king's meetings with Don Luís. It is even possible Las Casas played a role, along with the clergy and lords at court, in devising a plan to return the Indian to his homeland.[19]

Living in the royal palace, much of Don Luís's time was probably spent studying Castilian, Latin, and Christian theology. He may have visited Atocha and stayed at the monastery occasionally for special instruction. But if he had initially been intrigued by Spanish ways, after several months and as winter dragged on, it is likely his thoughts turned homeward. At some point about this time, he spoke to the king about his desire to go back to his people, and in the early spring, Philip agreed to his request. Captain Velázquez was directed to take responsibility for both him and an Indian named Alonso de Aguirre, one of the Florida Indians who, it was noted, had shown "much love" for Don Luís.[20]

Velázquez, Don Luís, and Aguirre were instructed to join the king's fleet, which was ready to sail for New Spain from San Lucar. As a further token of the importance of the mission, they were granted the privilege of sailing on board the fleet's flagship, commanded by Pedro Menéndez de Aviles, who was in charge of the convoy, a significant development since Menéndez would subsequently play a major role in the Indian's life. Philip had instructed that on arrival in New Spain, a small group of Dominicans should join Don Luís, Aguirre, and Velázquez and sail together to the Chesapeake. Once there, the holy work of converting the young Indian's people, "his parents, relatives, and countrymen to the Faith of Jesus Christ," would begin.[21]

CHAPTER 2

Mexico City to La Florida

C APTAIN VELÁZQUEZ, WITH THE TWO INDIANS UNDER HIS care, set sail with the royal fleet at the end of May 1562 and after a voyage of about ten weeks landed at San Juan de Ulua, the principal Spanish port on the Gulf Coast of Mexico. There they met the Dominican friars as instructed and readied themselves for the next stage of the journey. In a major change to the king's orders, however, instead of proceeding by ship to the Chesapeake Bay, they were ordered to go first to Mexico City, the capital of New Spain, some two hundred miles inland. The news must have been bitterly disappointing to Don Luís who, although weary from the ocean crossing, was surely eager to complete the last stage of the voyage homeward. Who issued the instructions and for what reason are unclear. Possibly, the Spanish viceroy Velasco wished to meet the remarkable young Indian and personally offer his assistance to him and the Dominicans for the blessed work they were about to undertake in the Chesapeake. Yet, whoever was responsible, the outcome was to greatly complicate Don Luís's efforts to return to his land and lead to a prolonged sojourn in Spain's Atlantic world.[1]

The journey through Mexico was the beginning of the young Indian's education about Spanish society in America. From the hot and humid coastal region to large fields of maize and broad pastures of grazing cattle inland, Don Luís would have seen local Indian peoples everywhere, tending their crops, orchards, and livestock, working on the great estates (*estancias*) of Spanish and Indian lords, or carrying goods on their backs along dirt roads to neighboring towns and markets. In the large towns, Indian nobles (*pilli*) and high-ranking Spaniards occupied the most important government and municipal offices; wealthy merchants, skilled craftsmen, and lesser officeholders filled a middling position; and smallholders, petty traders, artisans, laborers, and working women made up the bulk of the commoners (*machuatlli*). Churchmen spanned the entire social spectrum, from important regional prelates to poor mendicant friars. Most principal towns by this time had their own church, even if it consisted of only a humble structure, which served the townspeople and smaller surrounding communities. Despite the declining Indian population, to Don Luís's eyes the country would have appeared much more densely populated than his own land, and the towns, with their churches and municipal buildings, more akin to those he had seen in Spain than the small, woodland settlements of his own people.[2]

After several weeks, the small group exited the final high mountain pass (13,000 feet) and crested a ridge that overlooked the great expanse of the Valley of Mexico. They still had to travel another forty miles to reach Mexico City, once known as the fabled Mexica (Aztec) city of Tenochtitlan, conquered by Hernán Cortés and his army four decades earlier. Surrounding the city were "mountains, hills, and ridges of unequal slopes, some of which," Francisco Cervantes de Salazar, a contemporary, explained, "bristle with forests and abound in timber." The mountain slopes were remarkably fertile, suited to the cultivation of all sorts of crops and fruits, where wealthy Spaniards had their country estates. Dominating the vista before them was a series of lakes, including the massive Lake Texcoco on which the city was located. The entire lacustrine system stretched nearly fifty miles from north to south and twenty miles east to west at its broadest point, along which many of the most populous towns—Texcoco, Chalco, Azcapotzalco, and Coyoacan—were located. They were described by Bernal Díaz, one of Cortés's foot soldiers, as "great towns . . . rising from the water." Proximity to the lakes gave the valley's inhabitants access to the abundance of fish that thrived in the salty waters, to large flocks of water fowl that nested along the shore and on small islands, and to the convenience of waterborne transportation from one part of the region to another.[3]

ENTERING THE SUBURBS, the city would have appeared unmistakably Spanish to Don Luís and his companions. Yet, reminders of the old city were all around, notably in the tens of thousands of Indian people who lived and worked in the neighborhoods circling the inner city and the enduring layout of Mexica causeways, streets, plazas, and canals. By 1570, the city numbered approximately eighty-five thousand people, including Spaniards, Indians, mestizos, African slaves, and mulattos; a significant decline from overall numbers prior to conquest, but nevertheless on a par with many of the largest cities in Europe. Making up approximately 70 percent of the city's population, the presence of Nahuas and mestizos in the Indian quarters would have been particularly striking, complemented by nine thousand enslaved African and mulattos, and sixteen thousand Spaniards.[4]

Immediately following the siege and destruction of Tenochtitlan in 1521, the city had been cleansed and rebuilt at a frenzied rate. An eyewitness from the period, Father Toribio de Bonavente Motolinia, one of the first Franciscans to arrive, portrayed the scene in biblical terms: "More people [Indians] worked in building the great city . . . than upon the Temple of Jerusalem in Solomon's time." In the decades afterward, the transformation of the city slowed but did not cease. The first cathedral, a humble structure, was built in the great central square among the ruins of Mexica pyramids, and a palace for the archbishop was erected nearby. Churches and large monasteries were built for the Franciscans, Dominicans, and Augustinians, reflecting the need for central organizations to supervise the rapid expansion of the religious orders' work throughout Mexico. Soon after becoming viceroy at midcentury, Velasco ordered the construction of the University of Mexico and Royal Hospital of the Indians, by which time the city's principal municipal buildings fronted the former sacred plaza of the Mexica. If not complete, the Hispanicization of the city was well underway.[5]

Don Luís and Aguirre had little opportunity to experience the city, however. Shortly after arrival, they became dangerously ill, possibly of smallpox or measles, and were placed under the care of the friars of the Dominican convent of Santo Domingo. In February 1563, Fray Pedro de Feria wrote to Philip II informing him of what had befallen the two Indians over the previous months. He explained their illness reached such a point that it was thought doubtful they would "escape." But then a miracle occurred. Near death, the Indian had pleaded repeatedly to be granted the holy sacrament of baptism. Coming to trust his sincerity, the friars finally agreed to his plea and baptized him, confirming his name as that of the viceroy. Not long after, Don Luís gradually began to get better as did his companion, Aguirre, who had also been baptized.

Fray Feria's account of the two Indians' astonishing recovery is revealing. The Dominicans had brought them back from the dead and, by their demonstration of faith, into the holy community of the Catholic Church. Utterly convinced that Don Luís and Alonso were sincere about their conversion, Feria wrote to the king that he believed the Lord had arranged to bring the Indians to him and thereby enable his ambition to mount a large-scale Dominican mission to Florida as soon as possible, taking the Indians with them as guides.

Unfortunately for Feria, the commander of the New Spain fleet, Pedro Menéndez de Aviles, turned down the request. He explained he did not have sufficient resources to launch such an expedition and, despite the plan being approved by Viceroy Velasco, could spare only a small ship for Don Luís, Aguirre, and a few of the friars. This offer fell so far short of Feria's expectations that he decided to postpone the mission and keep the two Indians at the convent for the time being. He justified his decision by pointing out to the king that Don Luís could not be returned to his own land without ministers to ensure that he and Aguirre remained true to their faith. If the Indians were "to go back to their rites and idolatries and thus be lost, their baptism would have caused them a greater condemnation, committing it seems a greater inhumanity," he argued. For their sake and the benefit of their souls, Feria concluded, it would be better if they remained at the convent for the time being. He may have calculated also that Don Luís's "fine presence and mental capacity" would be of considerable help in teaching Indians in the city.[6]

The young Indian had no intention of abandoning hope of seeing his land again. Residing only a few hundred yards from the viceroy's palace, he must have spent many hours haunting the palace's antechambers, waiting for an audience with Don Velasco, his godfather and patron, to plead for his support to return to the Chesapeake. Velasco's death in 1564, however, was a major setback that resulted in the Indian having to wait two more years in Mexico City before prospects changed sufficiently to give him optimism once more.

DON LUÍS'S EXPERIENCES during his forced sojourn in Mexico City, his encounters with the Indians of New Spain, and his observations on his travels gave him a very good impression of how the Spanish conquered the peoples of Mexico. He did not speak Nahuatl but may have learned a smattering of words after a year or two or spoke Spanish to the Indians he met and taught in the city. Possibly

Aguirre, who was from Mexico, served as his translator. Even as the generation who recalled the conquest was passing away, it is highly likely he would have picked up information about the brutal fall of Tenochtitlan and enforced rebuilding of the city. Evidence of Spanish power was all around him in the shape of the city's defenses, monumental civic and religious buildings, and social segregation. As the godson of Viceroy Velasco and a special member of the Dominican community, Don Luís lived within the Spanish *traza*, the extensive, central area of the city where Indians were prohibited from residing. Whenever he left the convent, he would have seen the great buildings of the central square built by Indian workers from the rubble of the old sacred plaza. In fulfilling his pastoral work on behalf of the Dominicans, he probably visited the homes of Indians in the neighborhoods circling the *traza* as well as those who lived in the countryside outside the city and seen how they lived compared to the Spanish. He must have been aware of the labor services and taxes that the Spanish imposed upon the people and seen Indian men and women toiling on the estates of wealthy Spaniards or in grand Spanish mansions. Although important continuities in everyday life spanned the pre- and post-conquest period, indigenous peoples, including the high born, could never attain the social status of the Spanish. Most Indians were called simply *indios* by Spaniards, a racist term that stripped them of their rich cultural identity.

During his years in Mexico City, Don Luís could not have failed to notice the enormous influence of the Catholic Church and religious houses, ubiquitous throughout New Spain, on Indian lives. Conversion followed conquest. Idolatry and polytheism persisted, but the old gods, beliefs, and rituals were largely swept away or translated into hybridized forms of religion that borrowed from both cultures. The new Christian landscape signified by cathedrals and churches was a stark expression of the Indian peoples' subjugation. He had witnessed the power of the church in Spain and New Spain, knew of the devout faith of the king and of the viceroy, and had become

well aware of the desire to bring Catholicism to Indian peoples. The church, government, and military worked in unison to bring about colonization, submission, and conversion. It was a lesson the young Don Luís would not forget.[7]

ALTHOUGH THE DEATH of Velasco had left him temporarily in limbo in Mexico City, Pedro Menéndez's appointment as *adelantado* (military governor) of Florida in March 1565 proved the catalyst that would transform the Indian's fortunes. Henceforth, Don Luís would be closely involved in Menéndez's plans for Spanish settlement in North America, in which the Dominicans and other religious houses would play an important role. The apostolic work of friars was encouraged by the king and supported enthusiastically by Menéndez as a means of spreading the word of Christ among Indian peoples and helping to stabilize the garrisons he intended to establish. Don Luís was well aware that he was uniquely placed in furthering these plans. Joining the missions of mendicants might offer him an ideal opportunity to find his way home.

King Philip had rightly anticipated an attempt by the French to establish a colony on the Florida coast. A few years earlier, Jean Ribault, a veteran French pilot and privateer, set out from Le Havre with three small ships and one hundred fifty men to reconnoiter the region. He left a small garrison at a site he called Charlesfort (Port Royal), in present-day South Carolina, that did not last long, but in 1564 and 1565, the French tried again, this time assembling more than a thousand settlers and soldiers for the two large-scale expeditions. Rather than returning to the abandoned Charlesfort, the expedition's leaders chose instead an area about a hundred miles south on the River of May, near present-day Jacksonville. Here they had the benefits of a good defensive position, friendly local Indians, and the prospect of an easy route by river into the interior where they hoped to find gold or silver "in the mountains of Appalesse

[Appalachians]." Fort Caroline, as they called it, was to be a French bridgehead for the large groups of colonists that would follow.[8]

Informed of the news in early 1565, Philip II turned to Pedro Menéndez, then in Spain, for an assessment of the threat and how to deal with it. Menéndez quickly drafted a "Memorial," affirming the king's view that an enemy of Spain, whether French or English, who settled in Florida would be a potent menace to Spanish shipping and the security of Spanish possessions in the Caribbean and on the mainland. He told the king that depredations were already "being committed by packs of Lutherans and Englishmen," and if these interlopers gained possession of Florida, "they would easily be able to lord it over the West Indies, and the mainland of South America facing the Ocean Sea." In addition, he raised a greater concern that Philip might not have considered: any nation that established colonies in Florida would be ideally placed to discover the river passages he believed connected the Atlantic seaboard to the South Sea (Pacific), not only opening up trade with the Orient but also making the enormously valuable silver mines of New Spain and Peru vulnerable to attack from the Pacific as well as the Caribbean. In the long run, the entire Spanish enterprise in America might be endangered. It was imperative to act quickly, he believed, to ensure the French would not have time to entrench themselves and win over local Indian peoples as allies.[9]

In response, the king issued Menéndez an *asiento* (contract) to ready himself to sail in May with five hundred well-armed men. The new governor acted swiftly. After gathering ships, soldiers, arms, and provisions, his fleet sailed from Cadiz and arrived on the coast of Florida at the end of August. Three weeks later, he was ready to attack and led his forces on a daring overland march to storm Fort Caroline.

For the French soldiers and settlers, the end was swift and terrible. One of the few eyewitnesses to survive, Nicolas Le Challeux, recounted how the Spanish "led by the savage[s]" entered the fort with no resistance and began slaughtering everyone they could find, "each trying to outdo the other in slaying men, healthy and sick, women and babies," in such a fashion "that it is not possible to dream of a massacre that is equal to this one in cruelty and barbarity." The Spanish reported they put one hundred thirty of the French to death in the taking of the fort and hundreds more in succeeding weeks, for the French, as one of Menéndez's chaplains remarked simply, were "Lutherans, and against our Holy Catholic Faith." In mid-October, Menéndez wrote to the king with evident satisfaction that "I had Juan Ribao [Ribault] and all the rest put to the knife, considering it to be necessary to the service of God and of Your Majesty." Shortly after, the final remnants of French survivors had been killed or captured and the first phase of Menéndez's conquest of Florida successfully completed. He had won a brutal and ruthless victory that sent shockwaves across Europe and in the long run proved to be a decisive blow to French ambitions of becoming a major power in Florida.[10]

Menéndez's peculiar genius was a blend of personal fortitude, decisive leadership, and an aptitude to think on a grand scale. In the first flush of victory, he saw opening up before him no less than a complete reorientation of the Spanish empire in America, which henceforth would pivot not only on the gold and silver mines of Mexico and Peru but also on the great waterways of the northern continent that linked the Atlantic to the Pacific. In late December 1565, Menéndez informed the king that at Santa Elena a river extended 100 leagues (approximately 320 miles) inland as far as the Appalachian Mountains. The same distance north of Santa Elena was the Chesapeake Bay (Bahía de Santa María), the land of "the Indian Velasco, who is in New Spain," he wrote. Inland from the bay "are the mountains and beyond them there is an arm of the sea, that is navigated by [Indians in] canoes and extends to Tierra Nova." Another arm of the sea flowed "in the direction of China," which he stated confidently is "considered certain."[11]

The Chesapeake Bay was key to Menéndez's plans for fortifying and settling Florida. It was therefore imperative that the Spanish occupy and defend the bay to ensure neither the French nor English gained possession first. Using the Chesapeake as a base of operations, he wrote enthusiastically to Philip, fleets of Spanish galleys would patrol northern waters, ousting other nations from the valuable fisheries of the Newfoundland Banks and preventing any further attempts by the French to find a northwest passage to the Orient. A navigable route to the South Sea would establish a vital link with Spanish possessions in the East, stimulate trade with Spanish North America, and promote the further development of a Spanish global empire. Such a vision demanded colonies not expeditions. As commerce surged along the great rivers, so settlements would follow, encouraging an enormous influx of Spanish migrants, ultimately even greater than that to New Spain and Peru. In time, settlers would spread across the entire northern continent, radiating outward from the initial colonies on the Atlantic littoral. Following lines of trade deep into the interior, settlers would eventually reach the west coast and take possession of the whole of North America for Spain.[12]

The vision that Menéndez laid out for the king shrewdly integrated the different parts of Spain's American empire. He did not advocate simply adding another province to Philip's expanding American territories, no matter how opulent, but rather illustrated how New Spain and Florida would reinforce one another. The first priority was to establish a string of garrisons along the Florida coast that would ultimately stretch from the Chesapeake Bay to the Gulf of Mexico to protect the mainland from incursions by other European nations and to secure the Bahama Channel. From Yucatan via Havana, his garrisons would be provided with maize, "of which there is much in great quantity." The silver mines of Zacatecas, Mexico, he believed, were only a few hundred leagues from Santa Elena, "and the country of the Indians [Don Luís and Aguirre], and the way to New Spain will be easily kept open for trade and passage." Shipping silver from Mexico via the Chesapeake would be much easier and more convenient than from Veracruz, the current port of choice, where the navigation was treacherous. Menéndez argued that in the following years, colonists would move inland to settle at Coosa, a fertile valley province explored thirty-five years earlier by Hernando De Soto, where, Menéndez wrote, the Spanish would build "a fine city." So "will Your Majesty be lord of these great provinces, will enlighten the natives thereof, and greatly increase your kingdoms," he concluded enthusiastically.[13]

GOVERNOR MENÉNDEZ REGARDED the conversion of the Indians as an essential preliminary to the establishment of the Spanish colonies he envisioned. Once the local chief was persuaded, the people would follow. To that end, he quickly made the decision to involve Don Luís, still languishing in Mexico City, in an expedition to reconnoiter the Chesapeake Bay, which would entail making contact with local peoples. In March 1565, the king ordered officials in Mexico City and Archbishop Alonso de Montúfar to have the young Indian and the "other Indian, his servant" (Aguirre) placed in the custody of Menéndez. A couple of months later, Menéndez wrote to the king again, underlining that sending Don Luís as well as "certain religious" would be the most effective means of winning over the people.

Owing to the attack on the French and its aftermath, a year passed before the plan was put into effect. Don Luís, Aguirre, and two Dominicans arrived in San Mateo (a Spanish garrison on the site of the former Fort Caroline) at the end of June 1566, about the same time a large fleet from Spain reached St. Augustine, Menéndez's principal settlement in Florida. With 1,100 newly arrived soldiers and plenty of fresh provisions, the governor was able to reinforce St. Augustine and San Mateo as well as the new colony of Santa Elena. Don Luís and his companions would have been well aware of the influx of soldiers and possibly had an opportunity to discuss the prospective voyage to the Chesapeake with Menéndez, when the governor stopped briefly at the fort before returning to St. Augustine.

Menéndez gave orders for a small expedition to be dispatched led by the Dominican Pablo de San Pedro, who would serve as the spiritual leader and governor of the new colony in the Chesapeake. He was to be accompanied by another Dominican, Juan de Acuña, together with Pedro de Coronas, the commander of fifteen soldiers sent with the expedition, two officials directed to keep a record of what occurred, and Don Luís and Aguirre. Menéndez likely viewed the voyage as primarily a reconnaissance mission that would provide information about the friendliness, or otherwise, of the peoples of the region and a suitable location for a settlement.[14]

At the beginning of August 1566, Friar San Pedro's group set sail on *La Trinidad,* and within a couple of weeks, the ship was lying off the Virginia coast. Yet navigation proved difficult. The pilot was unable to locate the entrance to the bay, having gone too far north, possibly skirting the Eastern Shore, and before they could explore farther, severe weather drove them back out to sea. When they next returned to the coast, they found themselves too far south, off the Outer Banks of North Carolina. San Pedro and Coronas led a party ashore, and the friar took possession of the land, probably one of the barrier islands, in the name of the king, calling it San Bartolomé in honor of the saint's day when they landed. Don Luís did not recognize the area, however, which appeared deserted, and after several days of fruitless exploration, they decided to head back to the north where they had arrived earlier. Doubtless much to the Indian's frustration, once again the weather intervened. A severe storm that lasted for three days drove them out to sea, followed shortly after by hurricane-force winds that gave them no choice but to abandon any attempt to make landfall.

Events then took yet another turn for the worse. Instead of returning to St. Augustine as might be expected, the pilot argued

FIGURE 2.1. San Bartolomé. The image is a detail from *The Arrival of the English*, an engraving by Johann Theodore de Bry, plate 2, in Thomas Hariot, *A Briefe and True Report of the New Found Land of Virginia* (1590), which depicts the Outer Banks and Roanoke Island in 1585. Don Luís and the Spanish arrived twenty years earlier while searching for the entrance to the Chesapeake Bay and named the area San Bartolomé.

Courtesy of the Colonial Williamsburg Foundation. Gift of Mr. and Mrs. Richard F. Barry III, Mr. and Mrs. Macon F. Brock, Mr. and Mrs. David R. Goode, Mr. and Mrs. Conrad M. Hall, Mr. and Mrs. Thomas G. Johnson Jr., Mr. and Mrs. Charles W. Moorman, IV, and Mr. and Mrs. Richard D. Roberts.

forcefully in favor of sailing to Spain. He had important dispatches to deliver, and he assured the Dominicans that once out of the storm they would have a clear passage across the Atlantic. Putting the matter to the vote, the friars and most of the men opted for Spain; the two Indians did not have a say. Helpless as the coast gradually disappeared from view below the horizon, Don Luís must have wondered whether he would ever see his people again.

CHAPTER 3

The Spanish Mission

DON LUÍS ARRIVED IN SEVILLE AT THE END OF OCTOBER 1566, back to the city he had first visited five years earlier as Paquiquineo, the princely young Indian. With funds granted by the Casa de Contratación, he and his companions made their way to Madrid to report to the king about the failure of the voyage to Virginia and recent developments in New Spain. Thereafter, he and Aguirre may have stayed at the monastery of Atocha, perhaps joining the friars in mourning the recent passing of Bartolomé de las Casas. Staying close to the court offered him his best opportunity to petition Philip II to return him to the Chesapeake; he had few other options.[1]

While Don Luís remained in Madrid, Governor Menéndez was busy shoring up the numerous small garrisons he had established along the Florida coast in the wake of defeating the French. Many of the settlements were poorly provisioned and subject to frequent attacks from local Indians, which fostered a rebellious mood among the soldiers. The governor had made airy promises of friendly Indians, plentiful food, and riches yet to be discovered, but the reality was quite different, and his men were quickly becoming disillusioned by the harshness of life in the colony.

Menéndez's own arrangements also suffered setbacks. Supply ships had been lost at sea, and the expense of maintaining the garrisons, even with financial support from the king, had all but exhausted his own resources. Then, in the spring of 1567, he heard news of the failure of the Chesapeake expedition, which was blamed on the two Dominicans, Pablo de San Pedro and Juan de Acuña. The friars, a contemporary wrote, had already endured hunger and dangers in Florida and had no wish to expose themselves to further hardships in the Chesapeake where, notwithstanding Don Luís's assertions to the contrary, the fruitfulness of the land and response of local Indian peoples to the Spaniards were doubtful. Consequently, the Dominicans "secretly drew some of the soldiers into a conspiracy" and then persuaded the crew members to agree to a fabricated story about storms preventing them from entering the bay, which therefore justified their decision to sail for Seville.[2]

Nevertheless, despite the challenges, Menéndez remained encouraged by his progress and especially by the king's continuing support. Following his expulsion of the French, he had created settlements at St. Augustine, San Mateo, and Santa Elena that were seemingly taking root. Other small garrisons along the west and Atlantic coasts of Florida, although inadequately manned and provisioned, at least served to provide the Spanish with beachheads stretching nearly a thousand miles from Tampa to South Carolina. In addition, he had dispatched expeditions into the interior to determine whether river passages connected inland Florida to the Gulf of Mexico, the Pacific, and Newfoundland as he hoped. Lastly, he had attempted to befriend local Indian peoples with mixed results but a few notable successes. Traveling up and down the Florida coast, he had met with the chiefs of many peoples and sought to bring them over to his side by offering inducements or threatening force. He understood the value of Indian allies, such as the Timucuans who had aided him in the destruction of the French at Fort Caroline, just as he recognized the danger posed by hostile peoples. He was convinced that only with the long-term cooperation of Florida's Indians could he achieve his ultimate goal of winning North America for the Spanish.[3]

In mid-May 1567, Menéndez decided that his affairs were sufficiently settled in Florida to allow him to return to Spain and seek an audience with Philip II. The governor's most important objectives were to gain recompense from the king for his services, promote further royal patronage as well as private investment, and persuade religious groups, Dominicans or Jesuits, to send missionaries to existing and future settlements in Florida. In all respects, it is doubtful whether he could have dreamed how successful he would be, especially in view of the negative accounts of the colony about the worthlessness of the region and privations suffered by settlers that had begun to filter back to Spain. But if he had had any doubts, he would not have been concerned for long. Following his report to the king and court in late July, Philip showered him with honors that provided immediate financial relief as well as the promise of enormous riches to come. He was granted the governorship of Cuba in addition to his role as governor of Florida, which would enable him to leverage the strategic importance and prosperity of Havana to reinforce his settlements on the mainland.

Shortly before Christmas, Menéndez spoke "benevolently and zealously" at the Jesuit College in Seville about the fertility of Florida, its proximity to New Spain, and the holy work of saving souls. He described how he had traveled with his men from town to town, explaining "the Christian God" and offering salvation to the Indians once the missionaries came "to teach them." The following month, he wrote the superior general of the Jesuits, Francisco de Borgia, assuring him that "everywhere the Indians abandoned their idols and asked for the cross." They even brought gold and silver from their mines to the Spanish because they wanted to become Christians.

Other religious orders had petitioned him to send friars to Florida, but he had refused them because for "the present I wanted this Order and no other to instruct the natives." Referring to his planned return to Florida in the summer, he asked for six fathers and six brothers to accompany him, who, he assured Borgia, would be able to carry out their duties safely and with honor.

Then he came to a matter of great significance to him: the foundation of an Indian school in Havana where the eldest sons of chiefs dwelling along the Florida coast would learn to read and write and be instructed in the Catholic faith. After three or four years, the young Indians would be sent back to their provinces, and thereby, he confidently asserted, "each one will become an army" by bringing their peoples into the church. The school, he wrote, will become the mother college of all the missions founded in the New World where Jesuit priests would reside before going to their assigned ministries in Peru, New Mexico, and Florida. Menéndez's belief in the efficacy of an Indian school that would serve settlements throughout Spanish America was typical of the breadth of his thinking, an amplification of his own experiences with Don Luís and possibly other converts written large upon the emergent societies of Florida and beyond.[4]

GONZALO SOLÍS DE Merás, Menéndez's brother-in-law, had accompanied him during the conquest of Florida and subsequently became one of his first biographers. Writing about events in 1566, he mentioned that Don Luís had been with the governor for six years, a reference that suggests the critical importance of the Indian to Menéndez's plans for Florida. Don Luís provided a striking example of a highly intelligent young Indian from a family of chiefs who, as Solis put it, "was a good Christian with very good understanding." He offered living proof that indigenous peoples could be delivered from their "savage" ways and brought into the church. Consequently, Menéndez believed that Don Luís would play an important role in

persuading at least one of the religious orders in Spain to support his desire to send missionaries to the Chesapeake Bay.

When Menéndez arrived in the capital in the summer of 1567 to discuss his plans for Florida with the king, it is likely he also broached them with Don Luís and subsequently took the Indian with him on his visit later in the year to the Jesuit College in Seville. Quite probably he left him there to persuade the Jesuits of how indispensable Don Luís would be to their efforts to found missions in Florida and convert its peoples. A later account by Luis Gerónimo de Oré states that Don Luís resided at the college where he spoke to Rector Ignatius Fonseca and offered to guide missionaries to his land where, with God's help and his own efforts, the Indians "would be converted to the Faith." These words apparently aroused such an intense passion to save souls in the Jesuits' hearts that many begged leave of the king to "go to those parts, and take with them the *cacique* Don Luís," which Philip duly granted.[5]

Over the next few months, Superior General Borgia undertook the selection of those who would go. Father Juan Bautista de Segura, an experienced administrator who had been in charge of several colleges in Spain, was appointed vice provincial with authority over three other fathers and ten brothers. On April 10, 1568, they sailed with the royal fleet from San Lucar, Don Luís with them, and after nearly ten weeks at sea arrived at St. Augustine where, owing to serious food shortages, conditions were far worse than they had anticipated. Father Segura decided shortly after, therefore, to remove the Jesuits to Havana where he wrote to Borgia informing him that he had resolved to establish the headquarters of their ministry in the port so that "all may come for spiritual consolation and refreshment." He was initially impressed by the massive city-fortress. "This port is virtually Spain. The fleets from Peru and New Spain, as well as the military expeditions, such as those for Florida, and many private vessels usually stop over here for months. Persons of rank," he continued, "reside in this town which is growing daily now the King has fortified it against the attacks of pirates, so the fathers stationed here will have plenty to do." He affirmed Menéndez's opinion that a college in Havana would "be a seminary for Florida and all the Indies," as well as the local populace.[6]

At first brimming with optimism, Segura's outlook about the prospect of widespread conversions would falter the following year after several journeys along the Florida coast as far north as Santa Elena would fully reveal the Jesuits' limited results. Writing shortly before Christmas 1569, he informed Borgia that the missionaries' hard work and privations had resulted only in "slight benefit to the souls of the natives," and he was skeptical about the likelihood of achieving more success in the future, "judging by what has been seen up to the present." He wondered whether the missionaries' efforts might be better directed elsewhere. He had heard rumors, for example, that a route might exist from the lands of a chief named King Philip on the west coast of Florida through the land mass to China. Until they heard otherwise, however, Segura assured Borgia that the Jesuits would continue their ministries as best they could in those few areas such as Santa Elena where they might have at least some hope of success, but he was clearly beginning to consider other possibilities farther afield.[7]

It was about this time in Havana that Don Luís made a crucial intervention. Father Juan Rogel, one of the first Jesuits to arrive in Florida, described the Indian as "very crafty [clever]," for when he met Father Segura "he gave out that he was the son of a great chief, and as such our King in Spain had ordered him an allowance and clothing." Don Luís was educated and had received confession and communion, "and thus it seemed wise that the vice-provincial should take him on as an interpreter" and guide. More ominously, Rogel recalled that taking "the enterprise to heart, Father [Segura] did not wish to entrust it to any other [than the Indian]." Juan de la Carrera, one of the brothers who was with Segura on the voyage from Spain, added that the vice provincial met with Governor Menéndez who

FIGURE 3.1. Paquiquineo/Don Luís's American world. *Drawing by Jamie May.*

told him of a conversation that he had had with Don Luís about his homeland in which the Indian told him of the existence of "another sea in this region and another navigation of great importance for the discovery of great kingdoms such as Tartary and others contiguous to it." Carrera noted that Segura and Menéndez had "easily" reached the conclusion that a mission should be sent to the Chesapeake, after which there was no further discussion.[8]

OVER THE NEXT several months, meticulous preparations were made for the voyage. Father Segura chose a small group to go with him: Father Luís de Quirós, Brothers Gabriel Gomez, Sancho Cevallos, Juan Bautista Mendez, Pedro de Limares, Gabriel de Solis (a relative of Menéndez), and Cristobal Redondo. In addition, Don Luís was to serve as guide and interpreter, and a boy, Alonso de Olmos, who may have accompanied the Jesuits from Seville, was taken as a servant. Menéndez, who was fully supportive of the voyage, made available a frigate and an experienced mariner, Vicente Gonzales, to take them to the Chesapeake. They also took plenty of provisions for the initial year as well as planks and nails for a small house that would be built by the ship's carpenter once they arrived at their final destination. They were not accompanied by soldiers, however, despite an offer from the governor to provide them with a hundred men. A minor official of Santa Elena, Bartolomé Martinez, later wrote that the missionaries believed there was no need because "they had confidence in God and were bringing Don Luís . . . the lord and chief of that land." Segura was also concerned the soldiers would cause trouble and might hamper efforts to convert the Indians.[9]

Leaving Havana in July 1570, the group stopped at Santa Elena to rest and take on board additional supplies. There, Father Rogel and Brother Carrera met with Segura to discuss the mission and emphasize the risks he and his followers were taking. At the gathering, Segura confided his "plans and designs and hopes for the journey." These, Carrera remembered, were all "praiseworthy, for they came from a holy, sincere Christian heart," and yet the plan had serious flaws. He told Segura that Don Luís "did not satisfy" him, and judging from what the Indian had told him about his land, he was convinced he "was a liar." Carrera did not believe the stories told by the Indian about the fertility of the land or friendliness of the people and entreated Segura to think through the plan more thoroughly. A mission going to "such remote and distant lands relying on an Indian, leaving everything behind, without a guard of soldiers or any people other than his own" seemed to him to be perilous in the extreme. Carrera suggested that, rather than risking himself, Segura should send another of the fathers ahead to scout the land and confirm whether the Indian was telling the truth, a proposal that all the fathers except Luís de Quirós agreed was a good idea. Fathers Rogel and Antonio Sedeño, experienced with the Guale Indians of the Santa Elena region, even offered to go with Don Luís to the Chesapeake themselves, but despite all their arguments, Segura declined. The vice principal, Carrera recalled, remained unshakable in his belief that the expedition was "in conformity with the will of Our Lord which he (Segura) desired to accomplish in everything." With that, Segura left the meeting, "firm in his high purpose."

Rogel's and Carrera's accounts were written decades after the event, and it is possible that in hindsight both exaggerated their own efforts to dissuade Father Segura from going. Yet the alternatives they put forward were based on common Spanish practice at the time, outlined by Menéndez to the Jesuits in Seville, whereby the governor and his men would make the first approach to Indian chiefs, and if they appeared willing to convert, he would call for missionaries to live and teach among their people. Few Europeans, other than occasional traders or explorers, had encountered the Indians of the Chesapeake; Segura and his companions were entering an almost completely unknown territory. Carrera recalled that when it was time for Segura to depart, several of his company came to say good-bye "with great tenderness and tears," telling Carrera they "were going to their death." To make matters worse in Carrera's opinion, Segura and Quirós had insisted on taking with them Santa Elena's best church plate and other rich furnishings, which he was certain would be another incentive for the Indians to kill them. Why, then, against all advice did Segura persist? The only plausible explanation, as the vice provincial himself confirmed on a number of occasions, was the great faith he placed in Don Luís. He was the catalyst for the mission, the essential member of the company who would afford "the help which Timothy gave to St. Paul" and pave the way for success. Without Don Luís's involvement in the mission, it is most unlikely Segura would have risked his own life and those of his compatriots.[10]

In late August, after a voyage of several weeks, their ship entered the Chesapeake Bay. Captain Gonzales sailed directly west and reached the mainland, somewhere near Point Comfort (modern-day Hampton). Six or seven miles farther along the coast, the Jesuits made their initial landing at the entrance of the Powhatan (James) River, where beyond a bluff near some pines they set up an altar and held Mass to give thanks for their safe arrival. "Our Fathers and Brothers disembarked in a great and beautiful port" wrote Carrera, who saw the river two years later, "men who have sailed a great deal and have seen it say it is the best and largest port in the world." From there, all the while taking soundings, Gonzales made his way slowly northwestward upriver for approximately thirty miles before entering the Chickahominy River, where they saw numerous towns lining both banks.[11]

At this point, descriptions of their movements become extremely vague. They may have disembarked near Mattapanient, about five miles upriver from the mouth of the Chickahominy, or possibly a few miles farther up. Here, two brother chiefs of Don Luís together with other Indians greeted him and offered lodgings "amid demonstrations of great joy." Nearly nine years had passed since the young Indian had been taken by the Spanish, and now he had at last returned. After they rested for a day or two and unloaded their supplies, Don Luís led them on the next stage of their journey, "crossing great swamps and marshes," traveling over land and by canoe for at least ten miles to a place described by a later commentator as "far distant from the sea and any human protection." Father Quirós gave only the slightest hint of where they were when he wrote that to reach them was "2 good leagues" (seven miles) by land and the same

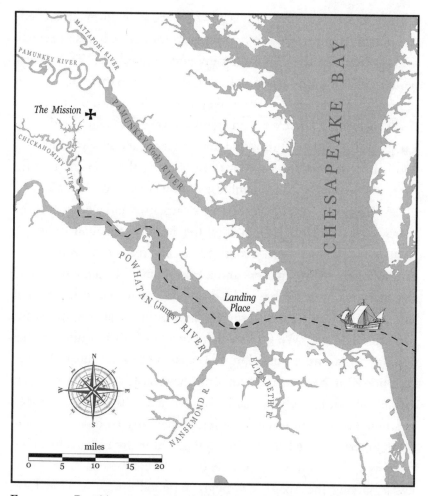

FIGURE 3.2. Possible route taken by the Jesuits in 1570 and location of their mission between the Chickahominy and Pamunkey (York) Rivers near Diascund Creek. *Drawing by Jamie May.*

or more along a creek, "so that the goods, which we have unloaded in this uninhabited place . . . must be carried by the Indians on their shoulders . . . and then embarked in canoes." He added that it "was not convenient" to return to them by the Powhatan River, obliquely criticizing the information they were given by Don Luís, but their pilot had gone in search of another river nearby that might offer a more direct route "to the place where we plan to make our encampment." Quirós's description suggests they ended up somewhere midway between the Chickahominy and Pamunkey (York) Rivers, perhaps inland from Diascund Creek. A relief ship carrying supplies returning by way of the Pamunkey (York) River would therefore reach them much quicker than the route they had taken with Don Luís.[12] But if Father Quirós had any concerns about why Don Luís had led them from the populous towns along the riverside to a remote place seemingly in the middle of nowhere, he did not show it.

As previously arranged, the ship's carpenter and a couple of the mariners accompanied them into the interior and constructed a small wooden house with a roof of thatched reeds that would serve as the fathers' living quarters and a tiny chapel.[13] Impatient to send the mariners away so he could dispatch a letter confirming their safe arrival, Quirós gave a brief description of local conditions the day after landing: "We find the land of Don Luís in quite another condition than we expected, not because he was at fault in his description of it, but because Our Lord has chastised it with six years famine and death, which has brought it about that there is much less population than usual." The Jesuits had arrived during a severe drought that affected the entire region, and many Indians had died or moved away. It quickly became obvious that instead of the Indians supplying the Spanish through the good offices of Don Luís, the missionaries would have to support the Indians by bringing in large quantities of corn by ship to sustain themselves and provide for the local peoples to sow. By cultivating the land, Quirós believed, it would be possible to cultivate their souls. If planting could begin in March or April, "many of the tribes will come here after being scattered over the region in search of food and there will be a good opportunity for the Holy Gospel." He added that "the chief has sought this very thing especially."

The situation in which the fathers found themselves was challenging but did not cause them undue alarm, and they did not appear to contemplate abandoning the mission. Unlike downriver, where the Powhatan River became brackish during the summer months, here the Jesuits had plenty of fresh water from nearby creeks all year-round. Local Indian peoples seemed delighted by the astonishing return of Don Luís, who they thought had been lost long ago. They believed he "had risen from the dead and come down from heaven," Quirós wrote, and consequently his people had "recovered their courage and hope that God may seek to favor them." They wanted "to be like Don Luís, begging us to remain in this land with them." Moreover, in a stunning piece of news, Quirós related that they had heard from the Indians specific information about a sea three or four days' journey inland, beyond a mountain range that might turn out to be a passage to the Pacific, which might confirm Governor Menéndez's theories about the geography of the North American interior. By way of concluding his letter, the father expressed great hope of the imminent conversion of the Indians and their "service to Our Lord and His Majesty and of an entrance into the mountains and to China." As long as Don Luís was loyal and the Jesuits had the good-will of the local people then all would be well. The Indian, Quirós added in a postscript, had turned out as well as they had hoped and "is most obedient to the wishes of Father [Segura] and shows deep respect for him, as also for the rest of us here."[14]

Yet, Segura's and Quirós's confidence turned out to be tragically mistaken. A few days after their ship had left, Don Luís asked for permission to go to his home village to see his relatives, telling the fathers that by returning to his home he would be able to persuade more of his people to come to the mission. He would travel by himself, he told them, because the terrain was difficult and he could journey much faster alone. The fathers agreed enthusiastically and set a time (unspecified in later accounts) for him to come back, perhaps within a few weeks. But Don Luís did not come back, and neighboring Indian people stopped visiting the mission, leaving the Jesuits to their own devices.

During a long winter, the missionaries eked out their remaining supplies and were then reduced to gathering roots and berries from the forest or bartering copper and tin for corn. They lived "in continual fright and alarm," according to Carrera, and awaited death every moment. Father Segura sent messages and had daily prayers said for Don Luís, convinced "that the devil held him in great deception." By early February, famished and suffering intensely from the bitter cold, Segura decided he could not wait any longer for the Indian and dispatched Father Quirós and two brothers to go to the village of a chief about fifteen miles away, close to where Don Luís was staying. According to Juan Rogel's account, they hoped to persuade Don Luís to accompany them back to the mission and barter for corn along the way.

Instead, on February 3, the Sunday after the Feast of the Purification, Don Luís ambushed them. He and a group of warriors attacked Quirós and Brother Solís with a volley of arrows and then finished them off with hatchets the Jesuits had brought with them to trade. Baptista Méndez fled into the woods bleeding heavily from his wounds but was discovered the following morning and slain. Their bodies were burned, and their clothing and possessions taken.

The killing of the Jesuits at the mission was equally swift and brutal. Led by Don Luís, a war party made up of fellow chiefs and relatives arrived at the mission the same day feigning friendship. Don Luís had positioned bowmen at the rear of the Jesuits' house to shoot anyone who escaped the slaughter within. Then, dressed in clothes taken from Father Quirós, he went inside with a small group of warriors and assigned each of them to kill one of the priests so that all would be dispatched at the same time. The first to die was Father Segura, killed by Don Luís while praying at the altar. Brother Carrera relates that just before he died, Segura saw the Indian approach him, wearing a cassock, and believed he had come to celebrate Mass, saying with joy, "You are very welcome Don Luís!" Before he was able to utter any more words, Don Luís struck him repeatedly with

Figure 3.3. *Don Luís and the Killing of the Jesuits*, an engraving by Melchior Kusell, in Mathias Tanner, *Societas Jesu usque ad sanguinis et vitae profusionem militans . . .* (Prague, 1675). The engraving depicts the martyrdom of the Jesuits in early February 1571. Don Luís is shown carrying out the killings alone. *Courtesy of Internet Archive.*

his ax, killing him and mutilating his body. The others perished in the same way, including Sancho Cevallos who had gone into the forest to collect wood. Only the boy, Alonso de Olmos, was spared. Warriors did not usually kill children, preferring to take them into their tribe. Alonso told the Indians that he wanted to die with his companions as it would be better for "him to die with Christians than live alone with Indians," but they would not do it. He managed, however, to persuade Don Luís to have his men bury the priests in a long ditch "with their crosses in their hands," first Segura followed by the others.

According to later Jesuit accounts, though "evil and hardened" in his sins, Don Luís was so moved by seeing his former companions dead in their graves that he wept freely and called them martyrs. After the missionaries were buried, the Indians began pillaging the mission. Expressing his contempt for the Catholic Church and the Jesuits, Don Luís handed out clothes, vestments, chalices, and patens, small plates used to hold Eucharistic bread, to his brothers and followers and carried away a small chest containing a crucifix and relics. Devotional books were ripped up and scattered over the ground. The mission was completely destroyed.[15]

It was predictable that Spanish writers would portray the killing of the missionaries as acts of savagery and wickedness. They were, after all, chronicling the martyrdom of Father Segura and his followers in one of the most devastating attacks on the Jesuits in sixteenth-century America, not seeking to comprehend Indian motives. Brother Carrera reported that he had no doubts but that the "wretched native" was a "second Judas," who, having nothing to fear from the Spanish after Segura dispatched their ship, "began to indulge in vices and sins publicly without fear of God or man." Acting "more like a pagan than a Christian in his manners, dress, and habits," Carrera continued, "he went off and lived with his uncle, a chief, in a country far distant from ours. There he allowed himself free rein in his sins, marrying many women in a pagan way." Other memorialists followed suit, calling him a renegade and the murders an "abominable act of treachery." Perhaps Carrera was right: Don Luís had fooled them all with his profession of faith and talk of helping to convert his people. Perhaps his life with the Dominicans and then Jesuits was a pretense sustained over the years to orchestrate his eventual return to Virginia. If so, it was a remarkable performance that fooled not only the Dominicans and Jesuits but also Philip II, high church and court officials, Governor Menéndez, and many others.

And yet Don Luís's true motives are not difficult to fathom. On a personal level, he understood that the killing of the Jesuits was vital to his own reaccommodation as a leading chief. When he first arrived back in his land, he would have looked like the Spaniards, dressed like them, and spoke their language. The very act of killing reestablished him among his people and symbolized his utter rejection of Spanish ways and his former life. Don Luís was no more; he was once again Paquiquineo.

Given his experiences with the Spanish, Don Luís was uniquely qualified to assess the possible futures that lay ahead in his own land. While in Mexico and Florida, he had learned that conversion to Catholicism and Spanish ways had followed brutal conquest. In Virginia, the reverse was meant to happen, conquest and colonization would follow conversion, but the eventual outcome would be the same. Don Luís, as Brother Carrera of Santa Elena perhaps guessed, was using the founding of a mission as a stratagem to return to his country and lure the fathers to their deaths. Having witnessed the condition of the vanquished in New Spain and given the strong possibility he knew something of Menéndez's grandiose plans for the Chesapeake, he could not possibly have allowed the Jesuits to establish a beachhead in the region. To do so would have inevitably led to a disastrous reduction in the power of his own family and other chiefs, if not their destruction. In time, Spanish soldiers and settlers would take their land and destroy their culture. As more and more came, their gods would be overthrown and replaced by the white man's god and church, and from wars and disease, their peoples would rapidly decline until ultimately their entire way of life disappeared. More immediately, he must have feared the Spanish would come looking for the fathers, and therefore it was imperative he leave no trace of what had happened. In that regard, his failure to kill the boy Alonso, who had survived the carnage at the mission and escaped to find sanctuary with another chief, was a blunder that would have serious repercussions.[16]

ALONSO'S SURVIVAL WAS of vital importance because it was he who eventually provided conclusive eyewitness testimony about the fate of the mission. By the summer of 1571, authorities in Havana were deeply concerned about what had happened to the fathers. A supply ship sent earlier could find no trace of them, although Indians wearing "religious robes" who tried to entice the Spanish ashore were spotted at a village not far from the mission. This was seemingly a ruse arranged by Paquiquineo/Don Luís to tempt the Spanish to land and then "overwhelm and kill them." None of the prearranged signals indicating the fathers were safe were seen from the masthead, however, and so the captain refused to land. In response, the Indians launched a furious attack in their canoes in an effort take the ship. Two Indian chiefs were captured by the Spanish during the attack, but they refused to provide any information about the whereabouts of the Jesuits, apart from indicating that Alonso was still alive.

An expedition under the personal command of Governor Menéndez, consisting of four ships and one hundred fifty soldiers, was organized the following year and entered the Chesapeake Bay in August 1572. The governor dispatched a small frigate with thirty soldiers upriver to search for Alonso and take hostages. Following a fierce skirmish with warriors firing arrows from the shore, the Spanish anchored off the mouth of the Chickahominy River where soldiers killed twenty and captured thirteen Indians, including "a principal chief." Using a combination of bribes and threats, the crew recovered Alonso and from him learned the story of the killing of the fathers. Menéndez told the Indians with whom he was bargaining that he would hang all the captives if they did not deliver

Paquiquineo/Don Luís to him within three days. When the Indian prisoner released to carry the news did not reappear by the appointed time, the governor ordered the hostages to be hanged from the ship's rigging, in clear view of any Indians looking on from the shore. An eyewitness reported that the "country remains very frightened from the chastisement the Governor inflicted, for previously they were free to kill any Spaniard who made no resistance. After seeing the opposite of what the Fathers were, they tremble. This chastisement has become famous throughout the land." Literally as a parting shot, the pilot of one of the ships steered toward land as if intending to speak to a crowd of Indians gathered by the river but instead the soldiers opened fire, killing "many."[17]

As for Paquiquineo/Don Luís, his fate remained a mystery; he had seemingly disappeared without trace.

PART TWO

War Chief

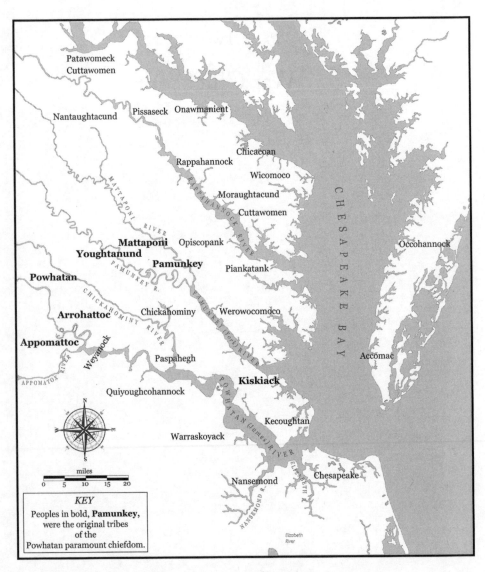

FIGURE 4.1. The Powhatan paramount chiefdom, about 1590.
Drawing by Jamie May.

CHAPTER 4

"King of Pamaunck"

P AQUIQUINEO RETURNED TO A LAND ON THE CUSP OF MAJOR
changes. A decade earlier, when he was taken by the Spanish,
the region had been characterized by small and midsize communities
as well as a few larger chiefdoms ruled by independent chiefs. The
transition from simple to more complex chiefdoms had been underway since at least the thirteenth century but had begun to gather
pace in the second half of the fifteenth and sixteenth centuries, owing to a dramatic intensification of raiding and warfare. In response
to threats posed by hostile peoples from outside the Chesapeake, settlements along the Powhatan (James) River and Pamunkey (York)
River Valleys began to evolve into chiefdoms capable of defending
themselves against increasingly frequent and violent attacks. Then,
sometime in the 1560s and early 1570s, by a strange quirk of lineage,
the man who would become the principal chief of the region, Powhatan (named for his people), inherited six chiefdoms: Powhatan,
Arrohattoc, Appomattoc, Pamunkey, Youghtanund, and Mattaponi.
The first three were on the Powhatan River, and the second three
and possibly Kiskiack were on the Pamunkey River. These territories,

perhaps with a couple of others, comprised the historic core of what was to become the great paramount chiefdom of the Powhatans.[1]

The rapid coaleasce of the chiefdom just a few years after Menén-dez's "chastisement" of 1572, however, suggests a highly significant additional explanation. Given his experience of the Spanish in New Spain and Florida and awareness of Menéndez's determination to establish a settlement in the Chesapeake, Paquiquineo must have believed the Spanish would return in force sooner or later. He was therefore likely an influential voice in Chief Powhatan's councils, arguing in favor of a rapid consolidation of tribes to confront the threat if it came. Separate clusters of chiefdoms would be unable to withstand an invasion and might well be persuaded to join with the Spanish to secure exclusive trade relations and gain advantage over one another. The Spanish, after all, were past masters of divide and conquer tactics, as illustrated by their conquests in Mexico. Only a powerful chiefdom, or an alliance of chiefdoms under the authority of a paramount chief (*mamanatowick*) such as Powhatan, would be sufficiently strong to ward off an invasion force of Spanish ships. It was a compelling argument.[2]

IN THE EVENT, Paquiquineo and Powhatan need not have been worried about the Spanish returning. The Spanish made no further attempts to establish Catholic missions or forts, apart from several reconnaissance voyages that were sent from Havana and St. Augustine to explore the bay and patrol the mid-Atlantic coast to guard against foreign interlopers, such as the English. About the time that Paquiquineo organized the killing of the Jesuits, Spanish settlements along the Florida coast and in the interior were already failing. A number of small garrisons located in the hinterland of modern-day South Carolina fell to Indian attacks, leading successive Spanish governors to abandon efforts to occupy the interior and focus instead on enforcing their control over coastal Indian peoples. The strategy was only partially successful from the Spaniards' point of view, and by 1587, when Santa Elena was abandoned, St. Augustine was left as the sole remaining Spanish settlement in Florida.[3]

Though the danger of a Spanish invasion faded in the last quarter of the sixteenth century, the threat from other European nations persisted, spurring on Powhatan's and Paquiquineo's efforts to persuade or force neighboring peoples to join their expanding chiefdom. As a young man, an English settler later recorded, Chief Powhatan was "vigilant, ambitious, [and] subtle to enlarge his dominions." In some cases, marriage and kinship alliances or diplomacy were used; in others, the deployment of warriors to mount frontal assaults, hit-and-run raids, and surprise attacks proved most effective. In the mid-1590s, the death of the chief of the Kecoughtans, a powerful people who lived near the mouth of the Powhatan (James) River, prompted Powhatan to organize an overwhelming attack. His warriors killed the new chief and most of the men and women, sparing only a few, who were taken and distributed among his own people.

A little over a decade later, Powhatan ordered the destruction of the Piankatanks, who lived along the river of the same name north of the Pamunkey River. In this case, he launched a surprise raid, probably commanded by the war chief Paquiquineo, after sending his men to lodge among them for a night. At the appointed hour, his warriors "fell to the spoil, 24 men they slew, the long hair of the one side of their heads with the skin cased off with shells or reeds, they brought away. They surprised also the women and children and the Werowance [chief]. All these they present to Powhatan" to serve him. A worse fate befell the Chesapeake people who inhabited lands along the southern shore at the entrance of the bay. Advised by his councilors that they posed a dire threat to the continuance of his rule, Powhatan commanded they be completely wiped out in an attack that involved the slaughter of men, women, and children. Powhatan strategically deployed his brothers and sons to rule over especially dangerous peoples or transplanted groups who had replaced the original inhabitants of an area.[4]

Powhatan was not an absolute ruler, however, but rather a chief of chiefs. An English eyewitness wrote in 1607 that there is "a king in this land called the great Pawatah, under whose dominions are at least 20 [the actual number was nearer thirty] several kingdoms, yet each king potent in his own territory." Lesser chiefs paid tribute, corn, and other goods, and the level of control he exerted over his numerous peoples varied considerably from one area to another. In outlying areas, such as north of the Rappahannock River or on the Eastern Shore, chiefs acted far more independently than those of the core area between the upper Powhatan and Pamunkey Rivers. Even in the core area, the Chickahominies, "coarse-pounded corn people," were an independent group who were at times allied with the Powhatans but never ruled by them. They were governed by a council of eight elders, not by a single chief. Elsewhere, semi-independent chiefs on the fringes of the paramount chiefdom might recognize Powhatan's authority and provide support in times of war or when called upon, but they would also pursue their own policies and trade opportunities and occasionally disobey or ignore his orders altogether when it suited them.

The growth of the Powhatan chiefdom was the most important political development in the mid-Atlantic region of the late sixteenth century. By 1600, the chiefdom stretched from south of the Powhatan River to the southern shore of the Potomac, and from the Atlantic Ocean to the foothills of the Blue Ridge Mountains, an area of approximately ten thousand square miles. Some fourteen thousand people inhabited Tsenacommacah, a Powhatan word that means "densely inhabited land," dispersed in several hundred communities throughout the region. Chief Powhatan's peoples belonged to the Algonquian language group, one of the three major linguistic

groups that populated the Chesapeake, the other two being Iroquoian and Siouan.[5]

Outside the boundaries of his chiefdom, a number of hostile peoples presented different levels and types of threat. Siouan-speaking
Monacans and Mannahoacs who inhabited the fertile river valleys
along the upper reaches of the Powhatan and Rappahannock Rivers
were ancient enemies of the Powhatans and orchestrated frequent
raids along their western border. To the north were the Iroquoian
Susquehannocks who lived at the head of the Chesapeake Bay along
the river that bears their name, described by the English as such
great and well-proportioned men that they seemed "like Giants."
Across the Potomac River was the Piscataway paramount chiefdom
and beyond them the Massawomecks (also Iroquoian) who periodi-
cally journeyed from the Great Lakes following the Indian Warpath
to plunder settlements in Virginia's piedmont and tidewater.[6]

In the long run, however, the greatest threat to Powhatan's and
Paquiquineo's rule would come from across the Atlantic. By the mid-
1580s, the Spanish had not yet reappeared, but a hundred Englishmen
had settled on Roanoke Island, North Carolina. Subsequently, a group
of them sailed to the Chesapeake Bay where they met Indian peoples who inhabited the southern shore. Soon after, they went a few
miles farther westward and discovered the mouths of the Powhatan
and Pamunkey Rivers, possibly making contact with the Kecoughtan
people, before crossing the bay to the Eastern Shore and then de-
parting.[7] News of the English from peoples of the Roanoke region
was grim. Virulent diseases had swept through their settlements and
taken many lives. The English were aggressive and unpredictable, and
by the spring of 1586, Indians of the entire region were ready to rise
up against them. The war that ensued claimed many lives before the
soldiers abandoned their fort in the summer and sailed for England.[8]

Twenty years later, another English expedition arrived in the Powhatan's lands and within a couple of weeks had set up an encampment

by the Powhatan River, occupying land on hunting grounds belonging to the Paspahegh people. The vital question for Powhatan and Paquiquineo, as for other chiefs, was what did the newcomers want and what might their arrival portend?

FIGURE 4.2. The capture of Captain John Smith by "the King of Pamaunkee and all his company," in John Smith, *The Generall Historie of Virginia, New-England, and the Summer Isles* . . . (London, 1632). In the lower half of the image, Smith defends himself against the Indian advance guard, and in the upper half, he is led from a frozen swamp ("Ooze") by his captors.
Courtesy of Special Collections, John D. Rockefeller Jr. Library, Colonial Williamsburg Foundation.

On a bitterly cold winter's day in December 1607, a remarkable encounter took place near the headwaters of the Chickahominy River. In a "vast and wild wilderness," a hunting party came upon three English soldiers cautiously exploring the area's many small creeks and marshy grounds. The Indians assumed the Englishmen had come from Paspahegh (Jamestown Island), where they had built a three-sided, wooden fort. Since their arrival, peoples who lived nearby had watched closely and become increasingly alarmed by the lack of any clear signal that the English intended to leave. A combination of disease and starvation had rapidly depleted their numbers, causing them to become desperate for food and leading to sporadic attacks on the Indians nearby to steal corn and other supplies. Now, however, in the lands of the Chickahominies, hidden among trees, the chief of the hunting party decided to capture the soldiers' leader to find out why the English had settled at Paspahegh.[9]

His opportunity arose soon after when a stocky, bearded man left his two companions to explore farther upriver alone. Following a brief skirmish during which the man held off the Indians' advance guard with his pistol, killing or wounding three of them, the entire hunting party arrived led by the "king of Pamaunck, called Opeckankenough" (Opechancanough), an older man of indeterminate age. His men quickly surrounded the soldier and drew their bows seemingly ready to shoot, but instead they placed them on the ground. Discovering the man to be a "captain," Opechancanough ordered him to throw down his weapons, assuring him he was in no danger. Through an Indian interpreter, the chief told the Englishman, whose name was John Smith, that his companions had been slain but him "they would reserve." Smith refused to surrender and demanded to be returned to his canoe forthwith. The standoff was soon resolved, however, when he stumbled backward into an icy quagmire and became stuck fast, rendering him unable to defend himself. Pulled from the ooze by a couple of warriors, Smith was brought before Opechancanough upon the chief's orders. Standing before the chief and having no better idea what to do, Smith opted to throw himself on the Indian's "mercies" and took from his pocket a compass dial, which he presented to the chief explaining as best he could how it worked.[10]

According to his later account,

Much they [the Indians] marveled at the playing of the Fly and Needle, which they could see so plainly, and yet not touch it, because of the glass that covered them. But when he demonstrated by that Globe-like Jewel, the roundness of the earth, and skies, the sphere of the Sun, Moon, and Stars, and how the Sun did chase the night round about the world continually; the greatness of the Land and Sea, the diversity of Nations, variety of complexions, and how we were to them the Antipodes, and many other such like matters, they all stood amazed with admiration.

How the Indian interpreter managed to convey the meaning of Smith's explanation of the cosmos or what the warriors thought of the white man's incomprehensible babbling is impossible to tell. In one version, Smith writes he was tied to a tree and about to be shot before the chief intervened once again by holding up the compass as a signal to let him live. In another account, possibly more reliable, he mentions that Opechancanough simply ordered his men to take him captive. Either way, the outcome was the same, and with a triumphant shout, the warriors led him into the woods, Smith all the while fearing for his life.[11]

He was taken to Rassawek, the "in-between place," a hunting camp about six miles away, where Opechancanough and his warriors made a dramatic entrance.[12] The chief was flanked by twenty men, five each front and rear and to the sides, each with a war bow and full quiver of arrows, while the rest of the warriors marched behind "in exceeding good order." Carried before the chief, Smith recalled, were the Englishmen's firearms and swords, trophies of the encounter. When they arrived at the camp, the women and children came out to see them. Then a group of warriors and Indian priests formed a ring and danced around him and the chief in "several Postures," singing and chanting in celebration of the slaying of the two Englishmen and capture of their captain. The warriors were dressed in fox and otter skins, their heads and shoulders painted scarlet, and had a piece of copper, bird wings, dried rattles from snakes, and shells tied in their hair.

FIGURE 4.3. Opechancanough's warriors dance in triumph around John Smith, in John Smith, *The Generall Historie of Virginia, New-England, and the Summer Isles . . .* (London, 1632). In the lower half of the image, Smith is tied to a tree about to be shot, and in the upper half, he is surrounded by warriors celebrating his capture. Note the warriors hold their bows, arrows, and war clubs, and the priests carry rattles as they dance.

Courtesy of Special Collections, John D. Rockefeller Jr. Library, Colonial Williamsburg Foundation.

Following the celebrations, Smith feasted with Opechancanough at his longhouse and afterward was taken to his lodging where his cloak, garters, and laces were returned to him along with his compass and writing tablet (notebook). Though closely guarded, he was treated well, and as they spent time together, Smith wrote of the growing "affection" between him and the chief. Opechancanough apparently showed much delight in "understanding the manner of our ships" and quizzed the Englishman: "*Casacunnakack, peya quagh acquintan uttasantasough.* In how many days will there come hither any more English ships?"[13] He questioned him on how the English crossed the ocean, about the earth and skies, and the white men's god. Then, in turn, he told Smith about his peoples' territories and the lands beyond, including word of "certain men clothed at a place called Ocanahonan."

"Clothed like me," Smith clarified, which perhaps indicated that some settlers of Sir Walter Ralegh's final attempt to found a colony in the Chesapeake Bay area twenty years earlier still survived in lands to the south. Finally, the chief mentioned that four or five days' journey from Rassawek was "a great turning of salt water," which Smith interpreted as credible evidence that the Pacific Ocean lay less than a week beyond the falls of the Powhatan River. The Englishman asked the chief if he could send a message to his compatriots at the fort, saying he wanted to assure his men he was well to avoid any possibility they might think he was dead and seek revenge. His actual intent, however, was to let them know what Opechancanough had told him, which if true offered news of astonishing opportunities awaiting them in the interior.[14]

Ignoring Smith's pleas to be returned to Jamestown, Opechancanough and his personal guard led him on a long trek across the frozen landscape, first north to the Youghtanund River and then to the Mattaponi. Along the way, they visited two hunting camps belonging to the peoples living along the rivers and the houses of the "Emperor of Powhatan," where tribute in the form of corn, deer skins, and other goods were stored. Opechancanough's purpose in showing the storehouses was probably to impress upon the Englishman the range and magnitude of their power, a stark contrast to the pitiful resources of the starving English at Jamestown.

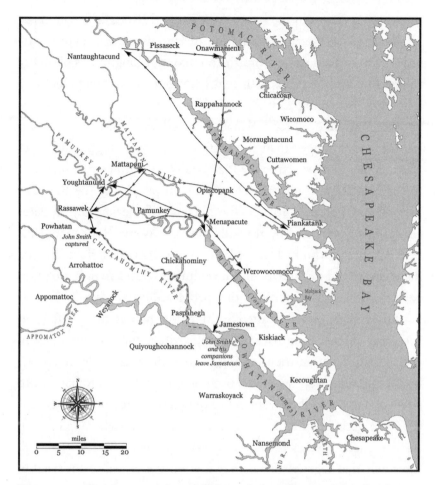

FIGURE 4.4. Opechancanough and Kekataugh lead Captain John Smith on a march across Tsenacommacah, December 1607. *Drawing by Jamie May.*

Smith voiced his desire to meet the great emperor as soon as possible but instead was taken back to Rassawek and from there, together with the entire camp, marched eastward to Menapacute, Opechancanough's principal residence located on Pamunkey Neck, called Sloping Hill by the Pamunkeys, at the confluence of the Youghtanund and Mattaponi Rivers.[15]

The large town was situated on a sandy hill that provided a pleasing vista of the surrounding rich lowlands and plains. To the west, the winding course of the lower Youghtanund River, "as broad as the Thames," had caused the formation of large marshes where multitudes of waterfowl nested. Smith counted four longhouses of eighty to one hundred feet in length that belonged to the great chief and a hundred belonging to the people. Transferred into the custody of another Pamunkey chief, Kekataugh, Smith was taken on a second journey, much longer than the first, back to the Youghtanund and Mattaponi and then east to the Piankatanks and after west and north to the Nantaughtacund and Onawmanient peoples of the Rappahannock and Potomac Rivers. The purpose of the journey, he later wrote, was occasioned by the kidnapping of some Rappahannocks by Englishmen who had entered the river a few years before. The Indians confirmed Smith was not the culprit, and Kekataugh took him back to Menapacute, visiting other peoples along the way.[16]

One further ordeal awaited Smith before he was allowed to meet the great chief: a lengthy and complex ritual that he described in vivid detail. Early in the morning, a great fire was made in a longhouse, and mats were spread on both sides of it. The guard had Smith sit on one mat and then went out of the house. "Presently came skipping in a great grim fellow, all painted over with coal, mingled with oil; and many Snakes and Weasels skins stuffed with moss, and all their tails tied together, so as they met on the crown of his head in a tassel; and round about the tassel was as a Coronet of feathers, the skins hanging round about his head, back, and shoulders, and in a manner covered his face; with a hellish voice and a rattle in his hand."

With "most strange gestures and passions," Smith continued, the priest "began his invocation, and environed the fire with a circle of meal," at which point "three more such like devils came rushing in with the like antique [antic] tricks, painted half black, half red: but all arrived and joined the singing and dancing." They danced around the Englishman "a pretty while," and then three more priests arrived and joined the singing and dancing. At last, all the priests "sat down right against him; three of them on the one hand of the chief Priest, and three on the other." Following more singing, "the chief Priest laid down five wheat corns [ears]," and then "straining his arms and hands with such violence that he sweat, and his veins swelled, he began a short Oration: at the conclusion they all gave a short groan; and then laid down three grains more." After that, they sang once again, which was followed by another oration, "ever laying down so many corns as before, till they had twice encircled the fire; that done, they took a bunch of little sticks prepared for that purpose, continuing still their devotion, and at the end of every song and Oration, they laid down a stick betwixt the divisions of Corn." Great cakes of deer suet, deer, and tobacco were thrown into the fire by the priest, accompanied by "many signs and demonstrations" and "vehement actions." Until night, "neither he nor they did eat or drink, and then they feasted merrily, with the best provisions they could make."

According to Smith, the ceremony continued for three days, "the meaning whereof the priests told him, was to know if he intended

FIGURE 4.5. Pamunkey priests' view of the world. *Drawing by Jamie May.*

them well or no." The circle of meal, he wrote, "signified their Country, the circles of corn the bounds of the Sea, and the sticks his Country. They imagined the world to be flat and round, like a trencher, and they in the midst." Having satisfied the priests, Smith was invited to the house of Opitchapam, another of Opechancanough's kinsmen and heir to the great chief, where he was lavishly feted.[17]

SHORTLY AFTER, SMITH was led to Werowocomoco, which means "place of the antler wearers," the great chief's capital on the Pamunkey River, where he was straightaway taken to the "Kings-house," all the while watched by more than two hundred "grim Courtiers" as if "he had been a monster." Once again, Smith described his experiences in detail. Before a fire, the "Emperor" lay proudly "on a Bedstead a foot high, upon ten or twelve Mats, richly hung with Many Chains of great Pearls about his neck and covered with a great Covering of *Rahaughcums* [raccoon skins]." At his head sat a young woman and at his feet another. On each side of the fire, the chief's men were ranged ten in a rank and behind them as many women, each wearing a great chain of white beads over their shoulders and "with all their heads and shoulders painted red; many of their heads bedecked with the white down of Birds." All the while, the great chief composed himself "with such a grave and Majestical countenance," Smith wrote, "as drove me into admiration to see such state in a naked Savage."

Chief Powhatan welcomed the English captain with "good words" and large platters of food and promised his friendship and to let him return to Jamestown within a few days. The "Queen of *Appamatuck*" brought him water to wash his hands, and another woman brought him a bunch of feathers to dry them. Powhatan had been greatly pleased by his kinsman Opechancanough's account of what Smith had told him and questioned the Englishman similarly.

In response to the question "Why had the English come?" Smith invented a story about having been in a fight "with the Spaniards our enemy" that had forced them to put into the Chesapeake Bay to make repairs. Directed upriver by friendly Kecoughtans who lived at the mouth of the Powhatan River, they continued traveling in their pinnace, a small boat, to replenish their water casks. But their pinnace sprang a leak, so they had camped temporarily at Jamestown to wait for the return of their leader, Captain Christopher Newport, whom Smith described as his father. Powhatan inquired why they had gone farther upriver in their boat, to which Smith replied that they had journeyed to "the other side of the main" or landmass, where there was salt water, to revenge the slaying of Captain Newport's child by the Monacans, ancient enemies of the Powhatans. By pretending to have already discovered the "back Sea" on a previous voyage, Smith was clearly hoping to learn more from the great chief.

Following a lengthy silence, Powhatan spoke. He described "Countries beyond the Falls" and other regions beyond his own chiefdom. Five to eight days away to the west, the headwaters of the Powhatan River "dashed amongst many stones and rocks" during storms that caused the waters to become brackish. Powhatan told Smith that the Anchanachuck people had slain Newport's son and that he, not the English, would revenge the killing. Upon the sea a "mighty Nation" called the Pocoughtronack, who "did eat men," made war against the peoples at the top of the bay, "under his territories," where the year before they had slain a hundred warriors. They shaved their heads and had long hair tied in a knot and carried swords "like Poleaxes." To the north of his lands were many kingdoms, and a great river flowed into the bay that issued from "mighty Mountains betwixt the two Seas," where men "with Short Coates, and Sleeves to the Elbows" passed in ships. To the south, Powhatan spoke of people clothed at "Ocanahonan," the countries of the "Mangoge" a day and a half away, "Chawwonock" two days, and the province of Roanoke six.

Near the southerly part of the "back Sea" was a land called "Anone" where, Powhatan said, "they have abundance of Brass" and walled houses like those of the English. "I requited his discourse," Smith wrote, "seeing what pride he had in his great and spacious Dominions, seeing that all he knew were under his Territories." In turn, Smith spoke of the large "territories of Europe" that were subject to his "great King whose subject I was," of their countless ships and manner of their wars. Captain Newport, he said, was the Werowance, king of all the waters, and at his greatness, Smith related haughtily, the chief "admired and [was] not a little feared."

FIGURE 4.6. Powhatan orders Captain John Smith to be slain, in John Smith, *The Generall Historie of Virginia, New-England, and the Summer Isles* . . . (London, 1632). At the bottom of the image, the famous scene of Pocahontas pleading for Smith's life is depicted. *Courtesy of Special Collections, John D. Rockefeller Jr. Library, Colonial Williamsburg Foundation.*

Following a discussion involving Powhatan, his councilors, and priests, two great stones were placed in front of the chief, and Smith was forced to lay his head on them. An illustration drawn years later shows two warriors standing over him with clubs ready to beat out his brains and another standing by with a bow and arrow. A large figure in the foreground indicates one of the great men, while Powhatan is seated in the background with his wives and warriors around him. At the bottom of the image, a diminutive figure almost obscured by the caption would play a major role in Smith's fable. "*Pocahontas* the Kings dearest daughter," he wrote years later, "when no entreaty could prevail, got his [Smith's] head in her arms, and laid her own upon his to save him from death: whereat the Emperor was contented he should live to make him hatchets, and her bells, beads, and copper." The chief then told Smith to abandon Jamestown and to live in a country called "Capahowasicke," a few miles downriver. He promised "to give me Corn, Venison, or what I wanted to feed us," Smith wrote. "Hatchets and Copper we should make him, and none should disturb us." Then he was released and permitted to return to Jamestown.

Another account by Smith from his *Generall Historie* offers a few additional details and several important variations. Two days after Smith's ordeal, Powhatan had him taken to a great house in the woods where he was left by himself. Shortly after, from behind a mat that divided the house, a dreadful noise was heard, at which Powhatan appeared painted black in a most hideous manner, "more like a devil then a man," Smith recalled. The chief told him they were friends and instructed him to go Jamestown and send him two great guns and a grindstone for which he would give him the country of Capahowosick and forever esteem him as his son Nantaquoud. Smith agreed, knowing that the Indians could not possibly transport cannons weighing a ton and a half to Werowocomoco, and was led back to the fort by a dozen guides early in the new year.[18]

SMITH'S INTERPRETATION OF his exchanges with Opechancanough and Powhatan, rich as they may be in descriptive detail, cannot, of course, be taken at face value. Besides conventional assumptions of European superiority that suffuse his writings, Smith took great pains to fashion himself as a resourceful and self-reliant leader, fully capable of managing "barbarous" Powhatans. Even in this he was frequently inconsistent, and his description and interpretation of events changed depending on when he wrote them. His earliest account, *A True Relation*, written only a few months after his capture, offers a far more sympathetic assessment of the Indians and what motivated them than his description in *The Generall Historie*, written a decade and a half later in very different circumstances. For much of the time he was in captivity, Smith could have been only vaguely aware of the significance of what was happening around him. With this in mind, an alternative version of Smith's ordeal may be proposed, one that retains much of the Englishman's narrative but drastically changes his interpretation of events by reversing the angle of vision and adopting instead the perspective of the two chiefs.

Opechancanough was probably sincere when he told Smith following his capture that he did not intend to kill him. He had likely heard reports previously of Smith from local peoples and knew that he was a principal leader of the intruders. It is even possible that Opechancanough and Powhatan had already decided on how they would deal with the English and the role that Smith would play in their strategy. Smith's impromptu discourse on the firmament, the skies and earth, multiplicity of nations, and sailing of ships across great oceans, a demonstration of European knowledge and his mastery of it, had nothing to do with his survival. Only the gift of his compass dial was significant, as Smith may have realized, for signaling his respect and entering into a social bond with the chief.

The well-established practice of gift giving throughout Indian communities of Virginia's coastal region allowed individuals, Indian and European, as well as peoples from different chiefdoms, to enter into social and political relationships, following a series of accepted conventions. First, a gift suitable to the occasion and person receiving it was offered; second, the gift and therefore the offer of a social bond was either accepted or rejected; and third, if the gift was accepted, the person or persons receiving it were expected to reciprocate in kind as a means of confirming the relationship. In Smith's case, Opechancanough recognized the compass as a formal gift appropriate to his status and reciprocated by sparing the Englishman's life and treating him as a man of high status, a captain. Smith mentioned several times the large quantities of bread and venison he was given, more than would serve "twenty men," he commented; he was granted extensive access to the chief, allowing each man to probe the other for useful information. Opechancanough wanted to know what the English were planning, and Smith was intent on learning about the potential riches of Virginia, themes that would be rehearsed again during Powhatan's meeting with the Englishman at Werowocomoco.[19]

The discussions the two chiefs conducted with Smith take on added meaning if one considers not only what was said (or apparently said) and what was not. Why did Opechancanough and Powhatan mention the proximity of a sea beyond the mountains, and "people clothed," clearly a reference to Europeans, possibly English, at "Ocanahonan," Chowanoc, and Roanoke to the south of their lands? Were they seeking to impress upon Smith the greatness of their territories and power? If they were hoping the English would leave in the near future, why would they provide the very sort of information that might persuade the English to stay: stories of a passage through the mountains to the South Sea and of the survival of settlers from Ralegh's colony, the lost colony of Roanoke, who, if they and their descendants still survived among Indian peoples, might also possess valuable information about gold and silver mines in the interior? For his part, why did Smith refer to being overpowered in a sea battle with the Spanish as an excuse for the English arriving in the Chesapeake Bay when he could have simply claimed that bad weather had forced them to find refuge? Had he already picked up from the Indians stories of the Spaniards' brutal incursion decades earlier? Smith also depicts the chiefs as largely ignorant of European technology. Opechancanough, he wrote, took great "delight" in learning about English ships and his description of the world and seas, just as Powhatan was "much de- lighted" by his brother chief's account of what Smith had told him.

Caution about what to reveal and what should remain secret was to be expected in such talks. Although Smith portrayed his conver- sations with the two chiefs as frank and open, even friendly, this can hardly have been the case. Too much was at stake. For Smith, the overwhelming priority was to stay alive, and in this regard, he had little choice but to agree to Powhatan's demands. At the same time, in his record of the exchanges, Smith could not risk being viewed by his countrymen as a turncoat. He therefore had to fashion his ap- parent cooperation with the chiefs as an inventive strategy to secure friendly relations, procure food, and obtain precious information. It is entirely possible, therefore, that he gave the chiefs far more detail about English objectives than appears in his writings.[20]

For Powhatan, one priority stood out above all others: the ab- sorption of the English within his chiefdom, which suggests the two chiefs had come to an agreement about how to deal with the English in view of the opportunities they might offer. In the great chief's longhouse at Werowocomoco, with Opechancanough present, Pow- hatan was explicit about his expectations. The English were to leave their fort at Paspahegh and "live with him upon his River," where they would inhabit a country in an underpopulated area of the York River at Capahowasicke. Smith would be the chief of the English tribe and be called Nantaquoud, thereby formalizing the social bond between the chief and Smith in a fictional father-son relationship.

This explanation also clarifies the meaning of Smith's experiences in the weeks before the meeting with Powhatan. The marches he was forced to make to various towns and hunting camps in the heartland of Powhatan's territories as well as the priestly ritual at Menapacute, as has been suggested by the anthropologist Frederic Gleach, were connected to an extended and elaborate reordering of the Powhatan world that allowed the incorporation of the English into the chief's territories. During the ceremony at Menapacute, priests' use of processed corn and unprocessed corn kernels together with small sticks in concentric circles illustrated the relationship between the Powhatans of the innermost circle of processed corn with non-Powhatan Indian peoples, represented by corn kernels, and the English of the outermost circle, depicted by sticks. During the three days of the ritual, the priests determined that the English did not pose a threat and could be safely brought into the Powhatan world.[21]

The remaining element of the Englishmen's incorporation focused on Smith at Werowocomoco. Historians have long debated whether Smith's account of his mock execution and rescue by Pocahontas actually happened or was merely a dramatic fabrication. The ceremony makes sense, however, in the context of the ritualized adoption of the English as a Powhatan tribe and of Smith as a Powhatan chief. Pocahontas would not have thrown herself impetuously across Smith's body to protect him; rather, her actions would have been carefully considered and scripted by Powhatan and his councilors. She was probably chosen because, as an intelligent young woman and daughter of the chief, she had been designated as one of the cultural mediators between the Powhatans and English, going back and forth from Werowocomoco to Jamestown. The mock execution, then, makes sense as a ritual that symbolized the death of Smith as an English captain and his rebirth as the Powhatan chief Nantaquoud of Capahowasicke.[22]

Two days later at a great house in the woods nearby, Powhatan made his demands clear. Now that Smith was bound by ties of family and duty to the chief, he was to go to the fort and arrange to send him two great guns and a grindstone, the latter for sharpening tools and metal weapons, as confirmation of their new accord. Here was the real reason why Opechancanough and Powhatan wanted to subordinate the English and bring them into their chiefdom: access to European weapons. They had witnessed the firepower of ships and knew the settlers had many cannons within the fort. In the long run, if they could secure a regular supply of weapons and gunpowder, they would not only prove a match for any hostile European newcomers but also for their formidable enemies to the west and north, the Monacans and Mannahoacs in the piedmont and Iroquoian peoples at the head of the bay. Employing European weaponry, the Powhatans' expansion of their territories would be limited only by distance and supplies. Given the weakness of the Englishmen's position at the end of 1607, the potential benefits from keeping them alive outweighed the danger they posed, at least for the time being.[23]

CAPTAIN SMITH WAS badly mistaken in assuming Opechancanough and Powhatan had only a limited understanding of European technology. The actions of the two chiefs point to a very different conclusion, one that underlines their acute perception of their severe technological deficit in weaponry and ships. Both were well aware of the increase of European voyages in American waters during their lifetimes; Powhatan hinted as much when he referred to men dressed in coats with sleeves to the elbows who sailed in ships in the far north, which was probably a reference to the Great Lakes and French traders. Both were familiar with the Spanish, as were the peoples who suffered from the retribution meted out by Governor Menéndez's warships in 1572. And both would have been aware of the devastating impact of successive Spanish entradas in the southeastern and southwestern provinces of North America.

Bearing in mind the challenges of communicating in a strange language and the highly selective sharing of information by the two chiefs, it is hardly surprising that Smith grossly misjudged the Indians' knowledge of Europeans. But what neither Smith nor any of the English leaders could have possibly imagined was that in the person of Opechancanough they confronted a chief who had experienced living among Europeans for nearly a decade. He had crossed the Atlantic many times, sailed in American waters from the Gulf of Mexico to the Chesapeake Bay, had lived in Spain and New Spain, was highly educated, and had witnessed precisely how the Spanish treated Indian peoples in their domains in Mexico, Cuba, and La Florida. The English interpreted his name as Opechancanough, but the Spanish had first called him Paquiquineo before giving him the name Don Luís.[24]

CHAPTER 5

Stratagems and Subterfuge

P OWHATAN AND OPECHANCANOUGH (PAQUIQUINEO) BUILT the paramount chiefdom together.[1] Powhatan was described by William Strachey, the colony's secretary, as tall and "of a sad aspect, round fat visage, with many gray hairs." In his youth, Strachey wrote, he had been "a strong and able savage, sinewy, active, and of a daring spirit." Like Captain John Smith, he emphasized the chief's natural authority but went further in describing him in quasi-mystical terms, contrasting his barbarous state with an "Impression of the divine nature" within him. The Englishman's reference to divinity was echoed by his peoples' own acknowledgment of him as a priestly as well as secular ruler, "one who dreams." Uniquely, his authority derived not only on his lineage but also his connection to the spirit world, which endowed him with great powers.[2]

Opechancanough was by far the most important of Powhatan's close relatives. His precise relationship to the great chief is unknown; he may have been a full brother, shared the same mother, or was a cousin of the chief. According to Indian oral history recorded at the end of the century, Opechancanough was thought to be a "Prince of a Foreign Nation" who "came to them a great Way from the South-West." Parsing their words, Robert Beverley, a wealthy planter-merchant who recorded their account, supposed him to have "come from the *Spanish Indians*, somewhere near *Mexico*, or the Mines of *St. Barbe*." The "mines of Saint Barbe," silver mines, were close to the border town of Santa Barbara, the northernmost Spanish settlement in Mexico in the 1560s that commonly served as the starting point for expeditions farther north into the vast interior later known as Texas and New Mexico. An English report from two and a half decades earlier provides additional evidence about Opechancanough's background in describing him as "no less a war captain than he who conquered all along from Mexico thither." Both descriptions were clearly references to his experiences in New Spain.[3]

Based on his knowledge of the Spanish and extraordinary leadership capabilities, Opechancanough occupied a vital position as Powhatan's war chief. As in the case of many Indian societies, the Powhatans were ruled by a peace chief and a war chief. The former was responsible mostly for internal matters related to the chiefdom and was the superior of the two, while the latter oversaw external affairs, advising on relations with outsiders, especially in cases of potential threats and conflict. Because Powhatan society was frequently on a war footing, his role as war chief gave him a commanding voice in all superior councils. He and Chief Powhatan, aided by lesser advisers and priests, would make all the major decisions impacting the chiefdom. Finally, in additional to his putative kinship with Powhatan and his role as war chief, Opechancanough's influence stemmed from being the principal chief of the Pamunkeys and their elite warrior corps of nearly three hundred men. Described as "of large Stature and noble Presence" who was "Perfectly skilled in the Art of Governing," Beverley wrote, he "caused all the Indians far and near to dread his Name, and had them all entirely in his Subjection."[4]

HE DID NOT have long to wait for an answer to the question he had put to John Smith at Rassawek: How many days until more ships come? On January 2, 1608, the *John and Francis* arrived at Jamestown Island, captained by the experienced mariner Christopher Newport, who had led the initial expedition to Virginia the previous year. The arrival of more Englishmen (there were no women) presented Chief Powhatan and Opechancanough with a conundrum. Given the new-comers' relatively small numbers and continuing dependence on his people for food, they did not yet pose a threat. If more came, how-ever, the balance of power might start to change. Powhatan opted to keep a close eye on the settlement and especially the movement of ships. "Watchful he is over us," Strachey remarked, "Concerning which he has his Sentinels, that at what time so ever any of our boats, pinnaces or ships, come in, fall down, or make up the river, give the Alarum." For the time being, the two chiefs chose to continue their diplomatic approach, watch and wait, and look for opportunities to bind the English closer to them and thereby channel their valuable trade goods into their treasure houses.[5]

Jamestown was managed and sponsored by the Virginia Com-pany of London. The legal instrument, a royal charter granted by King James I in April 1606, granted the company exclusive rights to establish a colony in the mid-Atlantic region centered on the Ches-apeake Bay, with the proviso that no other European nation had already taken possession of it. Indian peoples were not considered to have rights of occupation owing to what Europeans considered their heathen and savage nature. By the tenets of what passed for international law at the time, supplemented by the authority of suc-cessive monarchs and church prelates, only Christians were entitled to take ownership of "new lands" in America, the fiction being that by acquiring the Indians' lands Europeans would be able to convert them to the true faith. Although overseen by a royal council and the king's privy council, the company was not a state-sponsored ven-ture, such as the Spanish American colonies. Instead, it followed a corporate structure that gave its leading officers enormous latitude in conducting their own affairs, aided by the Crown's preference to remain largely disengaged.

The company was first and foremost a commercial venture. Investors looked forward to reaping handsome returns from the natural resources of the region, trade with Indians, and possibly the discovery of untold riches yet to be found in the interior. Led by some of the wealthiest merchants and influential statesmen of the day and inspired by a generation of promoters exalting the social and economic benefits of colonies, the company anticipated spectacular discoveries that might ultimately surpass those of the Spanish. Its leaders included Robert Cecil, earl of Salisbury, King James's first minister, and Sir Thomas Smythe, one of London's greatest merchants. These men were confident that, in the long term, thriving industries could be established in America and valuable products exported back to England, reducing the country's reliance on imported raw materials and manufactures from other parts of Europe. In the short term, like Spanish and French explorers before them, they looked to discover vast wealth in the unknown lands (to Europeans) of North America.[6]

Yet when Captain Newport arrived back at Jamestown in the opening days of 1608, rather than finding profitable commodities and a thriving settlement, he found the colony teetering on the brink of collapse. Of the one hundred or so men he had left behind when he returned to London six months earlier, only thirty-eight still survived, many in desperately poor health. Nothing of tangible value had been produced or discovered. Bitter infighting had broken out among the leaders, leading to the overthrow of the colony's first president, Edward Maria Wingfield, and the execution of a member of the colony's governing council thought to be a Spanish spy. Captain Smith would have shared the same fate when he returned to the fort after his captivity among the Powhatans, on suspicion of being a spy for the Indians, had he not been saved by Newport's timely arrival the same day.[7]

The *John and Francis* brought provisions and one hundred men, whom Newport quickly put to work constructing public buildings and the settlers' lodgings after a disastrous fire had burned much of the fort to the ground, leaving them dangerously exposed to an "extreme frost." After the setbacks, Newport was doubtless encouraged by news of Smith's discussions with Powhatan and Opechancanough, probably the only ray of hope in the generally dismal scene that confronted him. The two chiefs, Newport rightly believed, held the key to the colony's future. Powhatan sent small amounts of food once or twice a week, half for Smith and half for Captain Newport, the latter as a sign of respect for Smith's "father," and invited both men to Werowocomoco to accept more supplies of corn to help them and their men get through the rest of the winter. The chief did not want them to abandon the settlement just yet but rather sought an opportunity to get what he wanted from them and assess the potential of future relations.[8]

Wasting little time, Newport and Smith, together with thirty or forty armed men, sailed down the peninsula, rounded the headland to the mouth of the Pamunkey (York) River, and proceeded to Werowocomoco. Smith went ashore first with half the men to prepare the way for Newport. Surrounded by his wives and leading men who "made signs of great joy," Powhatan received the Englishman in his longhouse. Smith presented the chief with a red suit, a hat, and a white greyhound, all brought from England for the occasion, which, according to the Englishman, delighted the chief's councilors and affirmed their "perpetual" league and friendship with the English. Then Powhatan spoke: "Your kind visitation does much content me, but where is your father whom I much desire to see, is he not come with you?" Smith replied that Newport remained on board the ship, moored by the riverbank, and would come the next day. With a "merry countenance," Powhatan asked about the cannons that Smith had promised when he had been released and returned to Jamestown. Smith said that he had kept his word and offered Powhatan's men four demi-culverins, large cannons weighing more than a ton and a half each, to take back to Werowocomoco. But, he added drily, "they refused to take them." The chief laughed and asked for smaller cannons, which Smith granted, knowing the Indians would not be able to carry them either.

In turn, Smith requested the "corn and ground" he had been promised at their previous meeting when Powhatan had promised to make him a chief. Powhatan agreed he should have them but first demanded the soldiers lay down their arms at his feet, as did all his subjects. Smith objected, saying "that was a ceremony our enemies desired, but never our friends," yet if the chief doubted the Englishmen's friendship, "my Father," Smith said, referring to Newport, "would give him a child of his, in full assurance of our loves, and not only that, but when he should think it convenient, we would deliver under his subjection the Country of Manacam [Monacan] and Pocoughtaonack his enemies." According to Smith, his response so pleased the king that with "a loud oration he proclaimed me a weroance of Powhatan, and that all his subjects should so esteem us, and no man account us strangers nor Paspaheghans, but Powhatans, and that the Corn, women, and Country, should be to us as his own people." The *mamanatowick* (paramount chief) thereby seemingly affirmed Smith as one of his chiefs and the English as Powhatans. English guns, copper, and other prestige trade goods, which Powhatan and Opechancanough desired above all else, were far too valuable to be allowed to circulate among peoples outside their direct control.[9]

The next day, Newport landed at Werowocomoco and like Smith was greeted warmly. Thirteen-year-old Thomas Savage was presented to the chief, who said he would treat him "as his Son," and in return the chief gave the English his able servant, Namontack, who would subsequently travel to England with Newport. Both sides commonly employed adolescents to live with the other to learn their language and ways, which was of vital importance in providing an edge in negotiations. Trading took place the following day, but relations were less convivial than earlier. Powhatan once again inquired why the English came armed, at which Newport, conceding the chief might feel threatened, withdrew his men back to the river half a mile from the longhouse. Powhatan wanted to see all the hatchets and copper the English had brought before deciding how much corn he would give, making clear he held the upper hand: "Captain Newport it is not agreeable to my greatness, in this peddling manner to trade for trifles; and I esteem you also a great Weroance. Therefore, lay me down all your commodities together; what I like I will take, and in recompense give you what I think fitting their value." Despite Smith's advice to the contrary, Newport agreed, "thinking to out brave" Powhatan "in ostentation of greatness, and so to bewitch him with his bounty." As a result, Smith remarked, the chief "having his desire, valued his corn at such a rate, that I think it better cheap in Spain: for we had not four bushels for that we expected to have twenty hogsheads." Smith was concerned that the great chief might reasonably believe he had the measure of Newport and if he could trick him in trade he could fool him in war. Trade like diplomacy was a game of bluff and stratagems to best the opponent, and Powhatan had effortlessly outmaneuvered the English leader.[10]

Newport's response to Powhatan was not a matter of naiveté, however. His objective was quite different from Smith's. In contrast to Smith, who was generally concerned about terms of trade and the balance of power between the English and Indians, Newport had returned to Virginia to find precious minerals, and he needed the support and advice of the Powhatans to have any chance of success. He did not want to jeopardize good relations over a few barrels of corn and was therefore content to buy their goodwill with copper pots in return for information and possibly an alliance against the Monacans. He was likely pleased, therefore, by Powhatan's offer to send Opechancanough and one hundred Pamunkey warriors to assist the one hundred fifty English soldiers thought to be sufficient to undertake an expedition into the piedmont. The plan ultimately came to nothing, but Newport made his objective clear. He would continue to placate Powhatan in the hope they would help him find the gold or silver he believed lay somewhere in or near the western mountains.[11]

The encounter at Werowocomoco reveals important clues about each party's priorities. Powhatan had set out to impress Newport and Smith with his greatness. Each of the English was given enough food to feed twenty men. "Victuals you must know," Smith wrote, "is all their wealth, and the greatest kindness they could show us." Leading Smith to the river, Powhatan proudly pointed to his many large war canoes that he sent over the bay to collect tribute from chiefs on the Eastern Shore. Subjugated peoples were forced to pay regular tribute payments—pearls, beads, skins, venison, corn, and tobacco—which were stored in his temples and treasure houses at Orapax, Uttamussak, and elsewhere. Powhatan would in turn give tribute goods from his treasure houses to lesser chiefs, warriors, and priests, as an effective means of rewarding those he favored.

After leaving Werwocomoco, the English made their way upriver to Cinquoteck and Menapacute in the territory of the Pamunkeys. Opechancanough was also eager to display his generosity when he entertained Newport and Smith and came with his family to welcome the English personally. The two leaders and their men were honored with a lavish feast, and when it was time the next day for them to leave, Opechancanough, Smith wrote, said his good-byes with "what words or signs of love he could express."

Why such princely receptions? The two chiefs would not have believed Newport or Smith's professions of friendship as anything more than short-term and tactical, no different from their own. Their key objective remained to learn as much as possible about English plans and secure access to their valuable trade goods and, hopefully, firearms for as long as possible. The Spanish Jesuits had been killed with the axes they had given to the Indians, and likewise the English would eventually be slaughtered with their own firearms and swords. The two chiefs' aim from the beginning was to rid themselves of the English, but not before they had accumulated as many weapons and goods from the English as possible.[12]

IN THE SIX months that passed before Powhatan, Opechancanough, and the two English leaders met again at Werowocomoco, the entire complexion of their relationship was transformed. Powhatan was angered by the failure of Smith to supply the cannons and other weapons promised in previous meetings. At Newport's departure from Jamestown in early April 1608, to return once again to London, the chief had sent him twenty turkeys, "to express his love," in exchange for the same number of swords to be sent to him, which Newport ordered to be done. After similarly sending twenty turkeys to Smith, Powhatan was outraged when the Englishman refused to provide any swords. This refusal amounted to a grave insult and brazen challenge to the chief's authority.

The consequences of Smith's refusal were soon evident. Powhatan ordered those of his men who regularly frequented the fort to steal as many weapons and tools as they were able to carry, including axes, spades, hatchets, and swords. They took them by stealth or occasionally openly by force when the English were at work, Smith wrote. Two Indians, interrogated by the English, "Amocis the Paspaheyan," a spy of Powhatan's, and Macanoe, who was a councilor of the Paspaheghs, confirmed that the weapons and tools were then delivered to Powhatan and that he was plotting to kill the English leaders after Captain Newport returned to the colony. The chief would invite the English to Werowocomoco, "where with a great feast he would so enamor Captain Newport and his men, as they should seize on him, and the like traps would be laid for the rest." Meanwhile, Paspahegh and Chickahominy warriors would cut the throats of the men in the fort at Jamestown with their own weapons.

Whether or not Powhatan was plotting to kill the English at this time is uncertain. Against a background of rumors, half-truths, and deceit, the reality is impossible to untangle. Powhatan dispatched Pocahontas to the fort with an envoy named Rawhunt, "of subtle wit and crafty [clever] understanding," to deny any responsibility of wrongdoing. Rawhunt told Smith (according to Smith) that Powhatan "loved and respected" him and that "I should not doubt [in] anyway his kindness." Opechancanough also sent greetings and a "token" of his affection, his shooting glove and bracer (vambrace). Perhaps, as Powhatan suggested, some of his chiefs had acted on their own behalf in threatening the English. The Paspaheghs and Chickahominies in particular, Amocis said, hated them. Whatever doubt surrounded any plans to kill Newport, Smith, and the rest of the English, it is nevertheless clear that the two chiefs remained determined to acquire weapons and thereby make themselves invulnerable to future European incursions, whether English or Spanish.[13]

Shortly after Newport's departure, another ship, the *Phoenix* captained by Francis Nelson, arrived at Jamestown with an additional twenty men and provisions, raising the number of settlers in the fort to approximately one hundred sixty, a figure sufficiently large to cause the chiefs growing concern. A few months later, a group of men led by Captain Smith made two extensive explorations of the Chesapeake Bay in a single-mast barge, during which they encountered many of Powhatan's subject chiefdoms as well as powerful Indian peoples outside of his domains, such as the Massawomecks and Susquehannocks. Powhatan and Opechancanough would have been well aware of the risk such encounters posed to their own efforts to monopolize relations with Indians beyond their borders and the threat to their control of the region.

Meanwhile, news from the colony brought by Newport and Nelson to England in the summer and fall of 1608 would lead to another major threat to the two chiefs, one not easily assessed or countered.

Plans had begun in London about the future of Jamestown that would have an enormous impact on Powhatan and Opechancanough's chiefdom but which the chiefs had no possibility of discovering.

INITIAL REPORTS FROM the colony had painted a rosy picture of Virginia's unsurpassed fertility and abundance that seemingly promised "infinite treasure" to settlers and investors alike. Such was the optimism, it was confidently asserted that England would become in time "more Rich and Renowned than any kingdom in all Europe." Investors' hopes were soon dashed, however, when they learned the "ore" thought to be gold brought back to England was worthless, nothing more than "gilded dirt," Smith wrote. Even so, expectations of finding precious minerals did not entirely fade but switched instead to the possibility of discoveries in the interior, in the piedmont and mountains. Newport's accounts of his discussions with Powhatan and Opechancanough and a sketch map of the country by Captain Smith, which he combined with a lengthy written description of his adventures in Virginia, entitled *A True Relation*, sparked huge interest among Virginia Company leaders and led to renewed hope of great wealth.[14]

Smith's map, which he had drawn sometime before the summer of 1608, detailed the colony's major rivers, showing the Powhatan (James), Chickahominy, Pamunkey (York), and Mattaponi. Towns and villages visited by Smith during his march in captivity or on trading expeditions from Jamestown were marked along their upper courses. To the north, the crude rendering of the Toppahannock (Rappahannock) and Patawomeck (Potomac) Rivers suggest only a vague understanding of the landscape. But what would have caught the eye of London investors was not the lay of the land but a series of notations that seemed to confirm what he had been told by Opechancanough and Powhatan. At the very top of the map, along the edge of the paper, a roughly drawn coastline is labeled, "Here the salt water beats into the river amongst these rocks being the south sea." Where the Powhatan River flows into the sea it appears to take the form of a delta bordered to the immediate south by mountains. To the south of the Powhatan River (bottom left), a similarly crude rendering depicts the lands of the Chowanocs and Tuscaroras, who lived throughout the coastal plain of what is now North Carolina. It was in relation to this region that Smith's notations reveal specific information about the whereabouts of survivors of John White's 1587 colony. He wrote on the map on the southern bank of the Powhatan River "here Paspahegh and 2 of our men landed to go to Panawiock"; near what may be the Roanoke River, he noted "here the king of Paspahegh reported our men to be and went to see"; and farther south at Pakerackanick, he wrote "here remain 4 men clothed that came from Roanoke to Okanahowan." The map included new information derived from the report of two men sent by Smith south on an expedition led by the Paspahegh chief Wowinchopunck in January 1608.[15]

Although the search party was unable to make contact with survivors, Smith may have believed a future expedition would fare better. In any event, knowing that leaders of the Virginia Company would be most eager to locate one or more of the lost colonists, Smith considered such information sufficiently important to include on his sketch. Having lived in Indian country for twenty years, the colonists would have extensive connections with local peoples who had sheltered and traded with them. Indian peoples of "South Virginia" hostile to the Powhatans might well know of mines in the interior or a river passage to the great sea in the west. Finding survivors of the Roanoke colony would enable Jamestown settlers to draw upon their local knowledge and "open the womb and bowels of this country" to the great benefit of the company and the English nation.[16]

Consequently, when Newport arrived back in Virginia in early October 1608, he carried instructions from London to continue the search for precious mines, a river passage through the landmass to the Pacific, and survivors of the lost colony. First, however, he was to resume efforts to win over Powhatan and, if possible, garner more information about the interior. Captain Smith was dispatched to Werowocomoco with an invitation to the chief to visit Jamestown and receive gifts supposedly sent to him by King James. Smith returned Powhatan's young envoy, Namontack, and mentioned that the king's gifts would be the occasion to form an alliance against their common enemies, the Monacans. Powhatan responded bluntly: "If your King have sent me Presents, I also am a King, and this is my land: 8 days I will stay to receive them. Your Father is to come to me, not I to him, nor yet to your Fort, neither will I bite at such a bait." Fully aware why the English were keen to forge an alliance to attack the Monacans and march inland, he added, "as for the Monacans I can revenge my own injuries." Moreover, there was no salt water beyond the mountains, he said, "the relations you have had from my people are false."[17]

Smith returned to Jamestown with Powhatan's dispiriting message. Not to be deterred, however, Newport agreed to the great chief's terms and began planning an elaborate piece of theater that involved as the central scene the "coronation" of Powhatan. From the colonists' point of view, the ceremony was intended to confirm English recognition of Powhatan's preeminence among his own peoples while at the same time symbolizing his allegiance to James I. Yet when Newport and Smith, escorted by a well-armed guard of fifty men, arrived at Werowocomoco, they found the great chief unwilling to play his appointed role.

Smith described the farce that ensued. The gifts brought from England were laid before Powhatan and "his Bason and Ewer, Bed and furniture set up." The chief strenuously resisted wearing the scarlet cloak and other clothes brought for the ceremony until Namontack eventually persuaded him it was safe to put them on. "But a foul trouble there was to make him kneel to receive his crown,"

Smith observed, "he neither knowing the majesty nor meaning of a Crown, nor bending of the knee, endured so many persuasions, examples, and instructions, as tired them all; at last by leaning hard on his shoulders, he a little stooped, and three having the crown in their hands put it on his head." In response, Powhatan gave Newport "his old shoes and his mantel [cloak]" together with a few bushels of corn. Yet, he would not agree to help him discover the Monacans, "refusing to lend him either men or guides" other than Namontack.[18]

Powhatan had outwitted Newport once more and in so doing had barely concealed his contempt. He had made the English come to him, taken their gifts, and given them nothing of any worth in return. He completely subverted the meaning of the ritual by receiving the gifts as tribute, which afterward were stored in his treasure house at Orapax as potent symbols of his dominion over the newcomers. An English youth living with the Indians as an interpreter later recalled that every spring at the sowing of the corn, the chief went among his people wearing the crown and dispensing gifts to those he favored. Newport was no kingmaker, but as it turned out, any efforts to bring the chief into a mutually beneficial alliance were now too little too late. Even as he took part in the coronation charade, Powhatan was already making preparations to rid himself of the English for good.[19]

THE TRADE IN corn, so vital to English survival, was cut off. Aware that two hundred men lived in the fort short of provisions as another bitterly cold winter set in, Powhatan and Opechancanough believed the time was auspicious to starve them into submission. Additionally, the chiefs were now getting a steady supply of commodities they wanted from the fort. While Newport's ship, the *Mary and Margaret*, was in Jamestown, the mariners, some of the colonists, and local Indians had bartered for hatchets and all sorts of goods that had been brought over from London at the expense of the company. The sailors consumed stores meant for the settlers and sold to the Indians anything they wanted, including tools, pike heads, knives, and even powder and shot. Smith was infuriated. During the two months the ship was in port, "of two or three hundred Axes, Chisels, Hoes, and Pick-axes," he complained, "scarce twenty could be found."[20]

Cutting off food supplies was one component of Powhatan and Opechancanough's strategy; the other was killing their leader John Smith. With the departure of Newport in early December, the plan was put into effect. Smith was again invited to meet Powhatan, who promised to fill his barge with corn if he would build him an English-style house and bring a grindstone, fifty swords, cannons, and copper. Knowing full well he might be walking into a trap, Smith nevertheless opted to take the risk and dispatched a group of men ahead to build the house before setting off in a pinnace and two barges. Arriving at Werowocomoco the following month, Smith and his men found the river frozen nearly half a mile from the shore, forcing them to wade through icy water and mud to reach the shore. Powhatan was unwelcoming and asked why they had come and when they would be leaving, saying he did not send for them and had no corn for trade. Looking over the goods they had brought, including a copper kettle, the chief was unimpressed. He was not interested in any of the goods unless they were part of a trade that included guns and swords. He pointed out that a basket of corn was far more valuable to him than a basket of copper because he "could eat his corn, but not his copper."

Smith needed food and Powhatan wanted more English weapons, but there was much more at stake, as they both knew. Smith continued the bartering by emphasizing his "love" for the chief but ended with a thinly veiled threat:

Powhatan, though I had many courses to have made my provision, yet believing your promises to supply my wants, I neglected all, to satisfy your desire, and to testify my love, I sent you my men for your building, neglecting my own: what your people had you have engrossed, forbidding them our trade, . . . As for swords, and guns, I told you long ago, I had none to spare. And you shall know, those I have, can keep me from want, yet steal, or wrong you I will not, nor dissolve that friendship, we have mutually promised.

Powhatan reassured Smith that he and his people would supply them with what they could spare within two days but made his doubts of the Englishman's true purpose clear:

Yet Captain Smith . . . *some doubt I have of your coming hither, that makes me not so kindly seek to relieve you as I would; for many do inform me, your coming is not for trade, but to invade my people and possess my Country* [my italics], who dare not come to bring you corn, seeing you thus armed with your men. To clear us of this fear, leave aboard your weapons, for here they are needless we being all friends and forever Powhatans.

This conversation between Powhatan and Smith is the most extensive verbatim exchange between the two men and stands as one of the most remarkable recorded between an Indian chief and English leader in this period. Although we cannot know whether the voice of Powhatan as recorded by Smith is authentic, it is the closest we can come to hearing the chief's words from his own lips, and for that reason it is worth quoting at length. First, the chief reflected on peace and war:

Captain Smith, you may understand that I having seen the death of all my people thrice, and not anyone living of these three generations but myself; I know the difference of Peace and War better than any in my Country. But now I am old and ere long must die, my brethren, namely Opitchapam, Opechancanough, and Kekataugh, my two sisters, and their two daughters, are distinctly [respectively] each other's successors. I wish their experience no less than mine, and your love to them no less than mine to you. But this rumor from Nansemund, that you are come to destroy my Country, [did] so much frighten all my people as they dare not visit you. What will it avail you to take that by force you may quickly have by love, or to destroy them that provide you food. What can you get by war, when we can hide our provisions and fly to the woods? whereby you must famish by wronging us your friends. And why are you thus jealous of our loves seeing us unarmed, and both do, and are willing still to feed you, with that you cannot get but by our labors?

Powhatan had lived a long life, longer than any of his people, he pointed out, and had learned the benefits of peace compared to war through hard experience. This was a dubious claim given that he had been at war with neighboring peoples for thirty years as he had pieced together his extensive territories. He put to Smith stark questions: Would the English survive long without the help of his people? Could they provide for themselves? A similar argument was made by "Ocanindge," the orator (spokesman) for the Paspahegh chief, Wowinchopunck, a few months later: "We know you cannot live if you want our harvest, and that relief we bring you; if you promise us peace we will believe you, if you proceed in revenge, we will abandon the Country." But the most telling of Powhatan's speech was the reference to a rumor from the eastern part of his chiefdom, "that you are come to destroy my Country." Powhatan had been warned a year earlier by his *quioccosuks* (priests) that "from the Chesapeake Bay a Nation should arise, which would dissolve and give end" to his empire. The "devilish Oracle," as William Strachey later reported it, had led directly to the destruction of the Chesapeakes about the same time the English arrived in the bay. Many of his people, the chief told Smith, believed the English came as invaders not traders. How could they be trusted?[21]

Smith emphasized again his love for Powhatan and his people despite their failure to supply the colony with food as had been promised. He disregarded the chief's view of the English as adopted Powhatans and questioned the assertion the English could survive only if they remained on friendly terms. They could take what they wanted by force if they chose but preferred to live in peace. Knowing the colony was once again on the brink of starvation, Powhatan was hardly persuaded by Smith's argument and spoke of his disappointment in him:

> I never used any Werowance so kindly as yourself; yet from you I receive the least kindness of any. Captain Newport gave me swords, copper, cloths, a bed, tools, or what I desired, ever taking what I offered him, and would send away his guns when I entreated him: none doth deny to lay at my feet (or do) what I desire, but only you, of whom I have nothing, but what you regard not, and yet you have whatsoever you demand. Captain Newport you call father, and so you call me, but I see for all us both, you will do what you list [want], and we must both seek to content you: but if you intend so friendly as you say, send hence your arms that I may believe you, for you see the love I bear you, doth cause me thus nakedly to forget myself.

By this time, both men saw little point in continuing negotiations. Smith was convinced (rightly) the Powhatans were simply waiting for an opportunity to "cut his throat." Meanwhile, he had decided that his best course was to surprise the chief, take him hostage, and make his escape with as much corn as possible. Dissembling until his men were ready to leave, he replied:

> Powhatan, you must know as I have but one God, I honor but one king; and I live not here as your subject, but as your friend, to pleasure you with what I can: by the gifts you bestow on

me, you gain more then by trade; yet would you visit me as I do you, you should know it is not our customs to sell courtesy as a vendible commodity. Bring all your Country with you for your guard, I will not dislike of it as being over jealous. But to content you, tomorrow I will leave my arms, and trust to your promise. I call you father indeed, and as a father you shall see I will love you, but the small care you had of such a child, caused my men [to] persuade me to shift for myself.

These were the last words the two men spoke to one another. Powhatan left Werowocomoco with his wives and children while Smith, having failed to seize the chief, escaped ambush and fled back to his pinnace with his men and some provisions.[22]

The chief had decided that Smith's usefulness had come to an end. He had managed to win over four settlers, the "German" wood-workers who had built his house, and offered them much the same incentives as he had Smith a little over a year before. They would have food, shelter, and safety and avoid the fate of those who remained at the fort. In return, they would bring him all the weapons and tools he desired. Returning to Werowocomoco, the chief immediately dispatched two of the Germans to Jamestown to take as much as they could carry and persuade others to join them. If Powhatan could not get what he wanted from Smith, he would look to Smith's men instead and steal weapons just as Smith stole the Indians' corn. As a consequence, the chief quickly amassed some three hundred hatchets, fifty swords, and eight small cannons.[23]

Instead of returning to the fort, Smith chose instead to go up-river to Cinquoteck to seek corn from the Pamunkeys. He knew the settlers did not have enough provisions to get through the next couple of months, and another supply ship would not arrive until the spring or early summer. In Cinquoteck, he found Opechancanough, who was completely taken by surprise at the Englishmen's arrival. Scrambling to improvise adaptations to his plan to cut off Smith and his companions, he agreed to trade corn but said he needed a day to obtain supplies. The next morning, he returned with plenty of food and also hundreds of warriors, who quickly surrounded the house where they were lodging.

An extraordinary confrontation followed. First, Smith brazenly challenged the chief to single combat:

> I see Opechancanough you plot to murder me, but I fear it not, as yet your men and mine, have done no harm, but by our directions. Take therefore your arms; you see mine; my body shall be as naked as yours; the Isle in your river is a fit place, if you be contented: and the conqueror (of us two) shall be Lord and Master over all our men; otherwise draw all your men into the field; if you have not enough, take time to fetch more, and bring what number you will, so everyone bring a basket of corn, against all which I will stake the value in copper; you see I have but 15 men, and our game shall be, the conqueror take all.

Opechancanough ignored the challenge and approaching the door of the house with his personal guard attempted to draw Smith out to make him an easy target for his bowmen. Smith dashed from the house, grasped the chief's long scalp lock, and aimed his pistol at his chest, forcing him to surrender and order his warriors to put down their weapons. Smith threatened the assembled Indians, who must have been stunned by the affront to their chief, declaring that if they did not fill the Englishmen's barges with corn he would fill them with their dead carcasses. "I am not now at Rassawek (half drowned with mire) where you took me prisoner," he told them. "If you shoot but one Arrow to shed one drop of blood of any of my men, or steal the least of these Beads, or Copper . . . you shall see I will not cease revenge (if once I begin) so long as I can hear where to find one of your Nation that will not deny the name of Pamaunk."

FIGURE 5.1. "C[aptain] Smith taketh the King of Pamaunkee prisoner, 1608," in John Smith, *The Generall Historie of Virginia, New-England, and the Summer Isles* . . . (London, 1632). Smith holds Opechancanough firmly by his scalp lock, aiming a pistol at his chest. In the background are depictions of subsequent attempts by warriors to kill Smith and his men. *Courtesy of Special Collections, John D. Rockefeller Jr. Library, Colonial Williamsburg Foundation.*

The English eventually made their escape, leaving Opechanca-nough to brood on the terrible insult he had suffered at the hands of the Englishman in full view of his people. No formal declaration was made, but by the spring of 1609, the Powhatans and English were effectively at war.[24]

OVER THE COURSE of two years since the English arrived in 1607, both sides had sparred to gain the upper hand, but after Smith's escape from Opechancanough, relations moved into a new phase. Powhatan and Opechancanough had managed to get what they wanted, a supply of English weapons and the increasing likelihood of the colony disintegrating. Newport and Smith had failed to se-cure peace, regular food supplies, or information about the interior. In London, the Virginia Company viewed Smith's bellicose actions as little short of disastrous and had already put in place arrange-ments for his removal and a thorough overhaul of the government of the colony. For their part, the two chiefs decided to withdraw from the English altogether and let events run their course. A report by the company later in the year asserted that the Indians had cut off "all commerce and traffic [trade]" with the settlers, "cunningly mak-ing a war upon them . . . who dare no other way appear an enemy." In a highly symbolic act, Powhatan abandoned Werowocomoco, the seat of chiefly and spiritual power, and moved inland to Orapax, while Opechancanough remained at his longhouse on the Pamun-key (York) River. Both chiefs knew the colonists were starving and becoming increasingly rebellious. The chiefs did not fear the English and had no need to launch a large-scale frontal assault on Jamestown. It was only a matter of time, they calculated, before the settlers, perhaps urged on by the traitorous Germans, finally turned on their leaders and brought the colony down.[25]

CHAPTER 6

Starving Times

W HILE CAPTAIN JOHN SMITH STRUGGLED TO SAVE HIM-
self and Jamestown in the winter and spring of 1608 and
1609, in London the Virginia Company's leaders were putting the
finishing touches to a thorough overhaul of the venture. A different
scale of undertaking was required, which would translate the colony from a disastrous failure into a national enterprise that would
bring honor and profit to the realm. Sir Thomas Smythe, Sir Edwin
Sandys, and other leading statesmen and merchants remained confident that the colony would succeed if only a more effective form
of government and substantially greater investment could be put in
place. To ensure law and order in the colony, a military-style government would have to be imposed to be headed by lord governor and
captain general Sir Thomas West, Lord De La Warr, a high-ranking
nobleman and soldier. He was to be granted extensive powers, including authority to enforce martial law if necessary, and would be
supported by another experienced veteran of the wars in Ireland and
the Netherlands, Sir Thomas Gates.[1]

A broad appeal to potential investors and settlers was circulated throughout the country during these months promoting an expansive view of the colony's future. Alderman Robert Johnson, deputy of the company, returned to the refrain of the natural bounty of Virginia. The climate, he wrote in an influential pamphlet entitled *Nova Britannia*, was "wholesome, much warmer then England, and very agreeable to our Natures." Virginia was a pleasant land of "valleys and plains streaming with sweet Springs," of hills and mountains containing "hidden treasure, never yet searched," and of many sorts of rich soils and "minerals." It boasted great rivers and excellent harbors of which the "world affords no better for Ships of all burdens." There were "infinite store" of fish, fowls, and game, all kinds of trees, as well as fruits and roots good for nourishment. "What may we hope," he exclaimed, "when Art and Nature shall join, and strive together, to give best content to man and beast?" Peopled with sufficient settlers, the colony would supply England's copper and iron, glass, timber, fruits, vines to produce wine as good as any "from the Canaries," and mulberry trees for silk manufacture.

Establishing manufactures in Virginia would enable the kingdom to become self-sufficient in raw materials and manufactured goods and encourage the growth of a powerful mercantile marine. And if English towns were presently overrun by multitudes of vagrants and unemployed, as many local magistrates complained, in the colonies the poor would have no shortage of work that would serve the nation's advantage as well as their own. Petty thieves and rogues, who "for trifles may otherwise be devoured by the gallows" contemporaries pointed out, could save themselves by laboring in America. Work was available for all, "for no man must live idle there." Virginia would be a new commonwealth overseas, a settler society of industrious men and women. If "the Lord love us," Johnson wrote, "he will bring our people to it, and will give it us for a possession."[2]

Johnson, however, deliberately misrepresented Indian peoples, echoing caricatures that he must have known from his close association with the venture were wholly distorted. The country, he wrote, "is inhabited with wild and savage people, that live and lie [go] up and down in troops like herds of Deer in a Forest: they have no law but nature, their apparel skins of beasts, but most go naked." They have no arts or science, "yet they live under superior command such as it is, they are generally very loving and gentle, and do entertain and relieve our people with great kindness: they are easy to be brought to good, and would fain [rather] embrace a better condition." Such stereotypes had been commonplace in Europe for a century but allowed Johnson to introduce a theme that subsequently became central to the Virginia Company's appeal for broad support: the conversion of the Indians to Christianity and the Church of England, which would pave the way for them becoming English. "Our intrusion into their possession [of the land] shall tend to their great good," he explained, "yet not to supplant and root them out, but to bring them from their base condition to far better." If the Indians resisted, then the English could lawfully make war on them as long as the ultimate goal was to reclaim them from idolatry and sin. Conversion must follow conquest, or as Robert Gray put it, "those people are vanquished, to their unspeakable profit and gain."[3]

In a promotional masterstroke, Sir Thomas Smythe and his associates coupled the vision of a Protestant crusade in Virginia to a sense of national honor and calling. English settlers would be soldiers of Christ. The "Lord that called Abraham into another Country," the Reverend William Symonds declared, "does also . . . call you to go and carry the Gospel to a nation [the Powhatans] that never heard of Christ." Conversion of the Indians would ultimately lead to the full flowering of the English Church and nation in North America and the establishment of a Protestant empire in the New World that would counterbalance that of Catholic Spain. The outpouring of sermons from the pulpit and printing press offered a providential history of the English people that connected the nation's emergence as a Protestant bulwark against Catholic Spain to events unfolding in Europe and Virginia. Who could seriously doubt, ministers proclaimed, that the English held a special place in the affections of the Lord and were uniquely appointed to carry the gospel to the millions of Indians who lived in subjection to the devil and his minions?[4]

Sometime during these months, however, company leaders received unexpected and highly disturbing news. Credible information came to their ears that Powhatan's warriors had recently carried out a massacre of survivors of the lost colony of Roanoke, killing nearly all of them. The bearer of the bad news was William Strachey, the same man who later became secretary of the colony. Considering himself something of a writer, he had got to know leading playwrights such as Ben Jonson and William Shakespeare while honing his own literary skills. In need of money and having few better options, he had decided to try his luck in Virginia, taking upon himself the task of writing the first official history.

Hearing of the arrival in London of two Indians, Namontack and Machumps, sent by Powhatan to learn more about the English, Strachey sought them out to question them about their peoples' customs and way of life. Both, he discovered, were closely connected to Powhatan and might be able to offer valuable insights. What he learned from Machumps, in particular, came as a complete surprise, not in relation to Indian culture but to startling revelations about the fate of the Roanoke colonists. At "*Peccarecanick*, and *Ochanahoen*," two towns inland from the North Carolina coast, Machumps told Strachey, "the [Indian] People have houses built with stone walls, and one story above another, so taught them by those English who escaped the slaughter at *Roanoak*, at what [the] time this our Colony, (under the conduct of Capt. *Newport*) landed within the *Chesapeack* Bay." A local chief, "Eyanoco," who lived along the upper reaches of the Chowan River saved seven of the English, four men, two boys, and one young maid, "to beat his Copper, of which he hath certain

Mines" at a place called Ritanoe. Strachey was explicit about who was responsible for the killing of the lost colonists: the "men women, and Children of the first plantation at Roanoak," he wrote, "(who 20 and odd years had peaceably lived and intermixed with those Savages, and were out of his Territory)," were by "Commandment of Powhatan . . . miserably slaughtered without any offence given him." The shocking news was relayed to company leaders who in turn wrote a report, now lost, for James I.[5]

This attack was not a random act of violence. Since the arrival of the English at Paspahegh (Jamestown), Powhatan and Opechancanough had been determined to restrict opportunities for the new arrivals to make alliances with hostile neighboring peoples. But they recognized that a serious threat also existed to the south. The two chiefs rightly surmised that Roanoke survivors would be of great interest to the Jamestown colonists, not only for their familiarity with the country but also in helping to forge alliances between the English and the Indian peoples they (the lost colonists) lived with. Strachey confirmed the chiefs' fears when he remarked that Powhatan had been careful "to keep us by all means from the acquaintance of those nations that border and Confront him, for besides his knowledge [of] how easily and willingly his enemies will be drawn upon him by the least Countenance and encouragement from us, he does by keeping us from trading with them monopolize all the Copper brought into *Virginia* by the English." Smith's encounters with Indian peoples during his explorations of the Chesapeake Bay and Newport's efforts to establish contact with the Monacans represented threats to their authority, so, too, would any effort by the two English leaders to make contact with surviving English in the Roanoke region and hinterland of North Carolina.[6]

The Roanoke colonists were killed, Strachey emphasized, in lands outside Powhatan's chiefdom, "in the Territory of those Weroances which did in no sort depend on him, or acknowledge him." These peoples were most likely Chowanocs and Tuscaroras. In the fall of

1587, John White, the leader of a colony of 118 men, women, and children, had reluctantly left Roanoke Island to return to England to obtain supplies and recruit more settlers. Unable to return for three years, when he eventually reached the island, he found it deserted. Carvings on a post at the settlers' fort and on a nearby tree indicated some of the colonists, perhaps a couple of dozen, had moved to Croatoan Island about fifty miles to the south where the local people were friendly. The remainder of the colonists resettled inland at the head of the Albemarle Sound, possibly somewhere on or near Salmon Creek, and waited for White to return. As the years passed and no English ships came to find them, they merged with peoples who lived along the Chowan and Roanoke Rivers, building homes and raising families.[7]

For twenty years, the English had speculated about what had happened to the settlers. Now it appeared they had been killed in a large-scale raid by Powhatan warriors. No direct evidence exists about who carried out the attack, but as war chief, Opechancanough must have been involved and may even have led the assault in person. An echo of what might have occurred is found in an account by Edward Bland, who was part of an expedition to the falls of the Roanoke River in 1650. He was told by his Indian guides that many years earlier "the great Emperor, Appachancano" had led warriors and "several petty Kings" from Virginia to "make a War" upon the Tuscaroras, a powerful Iroquoian people. One of the petty chiefs was Parahunt, known as Tanx (little) Powhatan, a son of Powhatan, who held a grudge against the chief of the Chowanocs. While embracing the chief in greeting, Parahunt quickly wrapped a bow string around his neck and strangled him. This was probably a signal for an attack on the others assembled to greet Opechancanough. Farther south, Opechancanough "one morning with four hundred men treacherously slew two hundred forty" Tuscaroras at a place that was subsequently marked by "several great heaps bones," prompting Bland to name it Golgotha. The precise timing of Opechancanough's raid is not given, and there are no references in Bland's account to white settlers being killed. Yet, the reverend Samuel Purchas, while compiling a massive compendium of information about English overseas ventures in this period, claimed that Powhatan had boasted to John Smith that "he had been at the murder of that Colony" (the English Roanoke) and had "utensils of theirs to show," including a musket barrel, a brass mortar, and several pieces of iron. The presence of Chief Powhatan in the war party is highly unlikely, but it is quite possible his warriors brought back "trophies" from the raid.

The combined reports from Machumps, Strachey, and Bland suggest that the war party of elite Powhatan and Pamunkey warriors journeyed to the Roanoke region in the spring of 1607 with the intention of killing survivors of the lost colony together with the Indian peoples they lived with. Led by Opechancanough, they then returned to Tsenacommacah to undertake the destruction of the Chesapeakes, who were also perceived as a threat. If so, this suggests that in a crushing series of attacks shortly after the arrival of the English, Powhatan and Opechancanough moved decisively to cut off the leaders of the Chowanocs, reduce the Tuscaroras living along the Roanoke River, and remove any threat of a rising by the people living nearest to the mouth of the Chesapeake Bay, as they had been warned might happen by their priests.[8]

The seemingly strong possibility that the lost colonists had been killed on the orders of Powhatan and Opechancanough brought about an abrupt shift in the Virginia Company's approach to relations with the Indians, particularly the two great chiefs. James I ordered that retribution should be meted out to the priests, "being the ministers of Satan," who would be imprisoned or executed. Powhatan and Opechancanough would be imprisoned or carefully watched and forced to be tributaries (subordinate) to the English. Similarly, lesser chiefs would become tributaries and acknowledge King James as their lord, "and so we shall free them all from the tyranny of Powhatan," the company affirmed. Tribute that ordinarily would have been submitted to the chiefs would henceforth be rendered to the English governor albeit at a lesser amount, and in return, the Indians would be protected from their enemies and enjoy the many "commodities and blessings" of the English. Meanwhile, to advance the holy work of conversion, the company advised colonists to take Indian children into their own homes to be educated in Anglicanism and English manners. In this way, company leaders believed the "people will easily obey you and become in time civil and Christian."[9]

Company policy, therefore, turned away from seeking friendship with Chief Powhatan to a strategy set on putting an end to what was now construed by the English as a horrible tyranny over his people. Viewing themselves as liberators, the English were confident that oppressed Indians would willingly acquiesce to their rule because their lives would be immeasurably improved. Replacing Powhatan with English overlords would break the dominance of the chief and his warriors and instead encourage Indians to enjoy the fruits of their own labor and trade with the settlers, to the mutual benefit of the English and Indians alike.

By the late spring 1609, Sir Thomas Smythe could look back on a highly successful campaign to recruit fresh investors and colonists, restructure the company, and restart the colony. Scores of high-placed statesmen, wealthy aristocrats, gentry, and merchants had joined the venture, and hundreds of working men and women from all backgrounds flocked to sign up for the voyage being planned in the near future. Four major priorities had been identified by company leaders, which they believed would stimulate continuing investment and commercial success. Sir Thomas Gates, who was to serve as interim governor, was instructed to carry on the search for rich mines and a passage to the Pacific through the mountains, expand trade with Indians throughout the Chesapeake region, begin exacting tribute from local Indians who had been freed from Powhatan, and produce a range of profitable commodities of the sort itemized by Robert Johnson in *Nova Britannia*. Three important Indian towns were to be

occupied and developed as major new settlements, unitng the Roanoke region with the Powhatan (James) River Valley: one at the falls
of the Powhatan River and two, Ohonahorn and Ocanahowan, on
the Chowan and Roanoke Rivers respectively in North Carolina. In
mid-May, approximately five hundred settlers boarded seven ships
in London to begin new lives in North America. The entire enterprise was now on a more secure footing. Virginia would be a godly
commonwealth overseas, a "new Brittaine" populated by industrious
settlers who would benefit from the natural bounty of the land and
deliver God's word to the Powhatans.[10]

THREE MONTHS LATER, when Captain John Smith learned of a fleet
arriving in the Powhatan (James) River, he assumed it must be the
Spanish, little dreaming, he wrote, it could be another English supply.
Reacting immediately, he quickly put the fort into a posture of defense and noted in an aside that far from being in "any way negligent
or unwilling to aid and assist us with their best power," the Indians
offered to "fight under our colors." His comment was made with no
further elaboration and is impossible to confirm. Yet if true, it suggests that Powhatan and Opechancanough were far more alarmed
at the prospect of Spanish warships returning to the Chesapeake
than dealing with a demoralized group of Englishmen at Jamestown.
Even after three and a half decades, the prospect of a Spanish fleet
in the Chesapeake Bay was seemingly far more menacing than the
arrival of an English one.[11]

Nevertheless, the arrival of a large number of settlers including
women and children posed a threat of a different sort for the two
chiefs, notably by revealing the settlers' clear intent to establish permanent settlements in their land. The chiefs must have wondered,
too, how the newcomers would feed themselves. Did their arrival
portend an intensification of raids for corn on neighboring Indian
communities? Yet, from their point of view not all the news was bad.

Reports from their scouts along the river told of ships damaged and storm tossed, masts missing, yards broken, and what was left of sails hanging in shreds. From the Indians' close observation of the fort, it was clear the settlers remained in a state of disarray. Powhatan and Opechancanough were not inclined to launch attacks immediately but instead chose to wait and see what happened next among the fractious English.

During the summer, the settlers' provisions had already been in such short supply that Smith had been forced to send half of the men in the fort to oyster banks at the mouth of the Powhatan (James) River or to the falls, near present-day Richmond, to live off what they could scavenge. When the new arrivals eventually reached Jamestown Island in mid-August and approximately three hundred settlers disembarked, many seriously ill or injured, he was suddenly confronted with feeding four times the number of mouths with little in the way of additional provisions from England. A massive storm had battered the fleet, ruined their food supplies, and wrecked the admiral (leading ship), the *Sea Venture*, on Bermuda, together with the colony's entire newly appointed leadership. Having little choice if he was to alleviate pressure on remaining supplies at Jamestown and reduce the risk of disease sweeping through the settlement, Captain Smith once again opted to disperse the colonists to live off the land. The men were divided into two military companies and ordered to establish garrisons: Captain John Martin was sent downriver with approximately sixty to one hundred men to the fertile lands of the Nansemonds and Captain Francis West was dispatched with one hundred and twenty men to the falls. The remainder of the arrivals, including most of the women and children, camped in open fields around the fort.[12]

Hostilities with local peoples commenced soon afterward, precipitated by the Englishmen. At Nansemond, Captain Martin attempted to bargain with the chief, Weyhohomo, for a small island that he thought ideally suited for his needs. But the chief had no intention of selling the island, which was a sacred place, and wanted nothing to do with the English. Two messengers sent by Martin to negotiate were gruesomely put to death, "their Brains cut and scraped out of their heads with mussel shells," which led Martin to order his men to storm the island. George Percy, a prominent gentleman who was one of the leaders, reported that "being Landed and acquainted with treachery, we Beat the Savages out of the Island, burned their houses, ransacked their Temples, Took down the Corpses of their dead kings from off their Tombs and carried away their pearls, Copper and bracelets, wherewith they do decorate their kings' funerals." Following an attack on the mainland, Martin's soldiers captured the chief's son and another warrior and took them to the island as hostages. Shortly after, the chief's son was accidentally shot but somehow managed to escape from his captors and swim to the mainland, trailing blood from his wound. Having lost his most valuable captive and fearing retaliation, Martin decided not to risk further attacks but to retreat back to the island, abandoning any effort to plunder the large quantity of corn ripening in the Indians' fields.

Upriver at the falls, in the heartland of Powhatan's chiefdom, Captain West began constructing a fort close to the Powhatan (James) River that he anticipated would serve as the principal gateway into the interior where he expected to discover riches. Foraging in woods nearby, some of the men were attacked by Indian warriors and several killed or wounded. When Smith arrived to inspect West's progress, the two had a calamitous falling out. Smith claimed he had purchased the palisaded town of Powhatan from Parahunt with the intention of using it as an English fort and could not understand why West was constructing his own settlement at a different location. A "great division did grow amongst them," Percy wrote, and Smith conceiving "his authority and person neglected, incensed the Savages against Captain West and his Company, Reporting to them that our men had no more powder left them than would serve for one volley of shot." Another witness, the young Henry Spelman, who had been left with Parahunt, phrased the accusation more bluntly, saying that Smith "conspired with the Powhatan [probably Parahunt] to kill Capt. West." Not long after, warriors of the Arrohattoc people, allies of the Powhatans, attacked the fort, killing more Englishmen and taking with them the cloaks and swords of those they had slain. Over the next several weeks, sporadic fighting continued but neither side launched a general attack.[13]

By early October, five ships were ready to sail from Jamestown for England. Among the two dozen passengers on board was John Smith, grievously injured. The cause was an attempt on his life orchestrated by the colony's leaders, such was the bitter in-fighting that had overtaken the settlement. One of the leaders, John Ratcliffe, alias Sicklemore, took the opportunity to send a brief description of the state of affairs in Virginia in a letter to his patron, the earl of Salisbury. He first relayed the dreadful news of the disappearance of the *Sea Venture* and 180 passengers and crew, including Sir Thomas Gates, Sir George Somers, and Captain Newport. The men who were to bring about the comprehensive changes that had been in planning since the previous year had apparently been lost at sea. Instead of being led by men of authority fully conversant with the reforms the company was anxious to implement, the colony's government had dissolved into continual bickering among factions until Smith was finally removed and George Percy, one of the original settlers, was elected president in his place. While offering an overly optimistic account of the creation of new settlements, Ratcliffe also mentioned the colony's dire shortage of provisions and recommended the company send a year's worth of supplies immediately. Neighboring Indians had only enough corn for their own needs, and the woods around English settlements were as "yet so thick" as to make clearing sufficient ground for large-scale cultivation themselves utterly impractical.[14]

As THEY GATHERED information about English activities from peoples along the river and their scouts watching the fort, Powhatan and

Opechancanough consulted with their priests and chiefs to settle upon a strategy that would rid themselves of the intruders for good. Cutting off food supplies and waiting for the English to starve remained the central element of their plan, complemented by sporadic attacks to cut off settlers whenever the chance arose. War councils led by Opechancanough and Powhatan would have been held to communicate plans with principal chiefs involved, the Arrohattocs and Powhatans at the falls, perhaps supported by Pamunkey warriors, the Nansemonds, and the peoples living near Jamestown, possibly led by the Paspaheghs who had recently suffered from a brutal attack by the English. Once the strategy was agreed, chiefs or prominent warriors appointed as "captain" of their people dispatched subordinates to go from town to town recruiting men and telling them to be ready at a given place on a certain day "to serve the great king."[15]

The attacks began a couple of weeks after the departure of the fleet carrying Smith on October 4. An eyewitness reported the Indians "all revolted, and did murder and spoil all they could encounter." Their attacks were aided by the desperation and rebelliousness of many of the settlers. At Nansemond, seventeen men mutinied and stole a boat, "pretending" they were going to Kecoughtan to trade with the Indians for provisions. They were "served according to their desserts," George Percy wrote, "for not any of them were heard of after, and in all likelihood were cut off and slain by the savages." A few days later, Michael Sicklemore and a dozen men were killed by the Nansemonds, "their mouths stopped full of Bread being done as it seems in Contempt and scorn that others might expect the Like when they should come to seek for bread and relief amongst them." Percy recalled the legend of the Spanish general Pedro de Valdivia, killed by Indians of southern Chile by being forced to swallow molten gold, the Indians saying, "Now glut thyself with gold Baldivia [Valdivia]!" He "having there sought for gold as Sicklemore did here for food." The remainder of the men at Nansemond, about half of those who had set out a few weeks earlier, managed to escape and get back to Jamestown, where they were joined by Captain West's men who had suffered heavy casualties at the falls, also losing "near half" their number. Only Fort Algernon, as Percy had named a garrison established by Ratcliffe downriver at Point Comfort earlier in the year, remained as the sole English settlement outside Jamestown.[16]

The colonists' losses had been devastating, and with the return of the defeated settlers to Jamestown, numbers within the fort swelled to at least three hundred. Powhatan took advantage of this situation and deployed his warriors to seal off the island. Apart from fifty men at Point Comfort, the entire English colony was trapped and starving in the fort, with no prospect of relief from England. It was now November, and Percy was aware their provisions would not last much longer than three months and would be completely spent by February, in the middle of winter. He and the other leaders decided to dispatch John Ratcliffe and about thirty men in a pinnace to Orapax to trade for food. Earlier, before fighting began in earnest, Powhatan had sent Thomas Savage with four or five Indians to offer a gift of venison to the new president, Percy, and subsequently an invitation was delivered by Henry Spelman, another English boy with the Indians, whereby Powhatan promised to fill a barge with corn in return for copper.

The expedition was a disaster. Ratcliffe and his men were lured into an ambush on the Pamunkey (York) River and most of them killed. Following an argument about being given short measure, Chief Powhatan withdrew in anger, Spelman wrote, at which "a great number of Indians that lay lurking in the woods and corn about [around] began with an oulis and whoopubb [whooping and hubbub] and whilst our English men were in haste carrying their corn to their ships the Indians that were hidden in the corn shot the men as they passed and so killed them all saving one William Russell and one other." Ratcliffe was taken alive and suffered a horrendous death, "his flesh scraped from his bones," his limbs hacked off, and organs removed by women and thrown into a fire in front of him.[17]

Ratcliffe's death and failure to procure any corn left the settlers in the fort in desperate straits. "Now all of us at James Towne," Percy commented, "beginning to feel that sharp prick of hunger which no man [can] truly describe butt he which hath tasted the bitterness thereof." By November, his last hope was to send Francis West in the pinnace *Swallow* to the Potomac River to barter for corn with peoples who were largely independent of the Powhatans and potentially friendlier toward the English. Along the south bank of the Potomac, West managed to fill his pinnace with corn quickly but provoked the Patawomecks by "harsh and Cruel dealing," cutting off the heads of two Indians while bartering. On returning to the Powhatan River and learning at Fort Algernon of the desperate situation of the settlers at the fort, West's crew turned about and set sail for the open sea in the knowledge that having plenty of supplies on board they would be able to roam the ocean for months, preying on wealthy Spanish merchant ships rather than sharing the same fate as the starving colonists at Jamestown. William Strachey described West's deserters as "professed Pirates, with dreams of Mountains of Gold, and happy Robberies," who at one stroke betrayed the starving colonists, made the Patawomecks their enemies, and took away the settlers' best ship, "which should have been a refuge in extremities."[18]

Disease and starvation exerted a deadly grip on Jamestown. Some of those sick or injured from the voyage may have perished within a few days or weeks. One of the ships, the *Diamond*, had the plague in her when she left England, and pestilence, including serious intestinal illnesses, spread throughout the fort rapidly as sanitary conditions worsened and chronic malnourishment sickened the settlers. To satisfy their "Cruel hunger," Percy recalled, settlers went into the woods in search of "Serpents and snakes, and to dig the earth for wild and unknown Roots," where they "were Cut off and slain by the Savages." In desperation, they ate their horses, dogs, cats, and "vermin" such as rats and mice, and when they had eaten those, they even turned to their boot leather. Others, no matter what the risk, deserted. "Many of our men this starving Time did Run away to the Savages whom we never heard of after." The Indians killed as fast outside the fort, a settler commented, as famine and disease did within.

Powhatan's warriors looked on as the siege continued to take a heavy toll on settlers' lives through late fall and winter. They played their part by destroying the settlers' boats, driving deer from the island, and slaughtering their hogs. "And now famine beginning to Look ghastly and pale in every face," Percy wrote in harrowing prose, "that nothing was spared to maintain Life and to do those things which seem incredible As to dig up dead corpses out of graves and to eat them and some have Licked up the Blood which had fallen from their weak fellows." Some who were killed seeking help beyond the palisade were taken back to the fort and consumed by those who found their bodies. A young woman of fourteen who likely died before the end of 1609 had her skull cracked open and brains eaten. One of the settlers murdered his wife "as she slept on his bosom" and then "Ripped the child out of her womb and threw it into the River and after chopped the Mother in pieces and salted her for his food," for which unnatural act Percy had him tortured to extract his confession and then executed by burning. A letter by the Spanish ambassador in London, Don Alonso de Velasco, to King Philip III reported that the "Indians hold the English surrounded" and had "killed the larger part of them," while the rest were so lacking in provisions they would not survive long. The English were reduced to eating "dogs, cat skins and other vile stuff," as well as the dead. It would be "very easy to make an end of it [the colony] altogether," Velasco wrote with evident satisfaction, "by sending out a few ships to finish what might be left in that place."[19]

Powhatan and Opechancanough's tactics and the Indians' siege had been a spectacular success. By the spring of 1610, some 250 women and children had perished in the fort or been killed as they tried to run away. Including casualties at the falls and at Nansemond as well as Captain West's deserters, English numbers declined from a

high of approximately 450 in mid-August 1609 to 100 by the following spring. Indian losses, on the other hand, were minimal. Believing
that the remaining sick and famished settlers would shortly succumb
and having to turn to spring planting, Powhatan's warriors began
drifting away from the island in April and early May.[20]

With the departure of the Indians, Percy was able to leave the
fort and journey downriver to Fort Algernon to learn how Captain
James Davis and his men fared. To his surprise, he found the garrison well stocked with fish, crabs, and hogs. Davis was hoarding as
much food as possible with the intention of abandoning the colony
and sailing for England accompanied by the "better sort" in the two
pinnaces moored by the garrison. They, like West and his men, apparently had little scruple about leaving the Jamestown settlers to
die. Percy, however, did have scruples and decided to move half of
the fort's survivors to Point Comfort on the next tide, and when
they had regained their health, he would return them to the fort and
bring down the other half. If that did not prevent further deaths, he
would move all the survivors to Fort Algernon. But before Percy was
able to implement his plan, urgent news came from Fort Algernon's
lookout: two small ships had entered the Chesapeake Bay.[21]

THE TWO SMALL ships, the *Patience* and *Delivery*, were English,
built on Bermuda by the castaways using timbers, lines, and gear
salvaged from the *Sea Venture*. They had left Bermuda on May 11,
1610, and arrived at Fort Algernon a week and a half later. There,
Sir Thomas Gates and Sir George Somers heard the appalling news
about conditions at Jamestown. On the next tide, they arrived at the
fort and found a scene of desolation. "Entering the town, it appeared
rather as the ruins of some ancient fortification than that any people
living might now inhabit it." The church was ruined and abandoned,
palisades torn down, William Strachey reported, "and empty houses,
which [the] owners' death had taken from them, rent up and burnt"

for firewood to sustain survivors through a brutal winter. Gates and Somers "might Read a lecture of misery in our people's faces," Percy remarked, see for themselves the scarcity of provisions, and "understand the malice of the Savages, who knowing our weakness had many Times assaulted us" outside the fort. Jamestown was a charnel house. Only sixty or so settlers remained alive, and those so wasted they were "Lamentable to behold," looking "Like Anatomies [skeletons], Crying out we are starved We are starved." But Gates could do little to help them, only having enough food brought from Bermuda to feed his own company. And so the death toll mounted. Driven out of his wits by hunger, one Hugh Price "In A furious distracted mood did come openly into the market place Blaspheming exclaiming and crying out that there was no god," Percy wrote, "Alleging that if there were A god he would not suffer his creatures whom he had made and framed to endure those miseries." No story, Strachey lamented, "can remember to us, more woes, anguishes, then these people [the English], thus governed have both suffered and pulled upon their own heads."[22]

Gates, Somers, and Captain Newport concluded they had no choice but to abandon Jamestown. Their meager provisions were quickly running out, and there was no hope of getting food from the Powhatans. They would sail to Newfoundland where they would make contact with fishing fleets plying the cod-rich waters of the North Atlantic and from there return to England. Preparations for the voyage began immediately. The fort's cannons were buried in front of the main gate that faced the river, a sign that Gates believed the English would be back, and he ordered his men not to fire the fort, saying "my Masters let the town Stand [for] we know not but that as honest men as our selves may come and inhabit here." Then, discharging a volley of small shot in farewell, leaving the horror of Jamestown behind them, the settlers set off at midday on June 7, 1610, under the watchful eyes of Chief Powhatan's scouts.[23]

CHAPTER 7

"An Abundance of Blood"

I N ONE OF THE GREAT TURNAROUNDS OF AMERICAN HISTORY, while Sir Thomas Gates's little flotilla was anchored off Mulberry Island in the Powhatan (James) River, waiting for the ebb tide to carry them downriver, his men spotted a longboat coming rapidly upriver toward them. It was an advance party from three supply ships commanded by Lord De La Warr, the colony's recently appointed lord governor and captain general, who was with the fleet riding at Point Comfort. Gates was told to return to Jamestown immediately and prepare for their arrival. A couple of days later, on Sunday, June 10, 1610, De La Warr arrived with one hundred fifty settlers, many of them veterans from the wars against Spanish forces in the Netherlands, and enough supplies to last a year. Escorted by his personal guard, the lord governor paused before the fort to kiss the ground and give thanks for his safe arrival, and then proceeded to the church with as much pomp as could be mustered where, following a sermon, his commission was read, thereby formally installing the new government.[1]

What the colonists who had so nearly escaped the terrible conditions they had endured in the colony thought of their sudden reversal can only be imagined, but there is no doubt as to what Lord De La Warr expected of them. First was the establishment of law and order whereby men of rank, captains and other officers, governed with absolute authority. Second, according to the Virginia Company's instructions, he was to increase the number of English settlements and build more forts. Third, he was to liberate the Powhatans or, if they were unwilling to be freed and side with the English, subdue them by force.

Henceforth, the colony was to be run along military lines. Each captain would command fifty men whom they would train "in martial manner and warlike discipline." Throughout the day, the church bell would be rung to call the settlers together for work, meals, or rest. Order was to be enforced by a severe code of laws, the *Lawes Divine, Morall and Martiall*, a combination of martial and Mosaic law, which set out the duties of the settlers and penalties for disobedience. Officers were required to ensure all those under their command attended divine service twice daily and to punish anyone who blasphemed or challenged the authority of any minister. There was to be one God, one church, and one law; no dissension would be tolerated.[2]

Despite his martial temperament, De La Warr was initially prepared to negotiate with Chief Powhatan to bring about peace. Company leaders encouraged a moderate approach toward the Indians and emphasized, as they had to Gates, the importance of conversion to Anglicanism. Shortly before De La Warr left for Jamestown, a sermon preached by William Crashaw in London before the lord governor and leaders of the company made the point succinctly. The "plain necessity of this present action for Virginia: the principal ends [purpose] thereof," Crashaw stated, was "the plantation of a Church of English Christians there, and consequently of the conversion of the heathen from the devil to God."[3]

Accordingly, soon after his arrival at Jamestown, the governor attempted to open discussions with Powhatan. De La Warr sent messengers to complain about outrages committed by the chief's warriors against his men, which included killing some of his men and taking their weapons and fomenting "private conspiracies" encouraging settlers to desert. In a somewhat clumsy effort to flatter as well as threaten, the lord governor conveyed he was certain that being "so great and wise a king" these aggressive acts could not have been instigated by him or with his knowledge but rather by the chief's "worst and unruly people." He then demanded that Powhatan order his warriors to stop immediately, to punish or send to him the men responsible for attacking the blockhouse at Jamestown, and to return any English they had captured together with the weapons they had stolen. If he agreed to these terms, De La Warr promised to enter into friendship with him, which would lead to the chief becoming "a friend to King James and his subjects." Referring to the coronation ceremony of nearly two years earlier, he reminded Powhatan that he (the chief) "had formerly vowed, not only friendship but homage, receiving from His Majesty therefore many gifts, and upon his knees a crown and scepter with other Ornaments, the symbols of civil state and Christian sovereignty, thereby obliging himself to offices of duty to His Majesty." Among such duties, the most important, as far as the governor was concerned, required Powhatan to render obedience to him as James I's appointed representative in Virginia.

Chief Powhatan's reply amply illustrates the enormous cultural divide separating the two men. He likely met with other chiefs, including Opechancanough, to discuss the lord governor's demands. The situation was extremely serious. Within a month, during May and June, three hundred settlers and soldiers had arrived, tripling the colonists' numbers. Jamestown was being rebuilt, and two small forts were under construction downriver near the lands of the Kecoughtans. Nevertheless, Powhatan opted for an uncompromising response. He told De La Warr that the English were to leave "his country or confine themselves to James Town only, without searching further up into his land or rivers, or otherwise he would give command to his people to kill us [the English], and do to us all the mischief which they at their pleasure could and we feared." Lastly, the chief warned the lord governor not to send his messengers again, "unless they brought him a coach and three horses, for he had understood by the Indians which were [had been] in England how such was the state of great werowances and lords in England to ride and visit other great men."[4]

De La Warr was "much incensed" by the great chief's answer, which he considered hostile and insolent. Yet from Powhatan's point of view, his response was utterly justified. The English had invaded his land, taken his peoples' food, behaved violently, and were inveterate liars who could not be trusted. Over the previous two and half years, in talks with John Smith, Captain Newport, and now with Lord De La Warr, Powhatan had sought to define the relationship between them, insisting on limiting English occupation to Jamestown and offering to trade, so long as it was on his terms rather than those of the newcomers. His demand for a coach and horses, ludicrous to the English, was a way of underlining his expectation that he should be treated with the respect he believed was due to the paramount chief. As he saw it, this request was no more absurd than De La Warr's blithe assertion that the English had taken possession of his chiefdom and he and his peoples were subjects of James I. What the English described as Powhatan's "proud and disdainful" language was intended to remind De La Warr, just as he had made clear to Smith and Newport before, that he too was a king and this was his land.

Besides emphasizing matters of principle, Powhatan was also pragmatic and maintained a close watch on English activities. Indians who lived near the fort visited regularly and reported on the settlers' preparedness. Recent experience suggested that large numbers of settlers were especially vulnerable in the summer months, and after De La Warr's arrival, pestilent diseases, described as "calentures and fevers," began to take a rapid toll. Hundreds had already perished at Jamestown. Who was to say the current group would not suffer the same fate?[5]

Local Indians congregated daily near the blockhouse, a large fortified structure to the west of the fort used as an outer line of defense, or would gather outside the fort's gates, taunting the English. They also waited in ambush for settlers who went out to find fresh fruits or fetch fresh water, by which manner, William Strachey remarked, "they killed many of our men." His observation indicates that Powhatan and Opechancanough had ordered his warriors, or the Paspaheghs who lived near to the fort, to adopt debilitating hit-and-run tactics at Jamestown, killing the English and then retiring into the woods. The chiefs could not cut off the settlers entirely as they had during the winter months of the "starving time" because the English now had too many ships, but they could whittle away their numbers and thereby promote a climate of fear and hopelessness. Opechancanough may have informed Powhatan of the success of the strategy against Spanish garrisons along the Florida coast, which had been decimated by sickness, starvation, and the determined resistance of local Indians.

De La Warr warned the two chiefs that in future if any Indians approached the fort uninvited they would do so at their own peril. To set an example, two Paspahegh men who had been recently apprehended were taken in manacles before De La Warr for summary judgment. One of them, described as "a notable villain," who had made attempts on the lives of many in the fort, had his right hand struck off and was sent to Powhatan with a message reiterating the governor's demands or his men would destroy neighboring Indians' "cornfields, towns, and villages."[6]

The English commanders' reaction to the Powhatans was shaped in large part by conventional European thinking that held Indian peoples did not pose a serious military threat. Richard Hakluyt the younger, one of the foremost promoters of colonies of the period, looked to previous wars in Ireland for the sake of comparison and became convinced that "one hundred men will do more [damage] now among the naked and unarmed people in Virginia, than one thousand were able then to do in Ireland against that armed and warlike nation in those days." Based on his experience of living with the Indians, Henry Spelman observed that as "for armor or discipline in war, they have none." On the other hand, Captain Gabriel Archer, who had been slightly wounded during one of the first attacks on the English soon after the first colonists arrived in the Chesapeake Bay, offered a somewhat more informed assessment. Indian warriors, he wrote, "are proper lusty straight [well-built] men, very strong runners and exceedingly swift. They always fight in the woods with bow and arrows and a short sword. The speed they use in skirmishes is admirable." Settlers' own experiences bore out Archer's admonition. Following sporadic encounters during the first three years of settlement, and the sustained attacks over the previous six months, the English were well aware of the Indians' prowess but did not believe they could possibly overthrow them. English losses during the starving time were blamed on inept leaders rather than the battle skills and tactics of the Powhatans. In the long run, by underestimating the military capacity of the Indians, the English made a disastrous mistake and presented Powhatan and Opechancanough with a tactical opening of incalculable significance.[7]

IN EARLY JULY 1610, on the way downriver supposedly to trade with the Kecoughtans for corn, Sir Thomas Gates sent one of his men to recover a longboat that had drifted to the opposite shore of the Powhatan (James) River. The man, Humphrey Blunt, set off in a canoe but was quickly forced back by strong winds. He was soon seized by a group of warriors who dragged him into the woods where they "sacrificed" him. Gates held the Kecoughtans responsible for the gruesome killing and the next day landed his men near the Indians' town, ordering his taborer (drummer) to "play and dance thereby to allure the Indians to come to meet him," which they did. Waiting for the right moment to strike, his men drew their swords and swiftly fell upon the Indians, killing five and inflicting "Such extraordinary Large and mortal wounds" on many others, Percy recounted, that the soldiers were amazed any escaped. About a dozen of the people were killed and the rest fled, leaving the town and ripening corn to Gates and his company.

It is unlikely the killing of Blunt was the principal reason for Gates's assault on the Kecoughtans. George Percy does not mention it and states simply that Gates moved against them because he was desirous for revenge, without giving further details. Two months earlier, Percy claimed he planned an expedition against them because they "had treacherously slain" many of the settlers, possibly a reference to the killing of Michael Sicklemore and his men during the starving time. Yet, the most convincing reason for the English attack had little to do with revenge and more with the need to take possession of the Indians' extensive cornfields. A later description describes casually how in the building of two small forts near the town of Kecoughtan, the soldiers burned Indian houses they had no use for and killed twelve to fourteen Indians, taking "such corn as we found growing of their planting." The land was described as fertile and fair where vines, corn, and all sorts of fruits could be grown. At Kecoughtan, viewed as an ideal location for a city and chief fortification, the English also saw a spacious country perfectly suited to their hopes of developing an economy based on Mediterranean products that would thrive in Virginia to their great profit. By the attack on the Kecoughtans, the English made clear their intention to take the Indians' corn by force, kill as many warriors as possible, and, if feasible, occupy the land.[8]

The next month, English attacks escalated in number and ferocity. Focused on neighboring Indian peoples, De La Warr sent George Percy with seventy men to strike at the Paspaheghs and

Chickahominies. Strachey described the Paspaheghs as their "deadliest enemies," who had been hostile since the first arrival of the English. Wowinchopunck, their chief, had attempted to kill John Smith the previous year, and the Englishman, in turn, had captured and humiliated him and subsequently attacked his town, killing six or seven of his people. Percy transported his forces in two boats to the mouth of the Chickahominy River and on the night of August 10, guided by a captive Paspahegh named Kemps, led his men a few miles overland to the Paspaheghs' town. The soldiers were drawn up in files and ordered not to charge until the signal was given.

Percy described what happened next without sparing the horrific details. As at Kecoughtan, no warning was given, and at the signal the soldiers charged from several different directions attacking the Indians' houses and putting "some fifteen or sixteen [Indians] to the Sword." Many escaped, including the chief, but among those taken were the chief's wife and children, together with an Indian male. Percy demanded to know why they had not been dispatched already to which a lieutenant replied that they were his to do with as he liked. Percy ordered the male Indian's head to be struck off, his men to burn all the houses, and to cut down their corn. "And after we marched with the queen and her Children to our Boats again," he wrote, "where being no sooner well-shipped my soldiers did begin to murmur because the queen and her Children were spared. So upon a Council being called it was agreed to put the children to death, the which was effected by Throwing them overboard and shooting out their Brains in the water. Yet for all this Cruelty," he remarked, evidently shocked by the brutality, "the Soldiers were not well pleased and I had much to do to save the queen's life for that time." After the attack, Percy's men sailed a couple of miles up the Chickahominy where Captain James Davis led the soldiers in cutting down the Chickahominies' corn, setting fire to their town, and destroying their temples before returning once again to their boats and heading downriver to the fort.

De La Warr was pleased to hear of the success of the attacks but annoyed that the Paspahegh "queen" had not been killed. He therefore ordered her execution forthwith by burning, which he thought "best." Percy told the lord governor that "having seen so much Bloodshed that day, now in my Cold blood I desired to see no more." As for burning her, he "did not hold it fitting" and proposed instead she should be shot or put to the sword. Accordingly, one of the English captains, James Davis, took her into the woods nearby and killed her.[9]

Shortly after, the lord general dispatched Captain Edward Brewster with two companies of men against the Warraskoyacks. The elderly chief, Tackonekintaco, and his son, Tangoit, had been captured earlier by the English and on being freed consented to provide the settlers with five hundred bushels of corn, beans, and peas in return for copper, beads, and hatchets. Subsequently, when Tackonekintaco refused to deliver the provisions, De La Warr ordered his troops to attack them. Aware of the recent raids on their neighbors, the chief maintained a careful watch, and when the English were spotted coming downriver, he gave the signal for his people to abandon their towns and take refuge in surrounding woods. The soldiers did not venture into the woods but cut down the Indians' corn, burnt their houses, and then sailed back to Jamestown.

De La Warr's summer offensive against the Kecoughtans, Paspeheghs, Chickahominies, and Warraskoyacks indicated a significant hardening of attitude against Indian peoples. Using his ships, he put in place a strategy of moving his troops, one or two companies (fifty to one hundred men) at a time, along the rivers to surprise the Indians in their towns. Ignoring European rules of war, the soldiers gave no quarter and killed as many men, women, and children as possible before setting fire to their houses and taking their corn. They devastated their towns, ruined cornfields, and made off with the Indians' precious food stores. Indians, not English colonists, would feel the bitterness of starvation the next winter. The horrific violence perpetrated by the English was intended to sow terror among Indian peoples and to send a message to Powhatan that he should submit to De La Warr's demands and serve the lord governor. If not, the murderous and destructive attacks would continue.[10]

Other than forbidding his petty chiefs from supplying the English with food, Powhatan made no attempt to coordinate a response to the attacks. Each chief was left to his own devices. Given the speed and ferocity of the raids, effective defense was all but impossible, and their people were left with little alternative but to flee as the English approached. Indian fortunes would change dramatically later in the year, however.

De La Warr had decided to organize a large-scale expedition inland to search for mines and a river passage through the mountains. The first stage would entail repossessing the fort at the falls abandoned by his younger brother, Francis West. A group of German miners, recruited by the Virginia Company expressly for the purpose of finding and trying precious minerals, were sent on ahead upriver. Near a town of the Appomattocs, some of the men went ashore to refresh their water barrels, where they were invited to the village of the "Queen," Opossunoquonuske, to "feast and make merry." The Indians asked the men to come to their houses but to leave their weapons in their boat, saying that otherwise their women would be frightened. Like "greedy fools," Percy wrote, the men accepted, "more esteeming of A Little food than their own lives and safety, for when the Indians had them in their houses and found a fitting Time" they fell upon them and "Slew divers [many] and wounded all the rest." Only one man named Dowse, the drummer who had played and danced at Kecoughtan, managed to get back to the boat by sheltering under a makeshift shield as arrows rained down around him. The Indians, Percy observed, "be not So Simple as many Imagine who be not Acquainted with their Subtleties for they had not forgotten how their neighbors at Kecoughtan were allured and defeated by Sir Thomas Gates when he had the same Taborer [drummer] with him." Among the fourteen killed were all the Germans. Captain Brewster carried out reprisals with a second expedition for what the English characterized as "a treacherous Massacre," killing some of the Indians, burning the town, and wounding Opossunoquonuske with small shot as she escaped into the woods.[11]

Captains Brewster and George Yeardley were able to establish their men at the falls where they were joined by De La Warr but to little effect. During the winter, elite warriors, possibly Powhatan and Pamunkey, adopted similar tactics as the year before, raiding the English garrison and then retiring into the woods before the soldiers could counterattack. In the fighting, Captain William West (De La Warr's nephew) and several others were killed, after which, in one of the few examples of its kind, Strachey recorded the words the Indians sang in triumph:

1. *Mattanerew shashashewaw erawango pechecoma*
   Whe Tassantassa inoshashaw yehockan pocosack
   Whe, whe, yah, ha, ha, ne, he, wittowa, wittowa.
2. *Mattanerew shashashewaw, erawango pechecoma*
   Capt. Newport inoshashaw nier in hoc nantion matassan
   Whe, whe, yah, ha, ha, etc.
3. *Mattanerew shashashewaw erawango pechecoma*
   Thom. Newport inoshashaw nier in hoc nantion monocock
   Whe, whe, etc.
4. *Mattanerew shashashewaw erawango pechecoma*
   Pockin Simon moshasha mingon nantian Tamahuck.
   Whe, whe, etc.

They killed us for our guns (*pocosacks*), Strachey translated, and our swords (*monococks*), took Captain Newport's copper, and captured one of the sailors, Simon Score, for his hatchet. When they tortured him, he cried out "whe, whe, etc.," and the warriors sang scornfully, "Yah, ha, ha, Tewittaw, Tewittawa, Tewittawa." Strachey mentioned the Indians also had "a kind of angry song" in which they prayed to their god Okeus and to other "idols to plague the Tassantasses [English] and their posterities [future generations]." Okeus was their most important god for day-to-day affairs, a cruel deity, according to the English, who punished those who deserved it with sickness, famine, storms, and war. Indian priests' role in appealing to their gods for help against the intruders underlined once again the priests' central importance in efforts to defeat the English.

Powhatan's tactics defeated De La Warr's men at the falls in the winter of 1610–1611, just as they had defeated the English at Jamestown during the starving time. The settlers had been successful when raiding Indian communities close to rivers where they could maneuver their ships and destroy towns and cornfields, but once they began establishing garrisons, they became targets for sustained Indian hit-and-run attacks. In addition, English losses were multiplied severalfold by disease. The lord governor had been chronically ill since he arrived, which had seriously compromised his ability to command. During a sickly summer, approximately a hundred of his men died, and as a consequence he was forced to abandon the two forts he had established near the lands of the Kecoughtans to ensure he had sufficient men to repossess the fort at the falls. That effort, too, failed, and after a few months De La Warr and the soldiers returned to Jamestown.

At the end of March 1611, the ailing governor boarded his ship, together with more than fifty settlers, and left Jamestown, claiming that his health had so deteriorated that he had no choice but to leave. The day after he departed, according to George Percy, hundreds of Paspahegh warriors attacked the blockhouse outside the fort and killed about a dozen men. Once again in charge of the colony, Percy recorded that when the Indians let fly their arrows, they were as thick as hail and almost covered the ground where the soldiers were slain. They did so "Shout and hallow [holler] in Triumph of their gained victory that the Echo thereof made both the Air and woods to Ring," to make known their delight at revenging the death of Wowinchopunck, killed a couple of months earlier. Chanting "Paspahegh, Paspahegh," the warriors eventually withdrew into the woods when confronted by a large force hastily dispatched from the fort, leaving Percy's men the grim task of recovering the dead.[12]

Powhatan and Opechancanough probably assumed that De La Warr had left for good, but disappointingly there was no indication at Jamestown that the colony was about to be abandoned. In fact, although the two chiefs could not have known, the lord governor had planned only a temporary respite from his duties in Virginia. He meant to head for Nevis to regain his health in the island's wholesome natural springs and then return. Winds and tides swept him from the American coast across the Atlantic to the Azores, however, and from there he sailed on to England where he quickly penned an explanation for his departure for leaders of the Virginia Company.

Unsurprisingly, the lord governor painted an exceptionally rosy picture of the state of affairs in the colony at his departure. More than 200 settlers remained (the number was closer to 170), of whom most were in good health and well supplied with provisions, and the land was wonderfully fertile, their livestock thrived, and rich fishing grounds off the coast were within easy reach. Even after his experiences at the falls, he wrote that the Powhatans were "not able to do us hurt." He reported that Captain Samuel Argall, an experienced mariner familiar with the waters of the Chesapeake Bay, had made important discoveries along the Potomac River, which boasted "the goodliest Trees for masts . . . Hemp better than English, growing wild in abundance" and mines of antimony and lead farther north. More important in the long run was Argall's cordial meeting with Patawomeck Indians who were eager to trade despite Powhatan's embargo. The region would come to provide large quantities of corn, and the Patawomecks would later become powerful allies against the Powhatans.[13]

Nevertheless, had it been left to De La Warr's account alone, the colony may well have struggled to survive much longer. Investors chafed at the lack of profits or even favorable prospects, and confidence in the venture diminished to such a point that further attempts to raise funds for the colony appeared slim. Fortunately for the company, however, Gates's triumphant return to London in the summer of 1610 carrying news of the miraculous survival of the settlers on board the *Sea Venture* recast the colony's struggles into an epic narrative that reaffirmed God's special plan for the English. Who could deny "the Lords infinite goodness," the company proclaimed in *A True Declaration*, published later in the year, for if "He had not sent Sir Thomas Gates from the Bermudas, within four days they [the settlers at Jamestown] had almost been famished." If Gates had abandoned the fort and set sail sooner "and launched into the vast Ocean, who would have promised they should have encountered the Fleet of the Lord De la Ware?" Could there be any doubt, the company asked, that this "was the arm of the Lord of Hosts, who would have his people pass the red Sea and Wilderness, and then to possess the land of Canaan." Written in providential terms, the company was convinced that God was determined to "raise our state, and build his Church in that excellent climate [Virginia], if the action be seconded with resolution and Religion."

Planting Protestantism and more particularly the Church of England in North America was at the heart of the company's appeal to continue "the action." God had saved the colonists and the colony for a reason, which included the honor and profit of England but primarily, as Robert Johnson had emphasized earlier, to save the souls of millions of Indians who lived in thrall to Satan. Should not the gospel be preached "to all the world, before the end of the world?" The writer of *A True Declaration* wrote dismissively of the Spanish bringing the gospel to the Indians only after enslaving them. By contrast, the English had sought to trade fairly and live peaceably among the Indians, which the law of nations permitted, only to be met with relentless hostility. When Captain Newport visited Powhatan at Werowocomoco, the chief invited him to leave

Jamestown and possess "another whole kingdom, which he gave to him." This was a ploy, however, so he "might first gain by us, and then destroy us," which "makes our cause, much the juster [more just], when God turned their subtlety, to our utility: giving to us a lawful possession." Was there a holier work, the company concluded, than casting down "the altars of Devils that you may raise up the Altar of Christ: to forbid the sacrifice of men, that they may offer up the sacrifice of contrite spirits; to reduce Barbarism and infidelity, to civil government and Christianity?"[14]

Months before De La Warr's ineffectual campaign against the Powhatans at the falls and subsequent return to England, company leaders had already made the decision and raised the necessary funds to dispatch two large-scale expeditions to Virginia. They would be led by the seasoned military commanders Sir Thomas Dale and Sir Thomas Gates, who with hundreds of troops would inaugurate a new and terrible phase of the war.

DALE, APPOINTED MARSHAL of Virginia, left England in mid-March 1611 with three hundred men and sixty women and after a swift crossing arrived at Jamestown two months later. Among the "great store of armor and munition" he brought were one thousand arquebuses (a type of heavy musket), five hundred muskets, various types of swords, halberds, three hundred corselets consisting of breast and back plate armor, and five hundred helmets. Halberds and "bills," polearms typically six to eight feet long, were designed variously with vicious hooks, spikes, and axes and were employed to spear and hack the enemy to death; swords were used to sever heads and limbs, and short swords and daggers could be used to slash and thrust, causing massive internal bleeding and trauma. Musket balls were capable of smashing through cartilage and bone, causing terrible injuries that were usually fatal, killing by shock or infection if not by immediate blood loss. Firearms could be used singly or in massed ranks to devastating effect. Small ships, such as pinnaces or shallops, were capable of carrying swivel guns, aptly named murderers, breech loaded with small shot to pepper Indian settlements along the shores or at massed groups of warriors. Powhatan war bows were formidable weapons also capable of delivering fatal arrow shots or debilitating wounds, but stone arrowheads could not penetrate plate armor.[15]

Dale's strategy was straightforward, echoing that of his predecessor. He aimed to gain control of the Powhatan (James) River by establishing fortified settlements at the mouth and the falls as well as

Figure 7.1. Captain Samuel Argall meets with leaders of the Chickahominies, detail from an engraving by Johann Theodore de Bry after Georg Keller, plate 9, in *America*, part 10. Note the guard immediately behind him are dressed in coats of mail and carry swords and muskets. The sergeant at arms carries a halberd. Argall is dressed in a plate corselet and holds his officer's staff in his right hand denoting his rank. In the distance, soldiers are dressed in helmets and corselets and carry swords, muskets, and polearms. The Chickahominies are represented carrying only their bows and arrows.

Courtesy of the Virginia Museum of History and Culture (G159.C696 v.5).

at Jamestown and across the peninsula at Kiskiack on the Pamunkey (York) River. Just as Powhatan and Opechancanough understood from their experiences of the 1570s and 1580s that to withstand invasion by powerful European forces they needed to govern the peoples near the entrances of the major rivers, so Dale was convinced that only by controlling the Powhatan (James) River could he defeat the Powhatans. Building new forts along its banks would "so over master the subtle, mischievous, great Powhatan," he wrote to the earl of Salisbury, that either the chief would be forced to flee the country or accept an alliance with the English.[16]

Dale's first experience of battle in Virginia was against the Nansemonds, a powerful and numerous people who represented the only remaining threat to English mastery of the lower Powhatan River. Four chiefs, of whom Weyhohomo was the senior, ruled approximately eight hundred to one thousand inhabitants. In a series of skirmishes, as many as two hundred warriors put up fierce resistance and wounded many of the one hundred soldiers Dale had with him, including John Martin and Francis West. Percy reported that Dale himself narrowly escaped "for an arrow lit just upon the edge or Brim of his head piece, the which if it had fallen a thought [touch] lower might have shot him in the Brains and endangered his Life." Never having before encountered the English in plate armor marching in formation, warriors were astonished they did not inflict heavier casualties. Their priests helped by making strange "conjurations and charms, throwing fire up into the skies" and running up and down with rattles, making "many diabolical gestures" and "Spells and incantations, Imagining thereby to cause Rain to fall from the Clouds" to extinguish the soldiers' matches and spoil their powder. But, Percy commented grimly, "neither the devil whom they adore nor all their Sorcerers did anything Avail them for our men Cut down their Corn, Burned their houses and besides those which they had slain brought some of them prisoners to our fort." The Nansemonds were routed, and their towns reduced to ruins.[17]

Shortly after, when Powhatan learned that Dale was preparing an expedition to the falls, he forbade the commander to go or else, he warned, he would destroy the English in "a strange manner" by making the settlers drunk and killing them all. Dale was apparently greatly amused by the message and scoffed at his threat before setting out to find a suitable location for the colony's new capital. Encamped at the falls at prayer one night, the men heard a noise coming from the cornfields near their earthworks, "like an Indian *huphup* with an *oho oho*," and some saw an Indian leap over a fire and run into the corn chanting the same, at which the soldiers became much confused. All they could say was *oho oho* and picking up the wrong end of their weapons began to attack one another, "each man Taking one another for an Indian." The men awoke as out of a dream after seven to eight minutes and began to search for their enemies but realizing their mistake remained very quiet, shaken by the strange fantasy. "All which things," a young minister Alexander Whitaker concluded, "make me think that there be great witches among them and they very familiar with the devil."[18]

In early August 1611, Sir Thomas Gates arrived with another 300 settlers, cattle, and supplies. A total of 750 settlers were now in the colony, and once again the English were falling ill rapidly in the sultry summer heat, most likely from drinking polluted water and the unsanitary conditions caused by overcrowding. Gates, who as deputy governor outranked Dale, quickly took charge and began plans to move a large body of men off Jamestown Island as soon as possible. The following month, Captain Edward Brewster with 350 handpicked men, including many artisans who had arrived with Gates, set out overland to a site upriver where the new capital was to be built. The largest expedition yet mounted to the upper Powhatan River, the heartland of Tsenacommacah, could have left Powhatan or Opechancanough in no doubt about the increasingly grave threat their people faced.

The two chiefs could not overlook, therefore, an outstanding opportunity to inflict heavy casualties on the soldiers as they marched along the river. Brewster's men were repeatedly attacked by Powhatan and Arrohattoc warriors led by a charismatic warrior, Nemattanew, called by the English "Jack of the Feathers," owing to his practice of going into battle "covered with feathers and Swans wings fastened to his shoulders as though he meant to fly." Repulsing the attacks, the English eventually reached an area of high ground jutting into the river a few miles below Arrohattoc, where they joined Dale, who had followed by ship carrying timber and supplies. Over the following weeks, as the English erected a strong palisade across a neck of land to create a defensible island, the attacks were unceasing, the Indians approaching as close as possible to shoot directly into the fort, wounding many. Those working outside the palisade were even more vulnerable and were frequently forced back inside. But despite the Indians' dogged resistance, Dale's men pressed on building the town, named Henrico or Henricus in honor of another of Dale's influential patrons, Henry the Prince of Wales, eldest son of James I.

By late December, they had laid out three streets of framed houses and built a "handsome Church" and storehouses for the company's provisions and trade goods. Two miles from the fort they also constructed a stockade across the peninsula, guarded by sturdy blockhouses, to enclose acres of cornfields sufficient to supply the town and later neighboring settlements. Lastly, watchtowers were built at each corner of the fort's palisade to maintain a watch for Indian attacks and ships coming upriver. Besides English vessels, Dale and Gates had heard numerous reports from London about the possibility of an imminent Spanish assault on the colony. The previous June, a caravel sent by Philip III to discover where the English were located and assess their strength had attempted to enter the Powhatan River before heading back out to sea. Leaving behind several of their men, including a seasoned spy, Don Diego de Molina, who sent

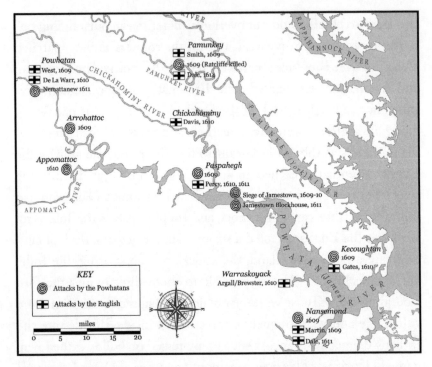

FIGURE 7.2. The siege of Jamestown and battles of 1609–1614. *Drawing by Jamie May.*

secret messages from Jamestown to Madrid for the next five years, company leaders in London and Dale and his council in Virginia feared a fleet of warships might arrive at any time.[19]

DALE'S SUCCESS IN creating a base of operations upriver near the falls, in contrast to earlier failures by Captain Francis West and Lord De La Warr, gave the English an enormous advantage in the campaign for control of the Powhatan (James) River Valley. From Henrico, Dale led a force late in the year to devastate the villages of the Appomattocs and make off with their corn supplies, which he explained was meant to "revenge the treacherous injury of those people, done unto us," a reference to the killing of the German miners. Admiring the fertility of their land, he immediately took possession of it and named the area the New Bermudas, in honor of the Bermuda Islands, which also had a reputation for fertility. In coming years, lands on both sides of the Powhatan River, from the mouth of the Appomattox River to Henrico and beyond the falls, were taken up by settlers, turning it into the most populous area occupied by the English in the Virginia colony. Although Virginia's commanders, with their ability to transport soldiers quickly by ship and superiority in weaponry, were confident about defeating the Powhatans in battle and defending themselves inside their fortified settlements, neither in 1612 nor the following year could they mount a decisive campaign to force Chief Powhatan to surrender or drive him out of the region.[20]

For his part, Powhatan could do nothing to counter the rapid expansion of English settlement. A frontal assault on the fort at Henrico would have been disastrous, costly in lives and playing into English hands. War bows, clubs, wooden "swords," and tomahawks were highly effective in hand-to-hand combat but no match for musket fire, steel swords, and daggers at close quarters. Powhatan's and Opechancanough's determined effort to acquire European weapons from the earliest days of English occupation speaks to their acute awareness of the carnage they could inflict. A crushing defeat would seriously deplete warrior numbers and also weaken Powhatan's authority, possibly encouraging those peoples who were allies through fear rather than friendship to join the English. All the great chief could do was maintain hit-and-run raids that gave the soldiers no peace and minimized his own losses and hope disease or possibly English disaffection would ultimately force them to abandon their settlements. For him as for other chiefs, the war was no longer an effort to expel the intruders from his lands or to contain and control them; it had become a desperate struggle for the survival of Tsenacommacah.[21]

CHAPTER 8

Betrayal

A T THE NORTHERN MARGINS OF POWHATAN'S CHIEFDOM lived the Patawomecks, the most numerous of the dozen or so peoples whose territories stretched along both sides of the Potomac River. The region had been a major border zone for centuries, its north bank containing peoples of the Piscataway paramount chiefdom and its south bank sustaining half a dozen chiefdoms, including the Patawomecks, loosely affiliated with the Powhatans. All of them, whether north or south, were subject to periodic raids by powerful "stranger" Indians, from the west the Mannahoacs and from the north the Susquehannocks and Massawomecks, described by Captain John Smith as "a great nation and very populous" who "continually tormented" peoples at the heads of the rivers. Patawomeck trade and diplomacy was therefore complex, requiring the war chief, Iopassus, to balance a variety of interests and challenges involving the Piscataway chiefdom, friendly peoples of the Potomac and across the peninsula on the Rappahannock River, attacks by hostile warriors, the demands of the great chief Powhatan, and latterly the arrival of the English, in a continuing effort to maintain their independence.[1]

Into this uncertain world of danger and opportunity sailed Captain Samuel Argall in the spring of 1613. He was not the first Englishman the Patawomecks had encountered. Captain John Smith had visited five years earlier while on his voyage of discovery around the Chesapeake Bay, the purpose of which, besides searching for mines and a passage to the South Sea, was to gather information about the relative strength of Powhatan's influence throughout the region. The reason for Argall's visit was somewhat different. He was primarily interested in trading for corn, although after four years of war, he too was interested in taking the pulse of Patawomeck-Powhatan relations. He was well liked by peoples of the region owing to his respectful conduct and fair dealing on previous voyages to the river, which had resulted in his bringing large quantities of corn back to Jamestown. Argall had successfully restored good relations with the Patawomecks following the disastrous visit of Captain Francis West several years earlier when the English were starving at Jamestown, and from then on both sides valued what each other had to offer: the English viewed the entire Potomac region as a granary from whence a steady supply of corn was forthcoming, and the Indians valued trade goods such as copper, glass beads, and iron tools.[2]

The timing of Argall's visit to the Potomac was auspicious. He was told by Indians farther upriver that Pocahontas was staying with the Patawomecks, having come ostensibly to "exchange some of her father's commodities for theirs" but more likely to collect tribute from the chief. Knowing she was a favorite daughter of Powhatan and a valued emissary, Argall quickly conceived a plan to take her prisoner and return to Jamestown, where she would be held as a hostage and used in negotiations to return English captives and the large store of weapons taken by Powhatan warriors. He approached Iopassus, a friend among the Patawomecks, and told him of his plan, urging his "brother" to help and reassuring him that no harm would come to Pocahontas or to them. If he helped, Argall told him, the

FIGURE 8.1. The betrayal and kidnapping of Pocahontas by Iopassus, engraving by Johann Theodore de Bry, after Georg Keller, plate 7, in *America*, part 10. In the foreground, Iopassus and his wife persuade Pocahontas to go with them on board Captain Samuel Argall's ship. On the right of the image, the story moves forward to Pocahontas having dinner with Argall, Iopassus, and his wife aboard the *Treasurer*. *Courtesy of the Virginia Museum of History and Culture (G159.C696 v.5).*

English would protect them against any reprisals from the Powhatans, but on the other hand if he refused, then they would no longer be brothers and the peace between their peoples would end.

Iopassus fully recognized the decision to join with the English would have far-reaching implications and immediately took the matter to the "great King of Patawomeck." A lengthy discussion ensued among the chief's priests and councilors that concluded with an agreement to help Argall. Shortly after, according to the plan,

Iopassus and his wife enticed Pocahontas aboard Argall's ship, the *Treasurer*, where they spent the night. The next morning, the two left, taking a small copper kettle as a token of the Englishman's thanks. Then Argall informed Pocahontas she would return with him to Jamestown. Little is known of her immediate response other than she became "exceeding pensive, and discontented." We may surmise, however, she was outraged at her treatment by the Patowomecks and Argall. She had once been a frequent visitor to Jamestown and had known the English leaders well, but she did not know the new commanders Dale and Gates or what they might expect from her.

While the *Treasurer* was still riding at anchor off the Potomac shore, the chief of the Patawomecks dispatched messengers to Powhatan, some eighty miles away in Orapax, where he was residing, to inform him about Captain Argall's abduction of Pocahontas. In return for his daughter, the messengers told him, Argall had laid out a number of demands. All English prisoners held by the chief should be freed forthwith and returned to Jamestown along with the weapons and tools stolen by his warriors, and in addition, the Englishman demanded a large quantity of corn. Other than accounts by Argall and Ralph Hamor, an eyewitness, there is no information about Powhatan's response, but it is certain that while he was apparently "much grieved" about his daughter's capture he was probably more distressed by his suspicion that the Patawomecks were directly involved in the plot and had betrayed him.

Powhatan did not hurry himself to recover his daughter, waiting three months before he replied and subsequently returning only a handful of prisoners and some broken muskets. He told Gates that "he made great use" of the prisoners and delighted in looking upon the weapons, which were highly valued trophies of his warriors' successes and English "shames." Powhatan did agree, however, to provide five hundred bushels of corn in compensation for the weapons and tools broken and, more important, when his daughter was safely returned promised to "be forever friends" with the English. Gates refused, telling the chief that his daughter was well treated and would remain with the English until the weapons were sent back. Much to Pocahontas's disgust, the return of weapons, not her, was viewed by both sets of leaders as the critical issue on which peace or the continuance of war hinged.[3]

Argall's trading voyages with peoples on the fringes of Powhatan's territories together with the exchanges concerning Pocahontas and the return of English weapons reveal a good deal about the shifting balance of power between the English leaders and the great chief. By the summer of 1613, as messages went back and forth between Jamestown and Orapax, Powhatan's control of Tsenacommacah was beginning to crumble. Argall was convinced the Patawomecks and peoples of the Eastern Shore, the Accomacs and Occohannocs, were desirous of peace as well as trade and were ready to enter into formal agreements with the English. At the same time, the peoples along the Powhatan River, from the Kecoughtans and Nansemonds to the Appomattocs and Powhatans, had either been defeated or subjected to devastating raids to which they had little answer. He had failed to dislodge the intruders at Jamestown, and new settlements had been established in the heart of his territories upriver. The threat of English alliances with hostile peoples to the west and south remained, and rumors had been picked up from the settlers of the possibility of an imminent attack by Spanish warships. The Powhatans' world was shrinking and so too was the great chief's authority.[4]

A LONG SILENCE ensued. Nothing was heard from Powhatan or Opechancanough until the following spring. All the while, Pocahontas lived in the fort at Jamestown learning English and being instructed in the precepts of Anglicanism. During this period, she met a young gentleman, John Rolfe. Eventually, to break the deadlock, toward the end of March 1614, Dale and Argall placed Pocahontas on board the *Treasurer* and with a frigate carrying 150 soldiers and an escort of a couple of smaller ships sailed up the Pamunkey River where the two chiefs' major settlements were located. Dale's intention was to force their warriors to fight for Pocahontas or exchange her for the English prisoners they still held, together with their tools and weapons.

The direction of the attack was influenced by several factors. Gates and Dale were already in control of the Powhatan (James) River but had not yet attempted attacks on Pamunkey (York) River settlements, hoping instead to persuade Powhatan to agree to peace rather than escalate the war by opening up another front. No English ships had ventured into Pamunkey territories since the disastrous expedition led by John Ratcliffe four and a half years earlier. Timing was also an important consideration, as the English commanders could not afford an inconclusive end to the fighting that would leave the English in limbo, neither at peace nor war. Between 1609 and 1611, twenty-four ships had arrived in Virginia carrying approximately 1,300 settlers and soldiers. However, owing to the enormous costs involved and continuing lack of return or any prospect of return to investors, settlers and supplies had subsequently dried up. Only five ships and less than a couple of hundred settlers arrived between 1612 and 1614. Quite likely, Powhatan and Opechancanough were aware of the dwindling number of ships arriving in the Powhatan River and calculated that maintaining the status quo was to their advantage. Gates and Dale therefore needed a decisive victory or a firm peace agreement, otherwise English settler populations would continue to decrease and eventually the colony would wither away. A similar assessment influenced the king of Spain's decision not to send a fleet to destroy Jamestown in these same years. Finally, the Pamunkeys were reputed to have the best warriors in the chiefdom; if Dale and Argall could defeat them, they would be able to take control of the Pamunkeys' lands and the war would be as good as over.[5]

In mid-June, Dale sent a lengthy letter back to England describing what happened. When his fleet arrived in the Pamunkey River, following the Youghtanund branch inland, warriors lined the banks shouting with "great bravado" and demanded to know why the English had come. Through interpreters, Dale told them they came to deliver Pocahontas and in return to retrieve their weapons and men or else, he told them, "to fight with them, burn their houses, take away their Canoes, break down their fishing Weirs, and do them what other damages we could." Some of the warriors replied that if the English wanted to fight they would welcome it, for they were well prepared and counseled "us rather to retire (if we loved our safety) then proceed." Ralph Hamor, an eyewitness and envoy, reported that the warriors bragged that the English "had ever had the worst of them in that River" and reminded them of the fate of Captain Ratcliffe who, with most of his company, had been killed.

Rather than fight, Dale chose initially to send John Rolfe and Robert Sparkes to discuss terms with Powhatan. They did not make any progress, however, being told by the Indians that the "great King" was three days' journey away but mentioning that Opechancanough was nearby and that whatever terms he agreed to Powhatan would confirm. Rolfe and Sparkes insisted they would meet with Powhatan only. When no further news of a meeting materialized, Dale decided to take action, putting his men ashore where they engaged a group of warriors, killing or injuring half a dozen, and then burning forty houses of the Indian town close by and pillaging as they went.

The following day, Dale continued higher up the river where more insults and challenges were exchanged. The Pamunkeys expressed fury at the Englishmen's behavior, while Dale replied they had come in a "peaceable manner" and had been attacked without provocation, which was clearly untrue. Calling from the riverbank, the Indians told Dale that they would help him recover what he came for and would immediately send messengers to Powhatan. After another couple of days passed and nothing was heard about the

FIGURE 8.2. Detail of the kidnapping of Pocahontas, from an engraving by Johann Theodore de Bry, after Georg Keller, plate 7, in *America*, part 10, showing the expedition of Sir Thomas Dale and Samuel Argall to the Pamunkey River in March 1614. A town is being attacked by English troops and set on fire, while Indian warriors assault the *Treasurer* and a barge.
Courtesy of the Virginia Museum of History and Culture (G159.C696 v.5).

weapons, the English disembarked close to one of Powhatan's major residencies, called Matchcot, where warriors mounted an impressive show of force, gathering hundreds of men ready to defend the town.

Tensions quickly rose as the Indians and English faced off, seemingly intent on a trial of strength. Then two of Pocahontas's brothers intervened and asked to talk to her. When she was brought ashore to meet them, according to Hamor, they "much rejoiced" at seeing her safe and well. However, she was less pleased to see them saying "that if her father had loved her, he would not value her less than old swords, pieces [muskets], or axes." Consequently, she told them she had decided to stay with the English.

At the last moment, hostilities were avoided. A message came from Powhatan that was sufficient to satisfy Dale and allow both sides to depart without losing face. The Englishmen's weapons and

FIGURE 8.3. The English arrive at Matchcot, a principal residence of Powhatan, where two of Pocahontas's brothers negotiate with Thomas Savage, the interpreter, for her release. To the left, Pamunkey warriors walk among Dale's heavily armed soldiers; in the center, hundreds of Indians mass in a show of strength and defiance. Matchcot is depicted in the background. Engraving by Johann Theodore de Bry, after Georg Keller, in *America*, part 10. *Courtesy of the John Carter Brown Library.*

tools would be returned to Jamestown within fifteen days "with some Corn," Dale was informed, and Pocahontas would be his "child, and ever dwell" with the English who would be the great chief's friend and live in peace. Given that it was early April, both sides were anxious to return to their communities to prepare for spring planting. With conditions agreed, the English returned to Jamestown and a few weeks later received a message from Opechancanough saying that he desired Dale to "call him friend" and "saying he was a great Captain, and did always fight: that I [Dale] was also a great Captain, and therefore he loved me; and that my friends should be his friends."

In this somewhat abrupt and confused manner, a settlement of sorts was reached, ending the first Powhatan-English war. It came after five years of sieges, vicious raids, brutal killings, and the systematic devastation of villages, livestock, and crops. Both sides could return to tending to their corn, fishing, and hunting, without fear of attack. Dale, a deeply religious man, had little doubt the outcome was a result of divine intervention. "Now may you judge Sir," Dale bragged to a friend in London, "if the God of Battles had not a helping hand in this, that having our Swords drawn . . . they [the Powhatans] tendered us peace, and strive with all alacrity to keep us in good opinion of them; by which many benefits arise unto us." The sudden turnaround in relations, however, may have had more to do with changes taking place among the Powhatan leadership than the Englishman's "God of Battles."[6]

ALTHOUGH PLANNED FOR some months, a highly consequential wedding conveniently set the seal on the peace accord. On April 5, Pocahontas, henceforth known by the English as Rebecca, married John Rolfe in the rustic splendor of the wooden church at Jamestown, witnessed by her elderly uncle Opachisco, two of his sons, and a throng of jubilant English commanders. Her relationship with Rolfe has been the subject of endless speculation in biographies, works of fiction, children's books, plays, and films. Were they in love, did they truly care about one another, or was it a marriage of convenience on both sides? Whereas Rolfe made his feelings plain in a long letter to Dale in which he examined his wish to marry her in painful detail, nothing was recorded about how she felt about the prospect other than her few words to her brothers at Matchcot, stating that she intended to remain with the English "who loved her." She may have found the freedoms offered by the English, who treated her with respect as the daughter of the Indian king, exhilarating, just as learning about the newcomers appealed to her intelligence and curiosity. However, in the absence of any written accounts of what she thought about her marriage to Rolfe, conversion to Anglicanism, and adoption of English ways, it is impossible to draw any firm conclusions. Only in London a few years later are a few clues forthcoming about how she positioned herself in the two worlds of the English and the Powhatans she inhabited.[7]

Whatever she thought, her father and Governor Dale both immediately saw major advantages from the union. Powhatan viewed the wedding as a marriage alliance that would lead not only to a cessation of hostilities but also halt the encroachment of English settlements on his peoples' lands. Additionally, his daughter would be located at the heart of the English leadership and might therefore find out what the English intended and were planning, valuable information that would help guide future relations. For Dale, the marriage represented a major breakthrough in achieving one of the Virginia Company's cherished objectives: the conversion of the Indians to Christianity and Englishness. My "principal care has been to get some of our savages to whom we may teach both our language and religion," he wrote to Sir Thomas Smythe, the leader of the company, from Henrico the previous year, but "the elders have been all too dead settled in their Ignorance, the children are so tenderly beloved of their parents that neither copper nor love can draw any from them." With Pocahontas's marriage, he could boast about converting the daughter of the paramount chief of Tsenacommacah, who he was convinced would play a vital role in the conversion of the great chief himself and his people.[8]

Toward the end of April, Dale received further good news. Messengers arrived from the Chickahominies inviting him to visit to negotiate their own peace accord. Dale set out once again with Argall to meet their leaders, accompanied by fifty men in case the invitation was an ambush. When the Chickahominy leaders told Argall of their desire to be friends, he asked whether they would accept King James as their king. Following a brief discussion, they agreed but with the condition that the English would fight their enemies if need be, to which Argall consented. At the conclusion of discussions, Argall gave each of the eight "great men" a large tomahawk and a piece of copper, assuring them of their people's freedom to move up and down the rivers and trade with the English without injury. For their part, the Chickahominies pledged themselves to a number of stipulations: to provide three hundred or four hundred bowmen to aid the English against the Spanish ("whose name is odious amongst them") or any Indians who attacked them; not to kill English settlers or their cattle nor to try to tear down their palisades; and to deliver annually two bushels of corn for every fighting man to the English storehouse, "as tribute of their obedience to his Majesty, and to his deputy" (the governor) in Virginia.

If the Chickahominies believed they were entering into an alliance more as equals than as subordinates, the English saw the relationship from a quite different perspective. The "chief men" who had governed largely independently were described by the English as "substitutes and Councilors under Sir Thomas Dale," in recognition of which they would each receive from James I every year "a red coat, or livery" and a picture "of his Majesty, engraved in Copper, with a chain of Copper to hang it about his neck, whereby they shall be known to King JAMES [as] his noble Men." By their willingness to call themselves English, fight in support of the colonists, and pay an annual tribute, they had become in effect James's vassals. Yet, no matter how the English commanders at Jamestown or leaders of the Virginia Company in London chose to interpret the new accord, by joining the English, the Chickahominy headmen had made a bold and unequivocal statement to Powhatan and Opechancanough about where their loyalties now lay.[9]

RALPH HAMOR TOGETHER with the young interpreter Thomas Savage were the last Englishmen to see Powhatan. Led by two Indian guides, they trekked overland to Matchcot in mid-May 1614, where the chief greeted them on the banks of the Pamunkey River. He was pleased to see Savage and asked why he had not returned after going to visit friends at Paspahegh (Jamestown) four years earlier. The chief used the occasion to inquire also about Namontack, sent to England with Captain Newport many years ago to meet King James, whom he had not heard from since despite the arrival of numerous ships from England. "How you have dealt with him I know not," he remarked tersely. Turning to Hamor, he placed his hands around the Englishman's neck and asked why he was not wearing the chain of pearls that was sent to Dale as a gift and to indicate that messengers were sent by him. Hamor was nonplussed since Dale had clearly not mentioned it but was able to reassure the chief that he had been accompanied from Jamestown by Powhatan's own men, one of whom was a trusted councilor, which he thought was sufficient validation.

Retiring to Powhatan's house, they first took a pipe of tobacco after which the chief inquired how "his Brother" Sir Thomas Dale fared and whether his daughter and "unknown son" (John Rolfe) liked living together. Hamor replied that Dale was very well and his daughter "so well content that she would not change her life to return and live with him, whereat he laughed heartily, and said he was very glad of it." Then, he asked what had led to their unexpected visit. Hamor formally relayed Dale's greeting of love and peace, which, Hamor confirmed, the English commander considered inviolable. As a token of Dale's love, he presented the great chief with several gifts, including two large pieces of copper, five strings of white and blue beads, and a pair of knives, also saying that if Powhatan would send men to Jamestown, Dale would provide him with a large grinding stone. Hamor then made the request that was the primary reason for his visit. Dale had heard of the "exquisite perfection" of Powhatan's youngest daughter, and if the chief would give his permission, he would gladly make the girl "his nearest companion, wife and bedfellow." Dale's request, Hamor said, was prompted by the fact that now "firmly united together, and made one people . . . he [Dale] would make a natural union between us," principally because he was resolved to remain "in your country so long as he lives," Hamor continued, "and would therefore not only have the firmest assurance he may, of perpetual friendship from you, but also hereby bind himself thereunto." This, of course, was a blatant lie; Dale had no intention of staying in Virginia for the rest of his life.[10]

FIGURE 8.4. Ralph Hamor visits Powhatan at Matchcot in May 1614, engraving by Johann Theodore de Bry, after Georg Keller, plate 10, in *America*, part 10. In the foreground, Powhatan feels Hamor's neck for a chain of pearls given by the chief to Dale to designate his envoys, while Thomas Savage looks on. The two Indians who had guided them overland from Jamestown are also present. In the middle of the engraving, Hamor presents chains of colored beads and other gifts to Powhatan at his house, who is attended by his wives and guarded by scores of warriors. Indians hunt deer and wildfowl peacefully in the background. *Courtesy of the Virginia Museum of History and Culture.*

Powhatan told Hamor that he was pleased to receive Dale's sal-
utations of love and peace, which he and his people would observe
and maintain, but as for his young daughter, she had been promised
to a great *weroance* within the past few days and had departed with
him. When Hamor pressed further, Powhatan replied that he loved
her "as dear as his own life," and although he had many children, he
delighted in her more than any other. If he could not see her often,
he said, he "could not possibly live." Moreover, he emphasized to
Hamor that he desired no firmer assurance of Dale's friendship than
the promises he had already made. From me, he said, "he has such a
pledge, one of my daughters [Pocahontas], which so long as she lives
shall be sufficient," and "I hold it not a brotherly part of your King
[Dale]," he continued, "to desire to bereave me of two of my children
at once." Then in a remarkable statement, he told Hamor that if the
English had no pledges at all from him or his people, they need not
fear. There have been too many of the English and mine killed, he
said, "and by my occasion there shall never be more, I which have
power to perform it, have said it." Repeating a comment made long
before to John Smith, he said that if the English should be the ag-
gressors, "my country is large enough, [and] I will remove myself
farther from you," for "I am now old, and would gladly end my days
in peace."

The following day, Hamor happened by chance to meet an Englishman, William Parker, taken by the Indians three years earlier.
He reported that Parker now looked more like a Powhatan than an
Englishman, so much so that if he had not spoken English, Hamor
would not have recognized him. Hamor demanded that Parker
should return with him to Jamestown. Powhatan responded with
anger: "You have one of my daughters with you, and I am therewith
well content, but you can no sooner see or know of any Englishman
being with me, but you must have him away, or else break peace and
friendship." The chief left in a rage, and it was not until late in the
evening that he met with Hamor again to discuss further gifts he

wished Dale to provide. Next morning, taking his leave by the riverside, Powhatan gave Hamor and Thomas Savage each a buckskin, "very well dressed and white as snow," and two more for Pocahontas and Rolfe. He looked forward to receiving the additional gifts from Dale and would in return send more skins, but if the English did not respond, he would move three days farther away and "never see *English* more."[11]

These discussions are suggestive about Powhatan's thinking after more than six years of negotiating and fighting with the English. The chief had come to accept that his warriors were incapable of dislodging the invaders from his lands for the time being, but he had not surrendered to the English and did not consider his people a conquered nation. His peoples far outnumbered the English, and he was doubtless aware that few English ships had arrived during the previous few years. His reluctance to return English men and women who had run away indicates his desire to take settlers into his own society rather than be absorbed by the English, and his rejection of Dale's suit to marry one of his young daughters suggests he was far from willing to agree to more conversions following that of Pocahontas. No evidence indicates that Pocahontas's marriage meant to him, any more than to Opechancanough, that the English and Powhatans were, as Dale put it, "made one people," other than in a purely rhetorical sense. As far as he was concerned, the marriage was merely a convenient means of sealing the accord. Powhatan was prepared to live and let live but had no wish to promote closer social or political ties between the English and his people. They were two peoples in one land, and despite his assurances, neither he nor Opechancanough were reconciled to living alongside the English in friendship. A truce in Powhatan's mind was an expedient, a means of ending the vicious cycle of killing and destruction that had dragged on for five years, which would be as beneficial to the English as it would be to his peoples.

For his part, Dale celebrated the end of hostilities as a decisive victory over the Indians. After early setbacks, the English had successfully repulsed Powhatan attacks, expanded their settlements along the Powhatan River Valley, and entered into important alliances with the Chickahominies, Patawomecks, and peoples on the Eastern Shore. By persuading Pocahontas to convert to Anglicanism, they had begun what they considered to be the great and holy work of converting the Powhatans to Christianity.

Surveying recent events in the summer of 1614, it appeared to Dale near miraculous that within just a couple of months, the colony's prospects had been entirely transformed. Following the establishment of peace, the natural abundance of the land could be fully exploited and God's church, a "Sanctum Sanctorum," would at last be built in America. No country in the world offered better prospects of infinite riches, Dale declared, while John Rolfe anticipated his marriage would be the catalyst for bringing tens of thousands of Indian peoples to the knowledge and worship of Jesus Christ. Virginia would shortly "come to perfection," Ralph Hamor concluded in his *True Discourse of the Present State of Virginia*, published the following year, "to the exceeding great comfort of all well affected Christians, and no small profit of the planters and adventurers: if it be well seconded and supplied with a good number of able men."[12] It was an ominous assessment for all Indian peoples of Tsenacommacah and beyond.

PART THREE

Prophecy Fulfilled

CHAPTER 9

Locust Years

IT WAS PROBABLY OPECHANCANOUGH, NOT POWHATAN, WHO made the decision to avoid bloodshed at Matchcot. None of the Englishmen who were there and sought a meeting with Powhatan were able to gain an audience, even though the great chief was likely in residence nearby. Indian messengers told two emissaries sent by Dale that Powhatan was three days away but that "Opochankano was hard by" and they should deliver their message to him, "saying that what he agreed upon and did, the great King [Powhatan] would confirm." This Opechancanough, Dale wrote by way of explanation to a friend in London, "is brother to Powhatan, and is his and their chief Captain and one that can as soon (if not sooner) as Powhatan command the men." This amounts to a remarkable statement. Dale may have harbored suspicions that the attempt to persuade his men to deliver their message to Opechancanough was a ploy designed to allow Powhatan to deny ever having received it. But another possibility is that Powhatan was no longer effectively in charge, which Dale was coming to realize. The great chief formally retained his role as *mamanatowick* and yet had been largely superseded by his brother in the influential councils of war and peace. Powhatan's resigned tone in his discussions with Ralph Hamor the following month suggests he had no wish to prolong hostilities, desiring instead to keep his distance from the English and end his days in peace.[1]

Opechancanough, by contrast, had a very different viewpoint. The reversals of war would have to be addressed or the entire chiefdom

FIGURE 9.1. Sir Thomas Dale, whom Opechancanough called a "great Captain," by Marcus Gheeraerts the younger. Painted 1609–1610 or 1616–1619. *Courtesy of the Virginia Museum of Fine Art, Richmond, Virginia, and the Adolph D. and Wilkins C. Williams Fund. Photograph by Travis Fullerton.*

might unravel, a concern given all the more credence by the Chick-ahominies' decision to make a treaty with Dale. A comprehensive short-term solution was unachievable, the damage done to the Powhatan chiefdom since 1610 was too great, and the colonists' grip on their new settlements too tenacious. Individual peoples along the Powhatan River, from the Kecoughtans to the Arrohattocs and Powhatans, had failed to drive off the English or even adequately protect themselves. Aside from several early successes, they had suffered a series of disastrous defeats, leading in some cases to being forced off their tribal lands.

Strikingly, neither Powhatan nor Opechancanough appear to have intervened directly to lead the war effort or arrange formal contact with English commanders even as hostilities intensified. Following the introduction of far more aggressive tactics by Gates, De La Warr, and Dale, local chiefs were left to their own devices to defend themselves. Powhatan could have organized a coordinated response but for some reason failed to act. His lack of leadership at a crucial moment caused irreparable harm.[2]

Gazing upon the scores of heavily armed soldiers making their way ashore at Matchcot, Opechancanough had probably already reached the conclusion that only a carefully coordinated strategy involving the most powerful peoples of the chiefdom would put an end to the English in Tsenacommacah. Precisely what such a strategy might entail would become clearer in succeeding years, but his decision not to engage Dale's men on the banks of the Pamunkey River suggests that an important part of any plan would be the avoidance of pitched battles in the open field where English superiority in weaponry and armor was optimal. Some other approach had to be devised to defeat the English, one that would give his men every advantage. The starting point was to gain the friendship of English leaders, just as he had skillfully managed to win the confidence of the late king of Spain Philip II, high-ranking Spanish authorities, and churchmen more than four decades before.[3]

IN THE SPRING of 1616, Dale and Argall left Jamestown on the *Treasurer* to return to London. On board were Pocahontas, John Rolfe, their infant son, Thomas, Pocahontas's sister Mattachanna, and several young Powhatan women whom the company wished to convert to Anglicanism and wed to suitable Englishmen. Giving his blessing to the departure, Opechancanough dispatched his trusted counselor and priest Uttamatomakkin (Tomakin), who was the husband of Mattachanna. He was instructed to learn more about the English and their homeland, gain an acquaintance with the king, and, if possible, seek out the Virginia Company's future plans.

The timing appeared auspicious. Dale and Opechancanough continued to be on good terms, and shortly before his departure, he picked up rumors that Powhatan "was gone Southwards, . . . some thought for fear of Opochancanough," who Powhatan believed was conspiring with the English "against him, thinking that he will not return." The news, if true, augured well for the colonists and confirmed Dale's earlier suspicions that a shift in power was taking place that might favor improved relations with the Indians.[4]

Opechancanough was also pleased by recent developments. Although he could not assume the role of *mamanatowick* while Powhatan and his elder brother Opitchapam still lived, he had consolidated his position as de facto ruler of the chiefdom and at the same time retained the trust of English settlers, including the new deputy governor, Captain George Yeardley. Several months after Dale's departure, the chief played an important role in a violent confrontation that erupted between the English and Chickahominies. Yeardley had sent to them a demand to provide the annual tribute of corn specified by their peace treaty, but they had returned a contemptuous reply saying they would not pay. Accompanied by one hundred of his best soldiers, Yeardley straightaway led an expedition of three ships to the Chickahominy River to exact revenge and take the corn if necessary. Passing by a number of towns along the riverside, according to an English account, his men were met with "scorn and contempt" from the Indians who told them that since Dale had left the colony they were no longer obliged to honor the treaty.

Yeardley put ashore at a town called Ozinies, which placed his men in the heart of the Chickahominies' settlements and extensive cornfields, and marched farther upriver to Mamanahunt (near modern-day Diascund Creek) where, after failing to reach an agreement, he ordered his men to fire upon the warriors and leaders gathered there, killing twelve and capturing twelve, including two of the ruling elders. He believed the show of force had put an end to the Chickahominies' resistance, having been promised the corn in return for the captives, but marching back to their ships, they encountered Opechancanough at Ozinies who told him that only he could broker a lasting peace. Subsequently, the chief made "much ado" about the trouble he had gone to in persuading the Chickahominies to agree. They now called him "King of the Ozinies," he told Yeardley, and had brought him "many presents of Beads, Copper, and such trash as they had," to his great satisfaction since hitherto neither he nor Powhatan had been able to bring them to obedience.

Another account of the confrontation was provided by an inveterate critic of the Virginia Company, Captain John Bargrave. According to him, when Yeardley became deputy governor Powhatan and Opechancanough plotted "to break the league" between the English and "Chickhomenes." Professing much friendship, Opechancanough alerted him to an outrage committed by a group of Chickhominies who had killed some of the settlers' cattle and hogs. As in the first version, Yeardley set out with one hundred armed men to meet the Indians, but Bargrave's description of what happened next was very different: "as it seems by correspondence [collusion] with Opichankano instead of parleying with the Chickohomenes," Yeardley ordered a volley of shot to "be delivered amongst them and killed 30 or 40." This "perfidious act" by the English, Bargrave concluded, "made them all fly out and seek Revenge, [and] they joined with Opichankano." Bargrave's purpose in writing his account years later, with the benefit of hindsight, was to underline the treachery of the two great chiefs and characterize Yeardley as woefully gullible. Yet, what stands out from both versions is the nimbleness of Opechancanough's stratagem (Powhatan was unlikely to have been involved) by which he established his personal authority over the Chickahominies, brought them back into the chiefdom, and at the same time demonstrated his eagerness to be a good friend to the English.[5]

Opechancanough met the third English governor in as many years when Samuel Argall returned to the colony on the *George* in the summer of 1617 to replace Yeardley. Adhering to his policy of maintaining friendly relations, the chief readily accepted an invitation to visit Jamestown, something Powhatan had never agreed to do. Powhatan had been cordial but distant in his dealings with the English after the end of the war whereas his brother openly courted English leaders, shaping a role for himself as a mediator between the settlers and Indians. Argall wrote to company leaders that Powhatan had left Orapax to visit the "King of Mayumps," whose people lived on the Potomac River and had "left the Government of his Kingdom to Opachanko and his other brother [Opitchapam]." In other words, both brothers were left in control of the chiefdom, but significantly Opechancanough was mentioned first. Argall reported that the priest Tomakin, who had returned on the same ship as him, "rails against England, English people, and particularly. . . . Thomas Dale," but his angry report had been dismissed by Opechancanough, and Tomakin was in disgrace.[6]

Pocahontas was meant to have returned to the colony with Rolfe and her infant son, Thomas, on board the *George* but fell ill and died at the small town of Gravesend as they made their way down the Thames to begin the voyage back to Virginia. In the six months before her death, much as the company had fervently hoped, she and the other Powhatans captivated Londoners, who flocked to catch a glimpse of the Indians, especially Lady Rebecca Rolfe. "The most remarkable person," court gossip and letter-writer John Chamberlain observed, "is Pocahuntas (daughter to Powatan a King or cacique of that Country) married to one Rolfe an Englishman." From their lodgings at the Belle Sauvage Inn on Ludgate Hill in the City of London—chosen not for its name but for its proximity to one of the greatest churches in Christendom, St. Paul's Cathedral—she and her husband set out daily to be feted by Sir Edwin Sandys, Dale, and Sir Thomas Smythe and ushered into the highest social circles. She was soon caught up in a whirlwind of "Plays, Balls, and other public Entertainments" and was "very respectfully received by all the Ladies about the Court." Throughout, the Reverend Samuel Purchas recalled, she "did not only accustom herself to civility, but still carried herself as the Daughter of a King, and was accordingly respected." Years later, planter-historian Robert Beverley commented that her deportment had so impressed those who met her at court that questions were raised as to whether John Rolfe should have sought the king's consent before "presuming to marry a Princess Royal." Beverley had no doubt that if she had lived to return to Virginia, she would have greatly reinforced the bonds of affection between the Powhatans and English.

Opechancanough's opinion of Pocahontas, her marriage, and her visit to London are unknown. He likely held views comparable to those of his brother, but he also had the benefit of hindsight from his own years among the Spanish and his several visits to the Spanish court. These may have led him to harbor strong suspicions about what the English actually wanted from his young kinswoman. Pocahontas's reaction to the English in their own country is equally opaque. An engraving of her, commissioned by the company in late 1616 to publicize her presence in the city, offers an unusually candid portrait. In portraying Pocahontas, the artist, Simon Van de Passe, made no attempt to Europeanize her features. Although dressed as a wealthy Englishwoman, she is obviously not English, which was precisely the message the company intended to convey: it was possible to "civilize" and Anglicize Indian peoples.

FIGURE 9.2. Frontispiece engraving of Pocahontas by Simon Van de Passe, 1616, in John Smith, *The Generall Historie of Virginia, New-England, and the Summer Isles* . . . (London, 1632). The inscription around the image says "Matoaka alias Rebecca daughter of the mighty Prince Powhatan Emperor of Virginia." Immediately below the image, her age is given as twenty-one in 1616. At the bottom, the bordering inscription is repeated with some additions: "Matoaks alias Rebecka daughter to the mighty Prince Powhatan Emperour of Attanoughskomouck alias virginia, converted and baptized in the Christian faith, and wife to the worshipful Mr. John Rolfe." *Courtesy of Special Collections, John D. Rockefeller Jr. Library, Colonial Williamsburg Foundation.*

Pocahontas appears to have been determined to complicate this presentation, however. If the company wished to emphasize her high status as daughter of the "mighty Prince" and emperor, Powhatan, she chose to underline her own identity as a Virginia Indian by placing her own name, Matoaka, before that of her English name, Rebecca. Only Rolfe and close friends were aware of her adult name (Pocahontas was a child's nickname that means, approximately, "little playful one"), and hence having Matoaka placed on her portrait was an opportunity to declare her true Indian name to the English public. Nor did she accept the modest countenance of a convert and wife in the portrait, which would have been expected of her in this period, and instead boldly looks the viewer in the eye. The message she wished to send was that she was both a Powhatan from the ruling family of Attanoughskomouck (a garbled effort to render Tsenacommacah) and a respectable English wife and mother. She was neither Indian nor English but both.

For company leaders, conversion of the entire Powhatan people was foremost in their plans to transform the colony, and hence the baptism of Pocahontas had represented a signal breakthrough. Captain John Smith, who was in London briefly during her visit while preparing for a voyage to New England, wrote a letter of recommendation to Queen Anne, the king's wife, praising Pocahontas's virtues. She had rejected "her barbarous condition" and was the first of her "Nation" to adopt Christianity, the first to speak English, and the first to have a child in marriage with an Englishman. In his opinion, her love of the English and devotion to the Anglican Church would be of incalculable benefit in bringing about the conversion of her people. Her death several months later, probably from tuberculosis, was therefore a huge loss to the Virginia Company, mitigated only by the "great demonstration of her Christian sincerity," the Reverend Purchas wrote, "as the first fruits of Virginian conversion."

Yet Pocahontas's death was not the end of plans to convert the Powhatans but rather the beginning of a renewed and more determined effort to redeem Indian peoples. It would be linked to a vision of a new type of English society in America, one that would embrace Indians as well as settlers in a peaceful "Christian Commonwealth."[7]

"BY THE NATIVES' liking and consent," the company proclaimed grandly in *A Brief Declaration*, in 1616, the English were "in actual possession of a great part of the Country." It was a bold statement that had little basis in fact. Only six settlements and 351 settlers remained in the colony, which represented less than half the number present five years earlier, and while the company touted the colony's peace and prosperity, other reports spoke of settlers enduring "wants and hardships." A few years earlier, Dale had written eloquently of the enormous potential of Virginia. "The more I range the country the more I admire it. I have seen the best countries in Europe: [and] I protest to you before the Living God, put them all together, this country will be equivalent to them if it be inhabited with good people." In London, John Rolfe wrote a short account of the colony that echoed Dale's assessment. With good and sufficient men, Virginia would become self-reliant in provisions, towns, and shipping, and explorations farther inland might reveal riches and valuable commodities. Many things, he concluded, "might come with ease to establish a firm and perfect Common-weal." Unfortunately for the company, potential migrants were far less convinced of Virginia's virtues than Dale or Rolfe. Rumors of harsh conditions were commonplace in England, especially London, and given the evident lack of profitable commodities, incentive to make the Atlantic crossing or venture further investments was diminishing. In the absence of news of riches or anything of worth other than some small quantities of sassafras, tobacco, pitch, and clapboard, John Chamberlain commented sourly, no present returns were to be expected. The colony appeared to be in terminal decline.[8]

Given the parlous state of affairs, *A Brief Declaration* was designed as more than simply another description of Virginia's promise but more significantly as an announcement of a new beginning offering tangible rewards to investors. A fresh group of company leaders had emerged who promoted ambitious and far-reaching reforms calculated to attract "multitudes" of settlers, the most important of which was a commitment to the widespread distribution of Indian lands to colonists and investors. Since its inception, securing title to vast regions in North America had been central to the company's vision of colonial enterprise. Successive royal charters gave the company exclusive rights to take advantage of the natural resources of the mid-Atlantic region and beyond. If English colonizers were prohibited from claiming lands "possessed" by other Christian monarchs, they were nonetheless, following the example of the Spanish and Portuguese, in no doubt that they had the moral and legal right to settle regions inhabited by peoples deemed "heathen" and "barbarous." Catholic and Protestant churchmen, legal scholars, and intellectuals offered any number of specious justifications for taking the Indians' lands, including the law of nations, which guaranteed the rights of Christians to trade wherever and with whomever they wished, and the "Law of God," which decreed monarchs should subdue "savage" peoples in pursuit of bringing Christianity to Indians who lived in servitude to their priests and Satan.[9]

Initially, English settlers had sought to avoid conflict with local Indian peoples and occupy what they considered to be vacant areas, even though they frequently were not, or else employ a self-serving fiction to buy land for a few pieces of copper or similar "trash." With the onset of fighting in 1609, however, settlers believed the use of force justified their occupation of prime Indian lands along the Powhatan River. Both sides clearly understood that the war had ultimately been about possessing the land. With the end of hostilities, and in light of the company's belief that Indian peoples had been reconciled to the English colony, leaders moved quickly to publicize their intention to enact a widespread distribution of land as soon as possible. Settler ownership was viewed as essential to unlocking the colony's and the company's own future prosperity.

In an effort to stem the company's financial decline, enormous land grants on extremely favorable terms were allocated to individuals and societies of "adventurers" made up of important financiers and merchants. Several leading company officers and colonists were quick to take advantage. In 1617, Governor Argall was assigned 2,400 acres close to Jamestown at "Paspahegh, alias Argall's town," and a grant of similar size upriver was given to Captain Yeardley in recognition of his services to the colony. The largest grants of the period, Smith's Hundred named for Sir Thomas Smythe and Martin's Hundred, each made up of 80,000 to 100,000 acres (125–150 square miles), were located along the north bank of the Powhatan River above and below Jamestown respectively. As with the deliberate placement of English forts and settlements on Indian lands during the war, the grants of 1617 were intended to secure some of the best agricultural land and to be punitive. The Chickahominies were forced off lands that bordered the new grants, Smith's Hundred and Argall's Town intruded upon the Paspaheghs' territories, and across the river a large grant awarded to Captain John Martin, who had been with the first expedition to Virginia, lay close to Quiyoughcohannock lands.[10]

Besides the enticing prospect of what the English saw as free land, the wholesale land grab was motivated above all by the emergence of a commodity able to command extremely handsome profits on the London markets: tobacco. "No country under the Sun," Ralph Hamor enthused, "does afford more pleasant, sweet, and strong Tobacco" as Virginia. Originally introduced into England from Spanish America, tobacco had quickly become popular among London's fashionable elite during the late sixteenth century and was then taken up by the middle and lower classes, both men and women, across England, creating a ready market for the much cheaper Virginia product. Hamor, like his friend John Rolfe, had experimented with the crop for a couple of years and accurately asserted it could be grown by anyone with access to a few acres. Along with planters already in the colony, the arrival of hundreds of new settlers sparked a tobacco boom. Governor Argall found Jamestown's marketplace and streets "and all other spare places planted with Tobacco." Elsewhere

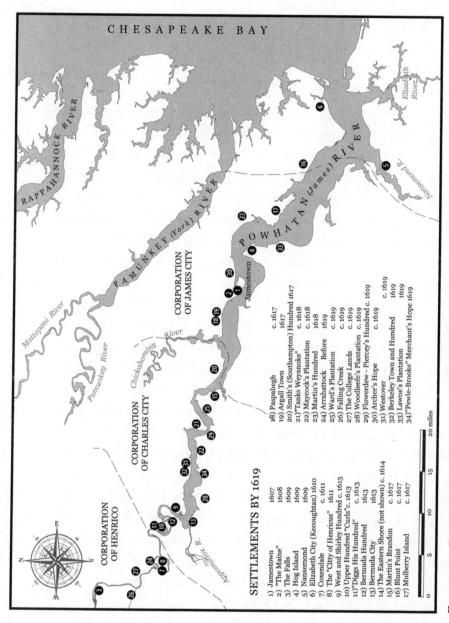

SETTLEMENTS BY 1619

1) Jamestown   1607
2) "The Maine"   1608
3) The Falls   1609
4) Hog Island   1609
5) Nansemond   1609
6) Elizabeth City (Kecoughtan) 1610
7) Coxendale   c. 1611
8) The "City of Henricus"   1611
9) West and Shirley Hundred c. 1613
10) Upper Hundred "Curls"c. 1613
11) "Diggs His Hundred"   c. 1613
12) Bermuda Hundred   1613
13) Bermuda City   1613
14) The Eastern Shore (not shown) c. 1614
15) Martin's Brandon   c. 1617
16) Blunt Point   c. 1617
17) Mulberry Island   c. 1617

18) Paspaheigh   c. 1617
19) Argall Town   1617
20) Smith's (Southampton) Hundred 1617
21) "Tanks Weyanoke"   c. 1618
22) Maycock's Plantation   c. 1618
23) Martin's Hundred   1618
24) Arrahattock   Before 1619
25) Ward's Plantation   c. 1619
26) Falling Creek   c. 1619
27) The College Lands   c. 1619
28) Woodleefe's Plantation c. 1619
29) Flowerdew - Piercey's Hundred c. 1619
30) Archer's Hope   c. 1619
31) Westover   c. 1619
32) Berkeley Town and Hundred 1619
33) Lawne's Plantation   1619
34) "Pewle-Brooke" Merchant's Hope 1619

FIGURE 9-3. Location of English settlements along the Powhatan River Valley and the four corporations in 1619. *Drawing by Jamie May.*

along the Powhatan River, planters were "dispersed all about" diligently tending to their crops.[11]

With the company's award of many more land grants over the next couple of years, colonists began taking up smaller grants and moving onto the traditional lands of the Nansemonds, Warraskoyacks, and Weyanocks, as well as occupying more land belonging to the Appomattocs, Arrohattocs, and Powhatans. By 1619, English settlers had taken possession of tens of thousands of acres along the Powhatan River Valley, much of it on the riverfront, and had established thirty settlements. Company leaders strongly disapproved of tobacco, which they considered a short-lived fad, and encouraged instead a diversified economy of crops and manufactures, but as plantations large and small expanded and returns from leaf remained, they would have at least derived satisfaction from the rapidly increasing numbers of settlers moving to the colony.[12]

Opechancanough was unlikely to have been prepared for the sheer scale of the English influx that followed the tobacco boom. Twenty-five ships carrying 1,500 settlers arrived between 1617 and 1619, hundreds of them intending to work their own land or labor on tobacco plantations as tenants or indentured servants, the latter serving fixed-term contracts of four to ten years. The first group of enslaved Africans (approximately thirty-two) also arrived in the colony in this period. They were first captured in Portuguese Angola and transported across the Atlantic in a Spanish slave ship, the *St. John the Baptist*. Two English warships attacked and looted the ship in the Gulf of Mexico and took the Africans north to Virginia. Both warships—the *Treasurer*, which had been plying Virginia waters for years, and the *White Lion*—were owned by Sir Robert Rich, an enormously wealthy nobleman who had large investments in the Virginia Company and took a great deal of interest in the colony.

How Opechancanough and the Powhatans viewed these African captives is unknown. The great chief had seen many African slaves on his Atlantic travels when a young man and perhaps regarded them as victims of European greed and ambition just like the *indios*, as the Spanish called them. Alternatively, he may have been troubled that, together with the hundreds of white settlers arriving regularly, the English now might intend to transport enslaved African laborers. Either way, he and his subordinate chiefs would certainly have been worried by the rapidly rising settler population, from three hundred fifty in 1616 to slightly less than a thousand by early 1620.[13]

Besides bringing passengers, ships brought European diseases. Argall reported a "great mortality" that swept through the settlers in the summer of 1617 but impacted the Indians far more severely. During the same months, a "murrain" seriously reduced deer populations, and a year later "a great drought" afflicted the area putting further pressure on food supplies and causing some peoples to be so depleted of food they were unable to pay their corn in tribute or debts to the English. During the torrid summer of 1619, another "great sickness and mortality" ravaged colonists and Indian peoples. Which European pathogens triggered the epidemics is unclear, but the most likely candidates were dysentery, typhoid, smallpox, and measles.

Opechancanough was familiar with the deadly potential of European maladies. As a youth, he nearly died while staying with Dominican friars at the convent of Santo Domingo in Mexico City and knew of the recurrent epidemics that had decimated Indian populations in Spanish American territories. Trails of virulent diseases left in the wake of Spanish or English soldiers caused havoc among Indian populations and led to the collapse of several powerful chiefdoms to the south of his territories. He understood better than most that if the company persisted in dispatching large numbers of settlers to Virginia, highly contagious diseases would continue to spread among his people and pose a threat to the very existence of his chiefdom.[14]

IN A LETTER to company leaders of March 1618, Governor Argall mentioned that Powhatan went from "place to place visiting his Country [and] taking pleasure in good friendship." The chief lamented Pocahontas's death but was gratified to hear her son lived and looked forward to seeing him when he was strong enough to return. Powhatan never saw the boy, however, since a month later he was dead as well. Without offering any details, John Rolfe reported his death and added that Opitchapam had become the *mamanato-wick* and taken as his official name Itoyatin. Little would change. Most important from an English perspective, both Itoyatin and Opechancanough gave assurances to preserve the peace with the settlers. English leaders paid little attention to Itoyatin who was a cipher and continued to work closely with Opechancanough, "one who has already the command of all the people," the real power in Tsenacommacah whom they believed they could trust.[15]

Opechancanough was as good as his word and continued to play his part as peacemaker. When a group of Pamunkeys killed five Englishmen trading with the Chickahominies as well as murdering several children in two separate incidents, he intervened to assure Argall that "the peace should never be broken by him." By way of reparation, he gave to Argall the Chickahominy town where the five men had been killed and promised to catch those responsible and send the governor their heads, which, as it turned out, he never did. He maintained the fiction that it was not the Pamunkeys but the Chickahominies that had committed the killings.

Opechancanough thereby protected his own warriors, at least one of whom had a musket and had used it to shoot and kill an Englishman named Richard Killingbeck. A year later in 1619 at the first General Assembly, the recently knighted Sir George Yeardley, the latest governor to arrive in the colony, and other assemblymen considered an appeal for justice sent by Opechancanough on behalf of the Accomac people. The Accomac chief had complained to the great chief that a group of Englishmen trading along the Eastern Shore had forcibly stolen quantities of their corn. Yeardley and the assemblymen were quick to condemn the English involved and to censure Captain John Martin who had employed them. By doing so, the governor confirmed that he and Opechancanough would work together if necessary to safeguard the peace, even if it meant punishing high-placed settlers. The Accomacs were on good terms with the English and were reliable trading partners, hence it was not lost on Yeardley or the assemblymen that their chief had appealed to Opechancanough rather than the English directly. To maintain the flow of corn to English plantations from across the bay, equitable dealings with the Accomacs were essential.[16]

Despite their common approach in dealing with the Accomacs, Governor Yeardley was struggling to maintain the warm relations that had marked the first few years immediately after the war. Unknown to Yeardley, of course, Opechancanough's strategy was to be conciliatory toward the English, emphasizing his peoples' acceptance of the peace and settlers and thereby lulling them into a false sense of security. But the previous four years had been very difficult for his people, especially along the Powhatan River, as land encroachments and diseases continued to take their toll. English leaders had enforced the payment of corn and in areas where Indian peoples had been removed from their land reduced them to dependence on settlers' provisions. Argall had prohibited trade with the Indians, specifically firearms and other weapons, and warned colonists against too great a familiarity "with the perfidious Savages," regulations repeated in part by the General Assembly. These developments made Opechancanough's role increasingly difficult to sustain, and he had begun keeping his distance. The English were beginning to notice the change. Since Yeardley's arrival, the governor's council remarked, the great chief had "stood aloof" and "would not be drawn [in]to any treaty at all, notwithstanding all the Art and endeavor the governor could use." To curry favor, the English even agreed to send eight to ten well-armed men with a Powhatan raiding party against the Monacans in the fall.

One other reason why the great chief may have kept his distance from Yeardley was uncertainty about the governor's position.

Sometime in the early summer 1619, the Indian interpreter Henry Spelman made his way to Opechancanough's court on the Pamunkey River to relay an important message. In front of another interpreter, Robert Poole, who had spent several years with Opechancanough, Spelman told the chief that "within a year there would come a Governor greater than this that was now in place." When the chief asked Poole who was "the great king shortly to come from England," he replied he did not know, at which Spelman said it was Sir Robert Rich, "who meant [intended] to plant at Kiskiack." Spelman went on to emphasize that Lord Rich was far greater than Yeardley, who would be "but a Tanx Werowance, that is a petty governor not of power to do anything." Opechancanough's frustration is evident when he told Spelman he wondered why so many governors were sent from England, "one upon the neck of another," which made it impossible to know who to trust, seeing that a new governor might well revoke decisions his predecessors had made. He might well have agreed with English leaders that Spelman's loose talk had placed their relations in danger of "slippery designs."[17]

Both sides remained committed to peace, however, at least for the time being. Company leaders were particularly keen to preserve good relations and released another promotional piece the following year emphasizing once again that Virginia only required honest, hardworking men and women, "bred up to labor and industry," to set free the country's full potential. Multitudes of settlers, the company declared, were already leaving English ports to make the Atlantic crossing, more than 1,300 in 1620 alone; the colony was sufficient in provisions, and an economy based on a wide variety of crops and industries was taking shape. With the adoption of recent wide-ranging reforms instigated by Sir Edwin Sandys and his supporters, colonists had now enjoyed a settled form of government, their own representative body in the form of the General Assembly, and would be governed by English laws rather than arbitrary military courts.

Working with leading colonists, Governor Yeardley had been successful in implementing the reforms, which had been well received, but greatly complicating his relationship with the Indians was company leaders' insistence on pursuing the holy work, as they saw it, of bringing the Powhatans and eventually all Indian peoples into the Church of England.[18]

Since Pocahontas's visit to London and James I's subsequent support for the mission of converting the Virginia Indians, charitable collections taken in hundreds of English churches across the country and gifts from pious individuals had flowed into company coffers. This "most Christian, honorable, and glorious" work, John Ferrar, deputy treasurer of the company, wrote, was of the "highest consequence to the Plantations . . . whereof both Church and commonwealth take their original foundation and happy estate." Company leaders believed that the conversion first of Powhatan children would be the means of converting the general population. Householders were enjoined to take in a certain number of children of which the most promising boys would be sent to an Indian College, yet to be built, that would prepare them to undertake the conversion of their elders. Located on the lands of the Arrohattocs, a huge tract of ten thousand acres was allocated for the college, where company servants would work, providing the supplies and profits to support the work of training Indian youths. Yeardley warned the company about unrealistic expectations. Indian parents were most reluctant to part with their children upon any terms. The "Spiritual vine you speak of," he wrote to Sir Edwin Sandys, "will not so suddenly be planted as it may be desired." Yet, he reported he had reached a compromise with Opechancanough whereby settlers would build houses and set aside grounds for planting corn in their settlements so that Indian families identified by the great chief could live among the English. Settlers would be able to teach the children Christian doctrine without having to take them from their parents, and with incentives, such as clothes, cattle, "and such other necessaries," parents and children might eventually prefer to stay with them.[19]

The approach received the enthusiastic backing of an influential colonist, George Thorpe, who arrived in the colony in the spring of 1620 and was soon put in charge of the Indian College project. Formerly a member of Parliament and gentleman of the king's privy chamber, he was a major investor in the company and well known to Sandys. Deeply religious, Thorpe was dedicated to the work of converting the Powhatans and believed the lack of progress was mainly the fault of the English. We are "not so charitable to them as Christians ought to be," he wrote to Sandys a year later, "they being (especially the better sort of them) of a peaceable and virtuous disposition." If the company provided gifts to show their "love and hearty affection," the Indians would be more likely to respond to conversion, since they began more and more to adopt English customs. The way to bring about the Indians' redemption was by providing more access to English goods and improving their material lives.[20]

THE COMPANY'S RENEWED efforts to gain his support for their Christian mission suited Opechancanough's plans well. He was aware that holding out the possibility of allowing his people to convert to the Church of England gave him enormous leverage over the English leaders in the colony. For the best part of a decade while living with the Spanish, he had promised to help the Dominicans and then the Jesuits convert the people of his homeland to Christianity. Half a century later, he adopted precisely the same role with the English.

The war had proved that his people could not defend their towns and cornfields from highly mobile and heavily armed soldiers able to move up and down the rivers with impunity in their ships. Now that the English were more numerous and better equipped, Opechanca-nough knew he could not engage them in frontal assaults that would leave his warriors vulnerable to musket fire. He had to discover a way of getting inside the English settlements, of gaining the set-tlers' trust, and then quickly striking them down using the settlers' own weapons and edge tools before they had time to defend them-selves. If the strategy was to be successful, he would have to take the English completely by surprise by waiting patiently until the right opportunity arose. No matter what the insult or provocation, it was vital his people appear to be compliant and receptive to the possibil-ity of converting to English ways.

In the spring of 1621, Opechancanough believed the moment had come. Putting into motion his final preparations for the attack, he sought to reassure Yeardley that all was well by confirming the league and peace the governor had been proposing for the last two years. But several months later, a serious misjudgment derailed his plans and nearly jeopardized his relationship with the governor.

Opechancanough intended to take advantage of a ceremony for the "taking up of Powhatan's bones" to gather large numbers of Indians, invite English leaders, and then murder them, signal-ing a general attack on the settlers. He had sent to the chief of the Accomacs, Esmy Shichans, for a "store of poison (naturally growing in his country)," probably spotted cowbane, which is highly toxic and lethal even in small amounts. Esmy Shichans was no friend of the great chief and valued his own peoples' independence and the Englishmen's trade. He vigorously refused to supply the poisonous plants and, worse, sent word to Yeardley about the plot. Opechan-canough quickly realized his mistake when the governor ordered every plantation in the colony to be on guard for an attack. The great chief "earnestly" denied any involvement in a plot, and when Yeard-ley could not find any conclusive evidence of his treachery, relations among the Powhatans and English gradually improved and settlers relaxed their guard.[21]

George Thorpe played a major part in ensuring there were no lasting repercussions following the aborted plot. Throughout the spring and summer, he had worked closely with Opechancanough in an effort to persuade him to convert. Putting into practice his own advice to the company, he had a house built for the great chief, which he claimed Opechancanough doted upon, and provided English goods such as clothing and "householdstuff." He urged that similar gifts be given to other chiefs who, like Opechancanough, would be most satisfied by them. In July, company instructions issued to Sir Francis Wyatt, Virginia's new governor, at that time in England, echoed Thorpe's approach. Wyatt was told to "have especial Care that no injury or oppression be wrought by the English against any of the Natives . . . whereby the present peace may be disturbed and ancient quarrels (now buried) might be revived." Indians well disposed toward the settlers and who lived among them should be rewarded accordingly so they would in time become drawn to civility and ultimately to the "knowledge and love of God and true religion." These converts would then serve as missionaries for the conversion of the Powhatans as a whole, "which we so much desire."[22]

By the end of the year, Opechancanough must have been satisfied by the turn of events. His misstep with Esmy Shichans had caused no lasting damage to his relations with the English, who had been more preoccupied with the possibility of a Spanish attack than by a threat from the Powhatans. Settlers had soon returned to their usual routines, focusing on their tobacco crop. When one of his great warriors, Nemattanew, was killed in a scuffle with a couple of settlers in the late fall, he still managed to maintain his composure and reassured Yeardley that "the Sky should sooner fall then Peace be broken." Although, as earlier in the year, relations soon returned to normal, with Indian and English people moving freely among one another, the governor warned settlers to be on their guard. Meanwhile, Captain Thorpe, as he was now called, continued to persist in his efforts to bring Anglicanism to the chief's people, and in November a new governor arrived who favored strengthening the peace.

In response, Opechancanough once again turned to preparations for the attack, finalizing plans with his war captains and confirming alliances with mercenary warriors. Sometime before the end of the year, he took the battle name Mangopeesomon. The long years of waiting and planning were nearly over.[23]

Chapter 10

World's End

I N A REPORT SENT TO LONDON IN EARLY 1622, GOVERNOR SIR Francis Wyatt and his council asked the company to send "men Skillful in the Art of fortifications" to advise on the location of the "most Defensible place for the seating of the Chief City of this kingdom, if they shall find James City a place not fit or proper for that purpose." The governor did not express any concern about the inadequacy of fortifications in the colony generally, and even his inquiry about strengthening Jamestown or some other place was more a reflection of continuing fears about a possible Spanish attack than a threat posed by the Powhatans. And yet the condition of the colony had been described as "ruinous" by Deputy Governor Samuel Argall only a few years earlier. In many settlements, palisades had either never been built or had been pulled down because settlers found the effort to maintain them too laborious. Jamestown remained strikingly vulnerable to attack. Although its inhabitants had managed to maintain sections of the settlement's five-sided palisade of 1608, up to fourteen feet high in places, and had placed three or four large cannons on its bulwarks, the rapidly expanding "New

Towne," a residential and commercial area beyond the settlement's walls, was largely unprotected, apart from the guns of ships moored in the river. Throughout the rest of the colony, a couple of cannons were placed at Point Comfort, at Wolstenholme Town in Martin's Hundred, and at Sir George Yeardley's plantation upriver at Flowerdew, but most plantations lacked heavy guns or fortifications of any kind.[1]

Opechancanough's prolonged strategy of reassuring the English of his peaceful intentions reached its culmination in a final meeting with George Thorpe shortly before the end of 1621. Wyatt had dispatched Thorpe with gifts and a message to Itoyatin (Sasawpen) and Opechancanough (Mangopeesomon) confirming the "League" of peace between them. The message was well received, and Opechancanough told Thorpe that he was much reassured. To underline his gratitude, he further indicated to Thorpe that he would allow some settler families to live with his people and Indians to live with the settlers. He also reiterated a former promise to send a guide to lead an English expedition to certain mines beyond the falls and gave his permission to settlers to take up land anywhere along his rivers except where his people were already living. Then in a stunning revelation, he confessed that he now believed his peoples' religion "was not the right way" and requested to be instructed in the English religion because "god loved us better than them." The chief ended by saying they would have an opportunity to discuss matters further at Pamunkey when he had finished his current hunting trip, a meeting that never happened.[2]

When, the following spring, the news of Opechancanough's apparent conversion reached company leaders in London, they were so pleased they immediately proposed a sermon be commissioned to give thanks to God. A month later, in April 1622, the Reverend Patrick Copland, a chaplain of the company, stood in the chancel of St. Mary-le-Bow and preached "Virginia's God Be Thanked" to a distinguished audience of company members, civic leaders, and merchants. There was "no danger," he confidently asserted, to those men and women leaving for Virginia either from war or famine, "for blessed be God, there hath been a long time, and still is a happy league of Peace and Amity soundly concluded, and faithfully kept, between the *English* and the *Natives,* that the fear of killing each other is now vanished away." He referred to George Thorpe as "that worthy overseer of your [Indian] College Lands," who had rightly chided company leaders earlier about not doing enough to convert the "Natives." Citing Thorpe, Copland said the Indians live peaceably among the settlers and "groan under the burden of the bondage of Satan wanting nothing more but a means to be delivered." This had been confirmed "by a discourse which he [Thorpe] had with Opachankano, their great King." But, in an astonishing turn of events, Governor Wyatt, company leaders, and the godly George Thorpe had been completely duped. Even as Copland spoke, English Virginia lay in ruins.[3]

ON MARCH 21, Opechancanough put his great attack into motion. Small groups of Indians, well known to the settlers in their localities, visited their plantations and settled down for the night. The elite of Opechancanough's forces were the Pamunkeys, who may have numbered from 500 to 600 bowmen. They were joined by warriors of the Powhatan (James) River chiefdoms—the Powhatans, Arrohattocs, Appomattocs, Weyanocks, Chickahominies, Quiyoughcohannocks, Warraskoyacks, and Nansemonds—supported also by the Kiskiacks from the Pamunkey (York) River and the Rappahannocks, or other Indians along that river, as well as several hundred mercenaries. John Bargrave, an influential planter-merchant and relentless critic of the Virginia Company, noted later that "the infinite trade they [the Pamunkeys] have had in this 4 years of security enabled Opichankanoe to hire many auxiliaries which in former times I know for want [lack] thereof Pohatan was never able to act the like." Opechanca-nough's total number of warriors and allies was probably between 1,400 and 1,600, of whom the majority were from the core chiefdoms of Tsenacommacah who had suffered greatly during the first war and its aftermath.[4]

Early the following morning, larger numbers of unarmed men carrying provisions or trade goods set off to nearby settlers' houses dispersed along the Powhatan River. Since many of the Indians had been trading with the English for years, casually dropping by when they had something to barter or perhaps sought to borrow tools, nothing appeared out of the ordinary. Then at eight o'clock, all along the Powhatan (James) River, Opechancanough's warriors abruptly fell upon the English, "not sparing either age or sex, man, woman, or child." Following the first waves of attacks made by local Indians known to the settlers, larger running groups of warriors, anywhere from fifty to several hundred, joined the fighting to finish off survivors and burn settlements.

Opechancanough's simultaneous attack was so overwhelming the settlers were unable to send warnings to other plantations. Applying English tactics used by Gates and Dale, his purpose was to destroy the settlers' buildings, equipment, and livestock in a massive attack on property as well as people. A bird's-eye view of the assault would have shown sheets of flames consuming houses and outbuildings and dense columns of smoke billowing up from burning plantations, wharves, and boats. Coming closer, dozens of men would have been seen grappling in desperate hand-to-hand combat and scores of Indians running toward the fighting, throwing themselves upon surviving English and killing them in their homes, fields, and yards. The screams of the injured and dying would have been clearly audible, mixed with the yells of warriors, shouts of alarm from householders and servants, crack of musket fire, and clash of steel.

So sudden was the attack, Edward Waterhouse, a company officeholder, wrote in an overtly racist account shortly after news reached London that few or none discerned the weapon or blow that brought them to their end: "In which manner they also slew many of our people then at their several works and husbandries in the fields, and without [outside] their houses, some in Planting Corn and Tobacco, some in gardening, some in making Brick, building, sawing, and other kinds of husbandry, they well knowing in what places and quarters each of our men were, in regard of their daily familiarity, and resort to us for trading and other negotiations, which the more willingly by us continued and cherished for the desire we had of effecting that great masterpiece of work, their conversion." And so, Waterhouse concluded, on "that fatal Friday" 347 settlers were clubbed, hacked, stabbed, or shot to death with their own tools and weapons.[5]

The attacks were devastating. Upriver, at Henrico and lands beyond, the Powhatans and Arrohattocs, supported by the Pamunkeys, swept through English settlements. Farthest to the west at Falling Creek, nearly the entire population was wiped out (twenty-two men, two women, and three children), including Captain John Berkeley, leader of a large-scale ironworks and a member of the governor's council. Only two children who, "with great difficulty hid" from the warriors, saved themselves. The ironworks, including a blast furnace, refinery forge, and other integrated workshops in which the company had invested thousands of pounds, was totally destroyed. Warriors broke down buildings and threw equipment into the creek.

At the Indian College Lands, another highly significant company project on the other side of the Powhatan (James) River, most of the tenant workers and indentured servants were killed. In discussions with the great chief, George Thorpe had described the hopes of company leaders as well as well-disposed Christians in England for the success of young Indian men taking Christ's message to the

Powhatans. Familiar with the recruitment of Indian novices and chiefs in the missionary work of religious orders in New Spain, Opechanca-nough had been quick to recognize the threat and was determined to extinguish it permanently. In this, his warriors were wholly success-ful, and as with the ironworks, the college project never recovered. A few miles downriver, as the attacks continued, nine men, two women, and two boys, probably brothers, died at Thomas Sheffield's property, and five men were killed on Henrico Island, which was devastated. John Proctor was absent from his plantation nearby, but his wife was able to organize their servants and drive attacking Indians away. Al-together, fifty-two men, four women, and five children perished in the Henrico region during the day, and the destruction of industrial works, buildings, and livestock was almost complete.[6]

At the same time, hundreds of Pamunkeys, Appomattocs, Weyanocks, Chickahominies, and Quiyoughcohannocks attacked nineteen settlements from the Appomattox River to the lands of the Chickahominies, killing 142 settlers. English casualties were heaviest in densely populated areas such as Bermuda Hundred and Charles City, where prime Indian lands had been taken by Dale and his men toward the end of the first war. At some plantations, Edward Water-house detailed entire families being wiped out, such as at William Ferrar's house, where Henricke Peterson, his wife, Alice, and her son, William, were slain, along with two maidservants, Mary and Eliz-abeth, and five men. At an adjoining plantation, Henry Milward, his wife, child, and sister were killed, as well as two men who were brothers, a boy, and "Goodwife Redhead," perhaps all inside or about the dwelling house when the warriors arrived and killed them within minutes of one another. The attacks indicate Opechancanough's re-solve to pursue a total war whereby his warriors were to slay every English man, woman, and child and take few prisoners.[7]

Captain George Thorpe was killed at Berkeley Hundred, a large plantation only recently established downriver from the Bermudas.

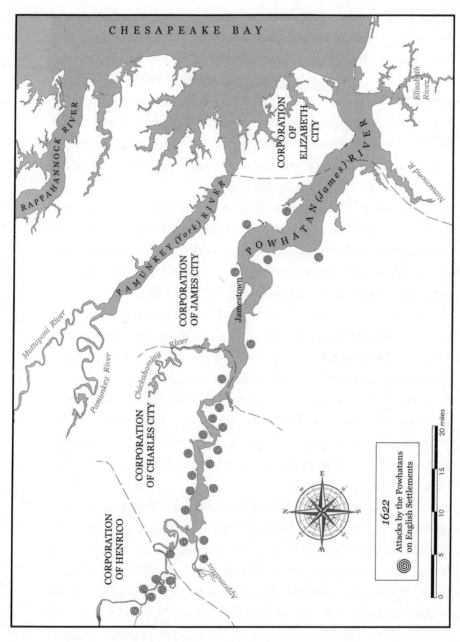

FIGURE 10.1. English settlements attacked by Powhatan warriors on March 22, 1622. Shown also are important settlements that were not attacked and the territorial bounds of the four corporations established in 1618. *Drawing by Jamie May.*

Thorpe, Waterhouse wrote, "thought nothing too dear for them [the Indians], and as being desirous to bind them to him by his many courtesies, he never denied them anything. Opechancanough and his people for the daily courtesies this good Gentleman did to one or other of them, did profess such outward love and respect to him, as nothing could seem more: but all was little regarded after by this Viperous brood, as the sequel showed: for they not only willfully murdered him, but cruelly and felly, out of devilish malice, did so many barbarous despites and foul scorns after to his dead corpse, as are unbefitting to be heard by any civil ear."

"One thing I cannot omit," he continued, "that when this good Gentleman upon his fatal hour was warned by his man (who perceived some treachery . . .) . . . [Thorpe] was so void of all suspicion, and so full of confidence, that they had sooner killed him than he could or would believe they meant any ill against him."

In fact, Thorpe was despised by the Pamunkeys who blamed him for trying to take their children from them to convert them to the English religion and because he was a high-ranking member of the colony's government. The mutilation of his body was intentional, designed to leave a clear message for other would-be missionaries or prominent English officials. He died alongside ten others at the plantation, as uncomprehending as the Jesuit father Segura half a century earlier about why Opechancanough and his people had turned against him.

Farther downriver, the Chickahominies and Pamunkeys made up the main strike force. At the West brothers' (Francis, John, and Nathaniel) plantations, called Westover, half a dozen men were killed together with twelve on Lieutenant John Gibbs's adjoining parcel. Nearby, a gentleman, Richard Owen, was slain in his house alongside his five servants, who included Francis, an Irishman, and an "old Maid called blind Margaret." Sir George Yeardley's plantation at Weyanock, a gift to him from Opechancanough, sustained the heaviest losses in the area and lost twenty-one people, probably

FIGURE 10.2. The attack of 1622, engraving by Matthäus Merian in *America*, part 8 (1628). The perspective appears to be looking downriver from the north bank of the Powhatan (James) River toward Jamestown, which is portrayed as a European walled city. Note the four war canoes full of warriors in the river and cannon fire from the bulwarks. *Courtesy of the Colonial Williamsburg Foundation, museum purchase.*

all company servants. The historian Frederick Fausz speculates that the ferocity of the attack may have been partly in revenge for the killing and capture of two dozen Chickahominies by Yeardley at Mamanahunt five years before. Directly across the Powhatan River at Flowerdew, another Yeardley plantation, warriors killed only six residents. All of the ten or so enslaved Africans living there appear to have escaped. Here, cannons and rudimentary defenses saved the great majority of the inhabitants.[8]

As Opechancanough's warriors swept from settlement to settlement during the morning, a coordinated attack was launched on Jamestown by land and water. An engraving from the late 1620s shows four war canoes approaching the fort, each carrying as many as twenty men armed with bows and clubs. The great chief had probably devised the plan in effort to take the English by surprise from an unexpected quarter, thereby aiding elite Pamunkey warriors who had massed outside Jamestown's walls to attack once they could get inside the fort. Although the weight of English settlement had moved upriver toward Bermuda Hundred and Henrico over the previous decade, Jamestown remained the colony's capital, the seat of colonial government, and the colony's leading port. A new church, where the General Assembly sat, had been constructed only a few years before, and nearby was New Towne, where wealthy planter-merchants had begun laying out their homes and businesses. Opechancanough planned to put the town to the torch, destroying public and commercial buildings and tearing down the fort and riverside wharves. The great chief calculated that by doing so, he would deal English leaders in the colony and London an enormous symbolic as well as material blow. Had he been successful, news of Jamestown's destruction and the deaths of hundreds of settlers would have reverberated around the capitals of Europe for years to come.

Success depended on maintaining secrecy so that local Indians could filter into the fort ready to launch the attack from within, but in this instance, Opechancanough's warriors were balked. An Anglicized Indian youth living in the household of a planter, Richard Pace, had been informed of the plot by another Indian bringing orders from their "King" to kill Pace. He was told that warriors would "come from divers [other] places to finish the Execution," that is, destroy the plantation and the rest of the household. Later that evening or during the night, the boy informed his master, and after securing his own house, Pace rowed across the river to Jamestown at first light to tell Governor Wyatt. Time was short, but Wyatt was able to call the townsmen to arms, ready the fort's defenses, and alert neighboring plantations. Under strict instructions not to attempt a frontal assault on the fort, or any heavily fortified enclosure, Opechancanough's warriors quickly withdrew and moved elsewhere.[9]

Forewarned, Jamestown avoided casualties, but seven miles downriver the largest number of fatalities of any single plantation occurred at Martin's Hundred, which was attacked by large groups of Pamunkeys and Kiskiacks possibly thwarted at Jamestown. Richard Frethorne, a young indentured servant living at the settlement, wrote the following spring that of "seven score, there were but 22 left alive." He exaggerated the numbers, but nevertheless the death toll was extremely high, some seventy-seven killed, including fourteen women and six children. Nine family groups perished and twenty settlers, mostly women, were captured. Wolstenholme Towne, the principal settlement of Martin's Hundred, was burned to the ground, and of the rest, only two houses and "a piece of a Church" were left standing.

An account of an attack at Ensign James Harrison's plantation across the river at Warraskoyack is a little confusing but nonetheless

FIGURE 10.3. Devastation of Wolstenholme Towne, at Martin's Hundred, March 22, 1622. Detail from a painting by Richard Schlecht.
Courtesy of the Colonial Williamsburg Foundation, Archaeological Collections.

provides an insight into specific Indian tactics. A group of Nansemonds and Warraskoyacks arrived near Harrison's house where Thomas Hamor (Ralph's brother) and half a dozen men were working. The Indians, carrying gifts, asked the men whether Captain Ralph Hamor would go with them into the woods to meet their "King" hunting nearby. In the house, busy writing a letter, Thomas did not respond, and a short time after, the warriors set fire to a tobacco barn, calling upon the English to put out the flames. All the men rushed to quench the flames, at which the Indians "shot them full of arrows." Thomas had not been with them, but hearing the shouting outside, he left the house and was immediately struck in the back with an arrow, causing him to retreat back into the house and barricade the door. The warriors then set the house on fire. Thomas, along with others, including women and children, managed to flee to a neighbor's house, a Master Baldwin, half a mile away, where they fought off the Indians with musket fire. As warriors broadened their assault, a number of buildings in the vicinity were set on fire, including Captain Hamor's new house under construction. Hamor and his men, who were at work on the house when they were attacked, fought with spades and axes and threw bricks until the warriors moved off. They then joined other survivors in the area, including Thomas, and seeing "all they had was burnt and consumed" abandoned their homes and left for Jamestown.[10]

Opechancanough did not expect that a single day's attack, even such a well-executed one, would succeed in expelling the English straightaway. A general withdrawal would probably take a few months and possibly much longer. Neither did he believe in a policy of containment, confining the English in Jamestown and other specific places, as several historians have argued. Ultimately, war was a contest for mastery of the land in which the winner would take all. At no point did he consider seriously the possibility of living alongside the English as a separate but equal people or of being a part of Sir Edwin Sandys's Christian commonwealth. His long experience with Europeans had taught him that there could be no accommodation with the settlers on terms that would adequately recognize the Powhatans' way of life and beliefs. Edward Waterhouse blamed the attack on "the instigation of the Devil" but referenced "the daily fear that possessed them [the Indians], that in time we by our growing continually upon them, would dispossess them of this Country, as they had been formerly of the West Indies by the Spaniard." Left unchecked, the English would keep coming and continue to occupy their lands, piece by piece, until his people would be reduced to ragged pensioners dependent on the settlers' largesse. His strategy was therefore based on achieving a victory so crushing that the English could not possibly recover. By destroying public works, plantations, and cutting off food supplies, he anticipated the English would eventually become so weakened and demoralized they would either eventually fall victim to his warriors or be forced to abandon the colony, as nearly happened during the harrowing "starving time" winter of 1609–1610.[11]

Above all, Opechancanough's strategy across eight bitter years following the end of the 1609–1614 war was premised on English leaders' unquestioning belief in their own cultural and military superiority. He correctly gambled that the likes of Yeardley, Wyatt, and Thorpe would not remotely suspect him capable of devising such a well-planned and audacious attack. Company officials in London responded, as he anticipated, by placing the blame for the disaster squarely on Sir Francis Wyatt's shoulders. "We have to our extreme grief understood of the great Massacre executed on our people in Virginia," they wrote, "and that in such a manner as is more miserable than death itself; to fall by the hands of men so contemptible; to be surprised by treachery in a time of known danger; to be deaf to so plain a warning (as we now too late understand) was last year given; to be secure in an occasion of so great suspicion and jealousy as was Nemattanew's death; not to perceive anything in so open and general conspiracy; but to be made in part instruments of contriving it, and almost guilty of the destruction by blindfold and stupid entertaining it . . . are circumstances, that do add much to our sorrow." George Wyatt, a veteran of the Spanish wars in the Netherlands, also noted in a letter to his son, Sir Francis, that he should not have been so trusting of the Indians. Had Francis been more on his guard, he could have avoided "the Pawn mate," which is "soonest given where least looked for." If it be "hurtful" to overestimate an enemy, George warned, it was just as dangerous to underestimate him. Similarly, in a declaration by "ancient planters" (those who had arrived between 1607 and 1616) still living in Virginia, the writers acknowledged that, owing to the settlers' insatiable greed for "present gain and profit," they had been too "trusting of a treacherous enemy." From long experience, Opechancanough recognized that the Europeans' arrogance was their greatest weakness.[12]

Though March 22 did not end in complete success for Opechancanough and his warriors, they nevertheless killed, by nightfall, between a quarter and a third of the settlers and reduced many settlements to smoldering ashes. Over the next couple of months, with the English in shock and disarray, warriors continued to conduct small-scale raids, killing even more settlers and destroying property. Settlers began abandoning their homesteads, seeking refuge at better protected plantations nearby, foreshadowing Governor Wyatt's order of late April to evacuate all outlying settlements and move to eight fortified locations at Kecoughtan, Newport News, Jamestown, Southampton Hundred, Flowerdew, West and Shirley Hundred, and Jordan's Journey, near Charles City. The sense of dread among settlers was palpable in their writings. "God forgive me," William Capps, an old planter, wrote, "I think the last massacre killed all our Country," and "besides them they killed, they burst the heart of all the rest." In June, John Pountis, vice admiral of the colony, complained to Wyatt that Southampton Hundred, where only five settlers had been lost in the attack, was so "often infested" by warriors they had been unable to plant tobacco and were starving with no "corn for the present to maintain life."[13]

Pountis's concern illustrates a vital if sometimes overlooked aspect of Opechancanough's strategy: the fighting not only destroyed settlers' food supplies but completely disrupted spring planting. Wyatt was faced with the immediate challenge of feeding hundreds of starving settlers sheltering in larger populations. Consequently, the first priority, after instigating measures to protect survivors, was to seek relief from England and send ships to the Patawomecks to negotiate for provisions. As it happened, Captain Raleigh Crashaw and Henry Spelman were already in the Potomac River on a trading voyage when they heard news of the attack. Somehow, news of their presence in the region came to the ears of Opechancanough who sent messengers and gifts to the Patawomeck chief, in an effort to persuade him to kill the English, boasting that "before the end of two Moons there should not be an Englishman in all their Countries." The chief refused the request or to join the Pamunkeys, whom he did not trust, and instead told Crashaw of the threat. He considered the English good trading partners and helpful as allies in local conflicts against Indian peoples farther up the Potomac River. With no hope of provisions from England for several months and severe shortages in the Powhatan River Valley, Wyatt and his advisers considered moving several hundred settlers to the Eastern Shore where they could buy corn from the friendly Accomacs, "since," the governor wrote to London, "there was never more cause to fear the miserable ruin of the Plantation [colony] by a relapse into extreme famine than at this time."[14]

From spring through fall, Opechancanough watched as the English struggled to save themselves, "oppressed with famine and sickness within, and engaged in a War" with his warriors without.

The continuing flow of corn to the English from the Patawomecks and Accomacs was a major source of frustration, however, making it impossible for him to entirely cut off food supplies to the famished settlers. His inability to exert his authority over powerful chiefdoms on the margins of his domains would ultimately prove costly, underscoring the critical damage done by the English in the hostilities ten years earlier.

CHAPTER 11

"War Without Peace or Truce"

I N LONDON, RECOVERING FROM THEIR OUTRAGE, VIRGINIA Company leaders quickly began formulating plans to rebuild the colony. The uprising had been a terrible setback, but Sir Edwin Sandys, the Earl of Southampton (who had been appointed leader of the company in 1620), and other leaders were determined to persevere. Wyatt was told to put aside any thoughts of creating another colony on the Eastern Shore. It would be "a Sin against the dead," they wrote, "to abandon the enterprise, until we have fully settled the possession [of the Powhatan (James) River Valley], for which so many of our Brethren have lost their lives." Restarting company projects, such as planting mulberry trees along with the ironworks, the Indian College, and the vineyards, was an absolute necessity, as was the production of other crops and manufactures. Settlements were to be fortified and repeopled as soon as possible, and hundreds of settlers were being recruited from all over the country to replace those who had been lost. To help protect the settlers and facilitate reprisals, the company petitioned the king to take possession of certain obsolete arms in the Tower of London, which "altogether unfit, and of no use for modern Service, might nevertheless be service-able against the naked people." One thousand halberds, hundreds of coats and shirts of mail, various types of muskets and pistols, two thousand iron helmets, and twenty barrels of powder were made ready to be shipped to Governor Wyatt for distribution among the settlers.[1]

During the six months immediately following the attack, Wyatt and his officers had focused their energies on survival, defending settlers from Indian raids, creating a military command structure throughout the colony, and seeking regular supplies of corn. By early September, they were ready to launch reprisals. "Our first work is expulsion of the Savages to gain free range of the country," Wyatt declared. Yet, he conceded the Indians would not be easily defeated. Opechancanough's warriors avoided battles in the open field, pre-ferring hit-and-run raids. The Indians' ultimate destruction would be a drawn-out affair, relying on the same scorched-earth tactics deployed a decade earlier: burning their towns, carrying away their corn, "and depriving them of whatsoever may yield them succor or relief."

WYATT'S COMMANDERS LAUNCHED their campaigns from mid-September onward. Sir George Yeardley, designated chief field commander, led raids of several hundred soldiers against the Weyanocks, Warraskoyacks, Nansemonds, and Pamunkeys. At Nan-semond, the Indians escaped, carrying away their possessions and as much corn as possible. At Pamunkey, Opechancanough's warriors played for time, promising to return twenty prisoners, mostly women taken from Martin's Hundred, and give up their English weapons. When Yeardley and his men realized the Indians' promises were made only to give them time to move their supplies, they attacked, burning houses and taking the remaining corn. George Sandys, the Virginia Company's treasurer in the colony, twice raided the

Quiyoughcohannocks, and Captain William Powell went against the Chickahominies, during which he was killed. Attacks were also carried out on the Powhatans and Rappahannocks.

Knowing they could not defeat soldiers wearing armor and wielding muskets and swords, the Indians responded by avoiding pitched battles and withdrawing as soon as the soldiers approached. George Wyatt noted in a letter to his son that for the Indians "flight is the manner of their fight" and praised them for their order and discipline. Indians would also occasionally ambush the English in quick and deadly attacks, and on at least one occasion, the Pamunkeys used firearms against Yeardley's raiding party. Governor Wyatt subsequently reported that, whereas in former times the Indians had been wary of English military capability, now they "dare maintain an open War with our people and being armed with our Weapons and having learned the use of our guns can brave our countrymen at their very doors." Shortly before his death, the illustrious warrior Nemattanew had been training his warriors how to fire muskets, yet for him as for Opechancanough, securing powder and shot from the English remained a challenge.[2]

Casualties on both sides had been relatively slight up until the end of the year when raids were halted, but as hostilities temporarily ceased for the winter, the English faced a tragedy of far greater proportions. During the terrible winter of 1622–1623, hundreds of settlers died of starvation and of diseases brought in ships. George Sandys reckoned that by the end of March, not less than five hundred old planters and new arrivals had died. So many had been carried off that the living were "hardly able to bury the dead," he wrote, a comment corroborated by sailors off the *Abigail*, who reported that people who "died in the streets, at James towne" were "so little cared for that they have lay [there] until the hogs have eaten their Corpses." Phoebus Canner lamented that "God's heavy hand had been here amongst us for we have had the sword, Famine, and great mortality: I beseech god to give me life and health that I may this year end this troublesome voyage. I am quite out of heart to live in this land, god send me well out of it." Cattle died as well as settlers, and provisions were in short supply. Peter Arundel, a silk maker, commented that he and his family were forced to subsist on oysters. Edward Hill, who had recently arrived in Elizabeth City, wrote to his brother in London that "We are all like to have the greatest famine in the land that ever was" and would return to England as soon as possible if he could. Men and women were described as "dying under hedges and in the woods," and corpses lying "for many days unregarded and unburied."[3]

Richard Frethorne, an indentured servant who lived at Martin's Hundred, provides a poignant case study. Shortly after arrival in early 1623, he wrote to his parish minister in England begging for food and clothes: "I am in a most miserable and pitiful Case [state], for want of meat [food] and want of clothes." He asked his minister to speak to his parishioners to raise a small donation on his behalf and begged "to be freed out of this Egypt." A few weeks later he wrote to his parents describing scurvy, the "bloody flux" (dysentery), and a shortage of provisions: "Since I came out of the ship, I never ate anything but peas and loblolly (that is water gruel)." It would be "most pitiful if you did know as much as I, when people cry out day, and night, Oh, that they were in England without their limbs and would not care to lose any limb to be in England again, yea though they beg from door to door." If "you love or respect me, as your Child release me from this bondage, and save my life," he pleaded. Whether his parents were able to save him is unknown but more likely he died in the summer or fall.[4] Opechancanough must have been aware of the horrors at Jamestown and elsewhere and planned to take advantage.

More good news arrived at the end of March. Captain Henry Spelman and twenty men, trading in the Potomac River for corn, had gone ashore at Nacotchtanks to meet the chief there when they were attacked by hundreds of warriors, cut off from their shallop (a light sailboat), and killed. Spelman was either unaware that

Captain Ralph Hamor had joined the Patawomecks on a raid of the Nacotchtanks the previous year, which resulted in several killings and the theft of their corn, or else he believed he could reestablish peace with them. Five men onboard the *Tiger*, a pinnace accompanying Spelman, barely managed to repel the Indians and get away, pursued by about sixty Nacotchtanks war canoes. News of Spelman's death and twenty men with their arms and armor was deeply troubling to English leaders. Indian warriors had never before directly attacked an English ship. The Indians had possession of a large cache of English weapons, which may have led Governor Wyatt to wonder whether Opechancanough would seek to join forces with the Nacotchtanks and cut off settlers' corn from the Patawomecks.[5]

SOON AFTER, WYATT received an unexpected visit from an Indian named Chauco, who had lived among the settlers, and Comahum, "a great man" who had taken part in the attack on Martin's Hundred. Chauco informed him that the "great King" Itoyatin believed that enough "blood had already been shed on both sides, that many of his People were starved, by our taking Away their Corn and burning their houses" and that accordingly he sought a truce to allow his people to plant their corn at Pamunkey and other places. In exchange, he promised that prisoners taken during the attack would be returned. As a sign of his good faith, Mrs. Alice Boyse, one of the wives captured at Wolstenholme, Martin's Hundred, was sent back to Jamestown in the attire of an Indian queen, which was meant to reassure the English she had been well treated. Wyatt and his commanders were content to appear in favor of a truce as a means of finding out where the Indians, especially the Pamunkeys, were planting their corn so they could plan their next series of raids accordingly. Several weeks later in May 1623, Itoyatin sent word a second time with a startling offer. If the governor would dispatch ten or twelve men as an escort, he would deliver the rest of the captives and also "his Brother Opachankano, who was the Author of the Massacre, into the hands of the English either alive or dead."[6]

Wyatt presumed the proposal was a ploy to lure a dozen English soldiers into an ambush and score a highly conspicuous victory. A similar tactic had been devised by Nemattanew several years earlier when he had requested Governor Yeardley to contribute eight to ten men "with their Arms" and armor for a raid on the Massitup-pamohtnocks, a day's march beyond the falls. Whether the English soldiers went or not is unclear, but later evidence suggests they did and never returned, probably having been killed for their weapons. Consequently, the English were on their guard, and yet here was an opportunity to set a countertrap for Opechancanough, Itoyatin, and their warriors, perhaps using the same tactic as that attempted by the chiefs two years before. Accordingly, the English agreed to parley at Patawomeck, a place that was viewed as neutral territory.

The politics that lay behind Wyatt's plan were intricate. For many years the English had been on good terms with the Pata-womecks until the summer of 1622 when, a few months after Ralph Hamor's successful voyage and attack on the Nacotchtanks, Captain Isaac Madison arrived at Patawomeck and, hearing rumors of a plot against him, captured the chief and slaughtered thirty or forty towns-people. The Patawomecks were incensed and had sought immediate reparations from the English. Ever since, Wyatt had been trying to repair relations, and now the proposed meeting with Itoyatin and Opechancanough at Patawomeck presented the ideal opportunity. If the English were able to kill or capture Opechancanough, they would strike a decisive blow against their leading enemy and one of the Patawomecks' greatest foes.

In May 1623, the experienced militia captain William Tucker was dispatched to the Potomac River with a dozen men, seemingly to retrieve the settlers and conclude a peace with Itoyatin. After numer-ous speeches and smoking of pipes, Tucker handed around bottles of sack (Spanish fortified wine) to the assembled chiefs and their men and offered a toast to the peace. Before the Indians drank, Tucker and his interpreter tasted it to show that no treachery was intended, but they drank from a different bottle while the Indians, including Itoyatin, Opechancanough, the chief of the Kiskiacks, their sons, and two hundred "great men" drank poisoned wine. How many died is uncertain, but most fell ill soon after drinking, and in the confusion that followed, Tucker ordered his men to fire a volley of shot that killed "some 50 more," including, he claimed, two kings.

Robert Bennett wrote to his brother Edward, whose plantation had suffered greatly in the attack of the year before, adding an intriguing detail. As Tucker and his men withdrew from the parley to their boats, an interpreter who was near "the king on a high rock" quickly dropped to the ground, which was the signal for the English to open fire. The volley killed the "great King Aponchanzion" (Opechancanough), as well as the chief of the Kiskiacks, "and many also," which Bennett was certain would "be a great dismaying to the bloody infidels." Tucker then returned to Jamestown with Indian scalps as proof of his success. The attack was hailed in Virginia and London as a signal triumph. Lord Southampton reported to company members with satisfaction that the settlers had regained the English captives taken the previous year and killed many "Indian Kings and great Commanders: Amongst whom they are confident that Opachankano was one." If this were true, the war would be as good as over.[7]

From summer through the fall, Wyatt's commanders followed up with another series of attacks on peoples of the Powhatan River Valley. As before, the English destroyed the Indians' towns and burned or took their corn. Late in the year, Wyatt led an expedition to the Potomac to attack the powerful Piscataway chiefdoms, another powerful enemy of the Patawomecks. With good relations restored and the assurance of corn from the Patawomecks, Wyatt was free to continue his war of attrition against the Powhatans. He reported to the Virginia Company in late January 1624 that his men had to their "uttermost abilities revenged themselves upon the Savages," having cut down their corn and burned their settlements along the Powhatan River. Wyatt also forcefully told company leaders that when dealing with such treacherous foes, he and his commanders held "nothing unjust that may tend to their ruin." Stratagems, he wrote, had always been used against enemies but, he continued ominously, "with these neither fair War nor good quarter is ever to be held."

The English were convinced Opechancanough and Itoyatin were dead, but as later events were to prove, both had survived. Itoyatin reappeared in the summer of 1624 when Wyatt and six soldiers in full armor attacked the Pamunkeys. Anticipating the English would sooner or later invade their territories to carry off their corn, Itoyatin had gathered a huge force to meet them, confident, as their "great brags" revealed, that they would emerge victorious. Wyatt estimated his men were confronted by approximately eight hundred Pamunkey bowmen and an unspecified number of allies, who encouraged by their own numbers and the "paucity of ours," he observed, engaged the English in open field and fought with great bravery to defend their cornfields.

Details of the battle are frustratingly vague and subject to distortions by the English to exaggerate their own success. The fighting lasted two days, which implies a series of pitched battles punctuated by tactical withdrawals on both sides to rest. Firing volleys in ranks to allow them to reload, the majority of Wyatt's men provided cover for the soldiers carrying off the Indians' corn. Despite their valor, the Pamunkeys were eventually beaten back by the concentrated firepower of the English, who had recently acquired snaphaunce muskets, an early form of flintlocks that were more effective than matchlocks. After sustaining heavy losses, the warriors eventually gave up "and dismayed, stood most ruefully looking on while their Corn was Cut down." By any measure, the battle was a decisive defeat for Itoyatin, which broke the half-century ascendancy of the

Pamunkeys and Powhatans and heralded a long period of largely unchallenged English expansion.[8]

HOSTILITIES CONTINUED ON and off throughout the remainder of the decade. Fighting fell most heavily on peoples of the upper Powhatan River Valley but also spread farther south into areas occupied by the Nansemonds and Chesapeakes and north to lands on the Pamunkey (York) River inhabited by the Kiskiacks. English expeditions followed much the same pattern as in previous years, whereby soldiers were transported along the rivers in their ships and landed to burn towns and cornfields with the intent of starving the Indians into submission and cutting off their trade. Legislation was passed to bolster settlers' defenses and to avoid casualties in Powhatan raids. Planters were ordered to construct palisades around their houses and were prohibited from going beyond their lands alone or working in the fields without an armed sentry. Yet, as the English sought to rebuild their settlements, sporadic killings ensured settlers continued to live in fear of attack.

Prosecuting the war and surviving the widespread food shortage were Wyatt's major priorities, but he also had to deal with dramatically changing English perceptions of the Powhatans. Hopes for the Indians' conversion and integration into settler society abruptly disappeared to be replaced by an outpouring of racist invective. Christopher Brooke, a company investor and member of Parliament well known to Sir Edwin Sandys, wrote a long poem in which he described Indians as "Souls drown'd in flesh and blood; / Rooted in Evil, and Oppos'd in Good; / Errors of Nature, of inhumane Birth, / The very dregs, garbage, and Spawn of Earth." Edward Waterhouse characterized them as "of all people the most lying and most inconstant in the world" and advocated adopting Spanish methods in hunting them down, using our "Mastiffs to seize them, which take this naked, tanned, deformed Savages, for no other than wild beasts." Similarly, the Reverend Samuel Purchas, who had welcomed Pocahontas and Tomakin in London years earlier, decried the Indians in venomous language as "Barbarians, Borders, and Out-Laws of Humanity" who were "more brutish than the beasts they hunt, more wild and unmanly than that unmanned Wild Country that they range rather than inhabit."[9]

A consistent theme in such writings emphasized that, owing to their "treachery," the Indians had not only forfeited Christian salvation and the earthly benefits of trade with the English but had also lost their rights to the land they inhabited. In "Virginia's Verger," a tract originally published in volume 9 of Purchas's multivolume work *Hakluytus Posthumus or Purchas His Pilgrimes* (1625), he adopted conventional European thinking about the laws of nature, nations, just war, and religion that justified taking possession of non-Christian uninhabited or sparsely inhabited lands. By "this last butchery," he argued, the Indians "had forfeited any rights to the land, and once rid of them a bountiful Virginia enriched by European plants and animals and populated by English settlers" would in time become "another England in America," adding for good measure the example of the earlier destruction of Sir Walter Ralegh's Roanoke colonies to make the extraordinary claim that by the "dispersed bones of their [settlers] and their Countrymen's since murdered carcasses, have taken a mortal immortal possession, and being dead, speak, proclaim and cry, This our earth is truly English, and therefore this Land is justly yours O English." The spilling of English blood had made Virginia English, freeing settlers to take full advantage of the region's natural abundance.[10]

Virginia became the first English mainland colony to enslave Indian peoples. Edward Waterhouse justified both the taking of Indian lands and their enslavement, writing that whereas before we "had possession of no more ground then their [the Indians'] waste, may now by right of War, and law of Nations, invade the Country, and destroy them that sought to destroy us: whereby we shall enjoy their cultivated places." The English would be free to exploit the Indians' prime agricultural lands and former hunting grounds, and prisoners of war could be "compelled to servitude and drudgery" and take the place of English laborers and workmen in such "inferior works of digging in mines, and the like." Captain John Martin agreed, arguing against destroying or expelling the Powhatans because the Indians were more "apt for work than yet our English are." The company discussed raising a colony-wide levy to support the war against the Powhatans, assuring settlers that Indian captives could be used as slaves to pay soldiers and defray costs. William Capps was confident he could bring in "3 or 4 score [Indian] slaves to work about [building] a fort or other servile work" at Point Comfort. William Claiborne, a member of the governor's council, announced he had developed a device that would prevent Indian slaves from running away (no details were given). Henceforth, enslavement of Indians became a regular feature of English practice in wartime.[11]

ENGLISH LEADERS AND Chief Itoyatin now had to reckon with the challenges that convulsed their respective societies. In the wake of damning reports about the Virginia Company's governance and conditions in the colony, particularly the loss of thousands of settlers from disease, malnutrition, and Indian attacks, a royal commission was established in May 1623 to investigate the allegations. A report from a special commission sent to Virginia to gather additional witness statements confirmed the company was bankrupt and the colony languished in a "weak and miserable" condition, persuading the king to instruct his attorney general to sue for the recovery of the company's charter. Legal proceedings dragged on for six months, until the charter was revoked on May 24, 1624. Following a year of uncertainty about what form the colony's government would take, the new king, Charles I, proclaimed that Virginia would henceforth be ruled directly by the Crown, thereby becoming England's first transatlantic royal colony. The attack of 1622 had not brought about the end of the colony, but it had succeeded in bringing down the Virginia Company.[12]

If Opechancanough's principal objectives were to cause chaos in the colony and sow discord among company officials, he succeeded spectacularly. And yet, after May 1623, he disappeared and was not seen or heard of by the English for seven years. His prolonged absence remains a mystery, which understandably gave English leaders confidence he had been killed by Tucker's men at the Patawomeck meeting. Perhaps his wounds were so grievous he needed years to recover and was therefore forced to retire to his quarters at Menmend far up the Pamunkey River, or possibly following his recovery, he opted to remain in seclusion and let his brother Itoyatin deal with the English, knowing that if he revealed himself he would be hunted down by soldiers. Whatever the reason, his absence came at a critical juncture in Indian-English relations. Having wrested military control of the region from the Powhatans and no longer constrained by company rule or the requirement to save Indian souls, settlers ruthlessly pursued their own interests, taking more and more Indian land.[13]

Following a lull in hostilities for more than a year, Itoyatin offered to negotiate a peace agreement. Governor Wyatt believed the chief had been heartened by English inaction, which was the result of the settlers' drastic shortage of powder and shot, and pleaded with government officials in London for munitions to be sent as soon as possible. The Indians, he wrote in 1626, were greatly desirous of ending the war, and he had given them cause for hope so as to encourage their return to planting corn. If "supplies of people, powder, and munitions come in time," he continued, "we may have fair opportunity to revenge their former Treacheries" by resuming raids and taking their food supplies. No English attacks occurred, however, and apart from a few skirmishes, one of which involved the Nansemonds capturing a couple of settlers, little transpired until the following year.

In early 1627, a rumor reported by friendly Indians came to the ears of the English that Itoyatin was planning a general attack that spring. Sir George Yeardley, serving again as governor, issued a proclamation repeating orders to settlers to reinforce their plantations and be on their guard. Whether the rumor had any basis in fact is unclear, but in July, Yeardley and his council decided to seize the initiative and "go upon the Indians and cut down their corn," which was to be organized against the Powhatans, Appomattocs, Weyanocks, Quiyoughcohannocks, Warraskoyacks, Chickahominies, Nansemonds, and so-called Chesapeakes, who were Nansemonds living in the territories formerly held by the Chesapeakes. The attack was planned to take place on August 1, and a ship was sent to the Pamunkey River as a ruse to suggest a raid was imminent. In fact, Yeardley was preparing to recruit men from the whole colony to go against the Pamunkeys in the fall, once again to steal their corn and to do "what other hurt and damage" they could.

Little is known about the outcome of the expedition, but evidently several Englishmen were taken captive, one of whom was sent to Jamestown in April 1628 with a message from Itoyatin that offered to return his prisoners in exchange for a peace treaty. The terms of the treaty, which have not survived, were apparently based on reciprocal pledges to halt the killings and refrain from encroaching on each other's lands and stealing livestock. With the death of Yeardley in October, another governor, Captain Francis West, seemingly went along with the treaty while preparing all the while to renege on it once the English prisoners were returned. Six months later he announced his withdrawal from the treaty to "prevent a second Massacre" and ordered settlers to return to unrestrained "enmity and wars with all the Indians of these parts." Accusing the Indians of breaking the treaty's conditions by committing outrages at several plantations,

West gave permission to settlers to kill them if either necessity or occasion arose.

In the summer of 1629, when the corn was ripe, the settlers instigated another series of brutal attacks on Indians along the Powhatan (James) River, which, according to English observers, did more damage than any other "since the great massacre." Later in the year, the General Assembly passed a measure ordering three attacks to be made in the spring, summer, and fall each year and divided the colony into "four divisions" to enable settlers to be recruited to carry them out. Clearly, the English were unconcerned about the Indians knowing when the attacks would come, an indication of their growing military confidence, and as historian James Rice has pointed out, these attacks were also a ploy devised by the colony's leaders to deliberately prolong the war and provide an excuse to take the Indians' corn. Freed from raising their own corn, the colonists could then devote more of their energies to raising tobacco and reaping greater profits.[14]

One of the attacks launched in the summer was a significant departure from previous years. William Claibourne led an assault on the Kiskiacks, who had moved from their traditional lands on the south bank of the Pamunkey River to a place called "Candanngack" (Cantaunkack) directly across the river. In earlier years, the English had sailed up the river on numerous occasions to engage the Pamunkeys in parleys or fighting, but they had never before attacked the Kiskiacks on their home territory. One reason for the novel direction of attack was to put into effect a plan that had been under consideration for several years. Governor Wyatt had proposed building a palisade across the peninsula from Martin's Hundred to Kiskiack to "Win the whole forest and make it inaccessible to the Savages." The same idea was suggested by Captain John Smith, still promoting colonial ventures while living in London, who explained how a fortified palisade from the Powhatan River to the Pamunkey River would create an enormous safe haven, capable of supporting ten thousand settlers and a vast cattle range. But nothing came of the proposals other than occasional expressions of encouragement to settlers to take up land in the area.

BY THE END of the decade conditions in Virginia were rapidly changing. The colony had stagnated for several years following the 1622 attack, but as the "scars of the massacre" gradually healed, larger numbers of settlers began to arrive, attracted by the booming tobacco economy. By 1630, the English population had doubled to approximately 2,600. The Powhatan River Valley was filling up, and the best lands had already been occupied by settlers, making the prospect of occupying other regions such as the Pamunkey River more appealing to newcomers. In addition, the Kiskiacks' former lands were viewed by colony leaders as potentially an important base from which to launch offensives against the Pamunkeys. About this time, also, word reached them that "their greatest enemy Appechankeno" (Opechancanough) still lived and was now the paramount chief by right of succession, his ineffectual predecessor having recently died. Entering into negotiations with the English, Opechancanough showed no inclination to renew hostilities. Instead, realizing the weakness of his people, he concluded a peace agreement with Governor Sir John Harvey in 1632. Occasional outbursts of violence continued and neither side remotely trusted the other, but large-scale attacks were avoided. It was a grudging peace, and yet it ended the long war.[15]

CHAPTER 12

The Last Stand

G OVERNOR HARVEY WAS PLEASED WITH HIS PROGRESS SINCE taking office the year before, a point he was eager to emphasize to government authorities in London. "We have now, blessed be God," he wrote in late December 1631, "arrived to that plenty which no foregoing times have attained" and have "banished that fear of famine which has always besieged us." The colony was well provisioned and had so much corn that it was likely to become "as Sicily to Rome, the Granary of his Majesty's Empire" in America. Planters had begun settling at Kiskiack and along the Pamunkey (York) River and were now in control of the entire eastern part of the peninsula from College Creek to Elizabeth City (Kecoughtan). He had encouraged a mixed economy of industries and crops, sought to limit tobacco cultivation, which he described as a "stinking commodity" albeit recognizing the profits, and reported the construction of a new fort at Point Comfort. Settlers were building better houses with gardens and orchards, brick rather than wooden buildings were becoming more common, and Jamestown was emerging as a small but busy Atlantic port that connected London and other parts of England to the colony's hinterland.[1]

The expansion of English settlement throughout the region continued apace. From approximately five thousand in 1634, the year when the colony was divided into eight counties, the settler population increased to eight thousand by the end of the decade. In 1635 alone, some two thousand migrants arrived from London, rapidly swelling the number of tobacco plantations dotted along the Powhatan (James) River and its major tributaries, both sides of the lower Chickahominy River, and the southern bank of the Pamunkey River from Kiskiack east to where the palisade crossing the peninsula had recently been completed. On the south bank of the Powhatan River, settlements were developing along the Nansemond and Elizabeth River systems, as well as bordering the bay where the Chesapeakes had formerly lived. In the late 1630s and early 1640s, planters began to take more interest in the region north of the Pamunkey River, extending to the Piankatank River and beyond to the Rappahannock. This vast area, uninhabited by Europeans, offered planters the pick of the best lands for themselves once the Indians were forced out. Finally, across the bay on the Eastern Shore, settlers were moving into lands owned by the Accomacs.[2]

Despite the spread of English settlements and consequent hardships suffered by his people, Opechancanough seemingly remained detached. Some Indian peoples disappeared in this period, the Warraskoyacks and Quiyoughcohannocks, for example, and others moved away from English settlements. Apart from a handful of appearances in the colonists' records, which show him working to maintain the peace accord, very little is known about what he was doing in these years. In 1634, another English colony was established north of the Potomac River, called Maryland, which caused considerable disquiet among Virginia's leaders who believed the colony infringed on their territory. The following year, a serious political crisis embroiled the leadership at Jamestown and led to angry mutterings raised by some of the councilors about Governor Harvey's incompetence threatening to "bring a second massacre among them." Nevertheless, the great chief stayed aloof. Even when Harvey was subsequently overthrown and forced to leave the colony for a couple of years, he opted not to seek advantage from the turmoil at Jamestown.[3]

Now in his nineties, Opechancanough chose only to engage with English leaders to keep the peace. They were free to assume that he preferred to spend the rest of his days living in the comfort of his own quarters out of the reach of the English, as his brother Powhatan had done twenty years earlier before he died. And yet, over the course of his long life, he had repeatedly shown his ability to wait for the right moment to strike.

WHILE OPECHANCANOUGH REMAINED remote from Jamestown, dramatic events unfolded on the other side of the Atlantic that eventually led to his final confrontation with the English. Civil war had broken out in England. After years of intense political struggle between King Charles I and Parliament, the two sides had reached a constitutional impasse. The king was adamant that his prerogative (absolute) powers conferred on him a right to govern as he saw fit, including the levying of taxes on his subjects, which ultimately did not require the consent of Parliament. He also vigorously defended the Church of England from efforts by proponents of reform, many of whom he associated with the House of Commons, to cleanse it of practices they viewed as too close to Catholicism and popery. On August 22, 1642, Charles abruptly left the capital and raised his royal standard at Nottingham, tantamount to a declaration of war, while Parliament rallied support in London. Over the next eighteen months, following a series of initial skirmishes, full-scale fighting between royalist and parliamentarian forces quickly spread across England, dividing the country into hostile camps and bringing widespread conflict and disorder to the shires.[4]

Here was the opportunity Opechancanough had been waiting for. Informed by settlers that "all was under the Sword in England," the great chief believed this was now "his time or never to root out all the English." The civil war would lead to major disruptions to trade and government in England, which would throw Virginia into chaos. Although his warrior strength, like his people generally, had been much diminished over the previous twenty years, he was nevertheless able to call upon some five hundred to six hundred warriors, including Powhatans, Appomattocs, Weyanocks, Pamunkeys, Mattaponis, Chickahominies, non-Christian Nansemonds, and Kiskiacks. His plan, similar to that of 1622, centered on an initial overwhelming attack followed by hit-and-run raids to starve and harry the settlers into submission, forcing them eventually to abandon their plantations. "For those that they could not surprise and kill under the feigned masque of Friendship and feasting," a commentator observed, "the rest would be [undone] by wants." Without supplies from England, the settlers would "be suddenly Consumed and Famished. The Indians Alaruming them night and day, and killing all their Cattle, as with ease they might do, and by destroying in the nights all their Corn Fields, which the English could not defend."[5]

The attack came at dawn on April 18, 1644, and once again the English were caught entirely off-guard. Most of the fighting occurred upriver in frontier areas where large numbers of English had moved over the past decade and a half. Robert Beverley, a wealthy planter and historian writing at the end of the seventeenth century, believed the "Massacre fell severest on the South-side of James River and on the heads of the other Rivers; but chiefly of York River, where the Emperor Opechancanough kept the Seat of his Government." Henrico and Charles City together with settlements along the York River west of Kiskiack, throughout the Chickahominies' lands, and along the Nansemond and Elizabeth Rivers on the southside suffered the largest number of casualties. The massive assault lasted two days, during which the Indians killed "near Five Hundred Christians."[6]

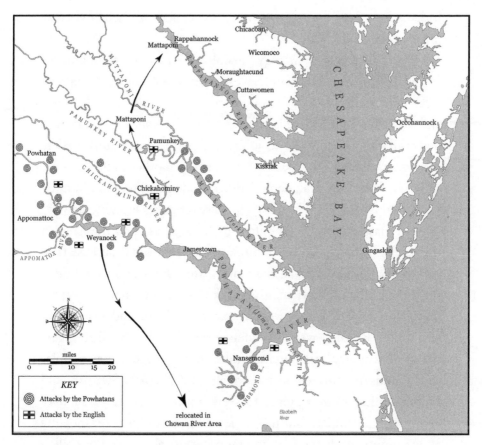

FIGURE 12.1. Major engagements of 1644. *Drawing by Jamie May.*

The high English death toll was a consequence partly of the settlers' inadequate defenses. Although improvements had been made
particularly in the case of large plantations, the majority of house-
holds, especially on the frontier, remained highly vulnerable. Robert
Evelyn, the colony's surveyor, noted that planters were "seated scat-
teringly in wooden clove board [clapboard] houses, where many
by fire were undone, and by two massacres in an instant fired." No
forts "or retreats" existed inland to provide "safety in time of danger,"
he wrote. Settlers continued to trade with the Indians, exchanging
mainly provisions, but also selling English weapons, and welcomed

Indians into their homes, who were "as familiar in their houses as those of the family."[7]

Opechancanough's strategy possibly also incorporated a broader regional dimension. He would have known about the simmering unrest among settlers and Indians across the Potomac River in Maryland and may have hoped that his attack in Virginia would encourage the powerful Susquehannocks to join forces with him against settlers throughout the Chesapeake. Possibly, he hoped other Indian peoples suffering from European depredations would also join him. In mid-May, a ship from Virginia arrived in Massachusetts bringing news of "a great massacre lately committed by the natives upon the English there." A Powhatan captive told them that "they did it because they saw the English take up all their lands from them, and would drive them out of the country; and they took this season [opportunity] for they understood that they were at war in England." Indians "within 600 miles," he said, "were confederate together to root all strangers out of the country." Six hundred miles encompassed Indian peoples of the mid-Atlantic region in conflict with English, Swedish, and Dutch settlers from Virginia to New York. No evidence survives about such a compact, but it is conceivable that Opechancanough's attack prompted discussions among other peoples, singly or collectively, about resisting the growing numbers of Europeans arriving on their shores.[8]

CRUCIALLY, BESIDES THE deployment of his warriors, Opechancanough counted on the colonists' own internal divisions to bring about the disarray necessary for his plan to succeed. A few days before the great attack, two London ships that supported Parliament opened fire on a Bristol ship crewed by royalist supporters in the Powhatan River, killing several men. The engagement, which was reported to Opechancanough, was a consequence of the London ships trying to prevent the Bristolmen from carrying off tobacco, the receipts of which would find their way into the king's coffers. Ironically, after decades of English fears about the possibility of a confrontation with Spanish ships in Virginia's waters, the first battle involved three English ships. At the same time, as supplies from England declined and exports were disrupted, Robert Beverley commented that settlers became increasingly "impatient to know what would be the Event [outcome] of so much confusion." His language, it should be noted, was eerily similar to fears raised by many people in England who spoke of the distemper, combustion, and distractions of the times.

War revived deep-seated religious differences among the English in Virginia. A settler of Puritan disposition wrote that "the massacre (though a judgment) did divert a great mischief that was growing among us by Sir William Berkeley's [the new governor] courses; for many of the most religious and honest inhabitants were marked out to be plundered and imprisoned for the refusal of an Oath [of Allegiance] that was imposed upon the people." Such was the opposition caused by the oath, the settler continued, that "if the Indians had but forborne for a month longer, they had found us in such a combustion among ourselves that they might with ease cut off every man if once we had spent that little powder and shot that we had among ourselves." John Winthrop, observing from New England, took a similar view and blamed the governor for "reviling the gospel" and the faithful ministers God had sent among them. Opechancanough, always an acute observer of the English, would have been aware of the trouble caused by religious divisions. The political crisis and bitter religious divisions in England had triggered "a great Disturbance" in Virginia, Robert Beverley confirmed. To "prevent the infection" of religious factionalism reaching the colony, Governor Berkeley passed severe laws against the Puritans that were very unpopular.[9]

What saved the settlers in 1644, according to John Ferrar, a former leader of the Virginia Company, was the Powhatans' failure to follow up their initial attack. If they had prosecuted their opportunity after "this second Massacre," he wrote, the colony would have

been "utterly deserted and ruinated." Instead, they removed themselves "many miles distant off [from] the Colony," which gave the
English time to organize an immediate response. Governor Berkeley
ordered a force of eighty men to be stationed in a fortified blockhouse at Middle Plantation (later Williamsburg), which reinforced
the palisade that crossed the peninsula, to raise the alarm if Powhatan warriors attempted to enter the settlers' safe haven. A month and
a half after the attack, the Grand Assembly (as it now called itself)
proclaimed the Indians had made themselves "our irreconcilable enemies by the late Bloody Massacre having most treacherously and
cruelly slain near four hundred of the inhabitants of this Colony."

During the spring and summer, Berkeley and the acting governor, Richard Kemp, issued orders to launch reprisals on all Indians
allied to Opechancanough and the Pamunkeys. Small-scale retal-
iatory raids took place in May and June and were followed by a
coordinated plan of attack against peoples of the James River Valley.
In the first half of July, soldiers destroyed the main town of the Weyanocks and attacked the Nansemonds, and in July and August, three
hundred well-armed soldiers led by Captain William Claiborne, the
commander in chief, marched on the Pamunkeys' towns, including Menmend, where Opechancanough lived. Evidently, given the
care in planning and equipping of the march, Claiborne anticipated
either killing or capturing the great chief. A diversionary action was
undertaken by the militias of Henrico and Charles City, two of the
hardest-hit areas, against neighboring Indians in an effort to prevent
them from joining the Pamunkeys, but although Claiborne's men
destroyed many Indian settlements, the chief eluded them. Finally,
in the last action of the summer before the English ran out of powder, an assault on the Chickahominies resulted in the loss of their
last town, Oraniock (Warreny).

Kemp reported subsequently to Berkeley that the opening shots
of the war against the Powhatans had been highly successful. They
had devastated their settlements, burned cornfields, and had even

managed to ransack the great chief's own personal quarters and trea-sure house. Soldiers had killed many warriors and taken numerous prisoners, he wrote, "the best and main of the service being per-formed by the horse Commanded by Captain Ralph Wormeley," he wrote dispassionately, which had been especially effective in pursu-ing Indians and executing them after they fled from their towns.[10]

Nevertheless, just how close Opechancanough's strategy came to succeeding can be judged by events during the remainder of the year. It is clear that the Indians did not withdraw after the initial attack as John Ferrar claimed. In fact, after weathering English reprisals, the great chief likely considered he still had a chance of victory. Real-izing the settlers' shortage of powder, Pamunkey warriors mounted a series of large-scale counterattacks along the York River, killing settlers, taking captives, and slaughtering cattle and hogs. So sud-den and destructive were the attacks that "the people cried out" for soldiers to retaliate, but owing to the colony-wide lack of powder, Kemp could do nothing to defend them.[11]

In the fall of 1644, another political crisis emerged in the col-ony that would have given Opechancanough further cause for hope. Captain Leonard Calvert arrived in the colony carrying a commis-sion from the king to seize "all London Ships and all London estates within the Colony," London being a shorthand for parliamentarian sympathizers. Kemp was understandably horrified knowing he could not possibly enforce the command and that any attempt to do so might pitch the colony into its own civil war. The situation was fur-ther complicated by Calvert's Catholicism and position as governor of Maryland, the colony being viewed by many high-placed Virgin-ians, Claiborne foremost among them, as an illegitimate fabrication of royal favoritism tainted by popery.

Kemp reported the matter to Berkeley bluntly. Any ill-conceived attempt to implement Calvert's (and the king's) orders could easily lead to ruin, especially bearing in mind the English were in the midst of war themselves. Had it not been for powder supplied by the ship that brought Calvert to the colony, he would have been reduced to a single barrel, which would have left the English almost defenseless. Kemp was outspoken about the rebellious temperament of the people generally, who had been greatly encouraged by news from Massachusetts that Charles's armies had been defeated. "I was not a stranger," he wrote, to those "people bent to better their conditions under any Masters." Rumors were circulating about valuable plunder to be had in the houses of wealthy planters sympathetic to the king, and many settlers considered the possibility of a parliamentarian government in the colony rather to be wished for than feared. These were the very conditions that Opechancanough had hoped would lead to the overthrow of the English.

As the wrangling between Kemp and Calvert continued, word of the royal commission became public and caused outrage among the settlers. "Whisperings and Rumors were spread among the people that the King had sent a Papist to be Governor," which gave credence to speculation already circulating in pamphlets in the colony that Charles I himself was estranged from the Church of England and had become a papist.

The colony teetered on the edge of rebellion when the Grand Assembly met at Jamestown on October 1 to address the shortage of provisions and improvement of the colony's defenses and to decide upon further marches and levies in support of the war. Only the timely arrival of a London ship of sixteen guns off Jamestown put an end to Calvert's efforts to enforce his royal commission. He fled the colony with the people's curses ringing in his ears, only to find a few months later that the calamity he might have brought down on Virginia became a reality in Maryland. Kemp wrote to Berkeley, with more than a hint of satisfaction, that another London ship, aptly named the *Reformation* and commanded by Captain Richard Ingle, had plundered Catholic estates indiscriminately in Maryland, which had led to the collapse of Calvert's government.[12]

CALVERT'S FATE SEALED that of Opechancanough. Parliamentary forces in England were gaining the upper hand, and a fleet of London ships arrived in Virginia at the end of January 1645 offering free trade, which allowed settlers to replenish their dwindling food supplies, powder, and ammunition. Kemp called another assembly, convened a couple of weeks later, to plan more punishing attacks against the Indians as well as the construction of three small forts on the major rivers in the heart of Indian territory: Fort Royal on the south bank of the Pamunkey, Fort Charles at the falls of the Powhatan, and Fort James overlooking the Chickahominy, west of Diascund Creek. Soldiers stationed at the forts, designed as palisaded blockhouses, would be the first line of defense against Indian raiding parties and provided forward bases from which to continually assault the Indians over the next six months. English commanders had also entered into agreements with the Accomacs and Rappahannocks to aid the English in the "further discovery of the Enemy," notably the Indians' cornfields and if possible the whereabouts of Opechancanough.

Suddenly, the tide had turned. During the fall and early winter, the momentum of the war had swung in favor of the Powhatans, but by the summer of 1645, the English were firmly in the ascendancy. Opechancanough's alliance began to disintegrate under the incessant English onslaught that took place from June to December. The Weyanocks had already abandoned the struggle and moved south to Wiccacon on the Chowan River, where they were pursued by the English in a large amphibious expedition. The Nansemonds also moved southward farther into the interior, and the Chickahominies left their traditional lands, moved closer to the Pamunkeys, and then moved again to resettle north of the Mattaponi River. Large numbers of Indians taken captive during the fighting were either enslaved by planters or placed on board the ship that had recently brought Governor Berkeley back to Virginia to be sold in the "Western Island," probably Barbados. In June, the great chief sent one of his prisoners, Margaret Worleigh, to Jamestown with an invitation to the governor to meet and conclude a peace. Berkeley agreed, and the meeting was arranged to take place at Fort Royal. Yet, as in 1623, English leaders had no intention of concluding peace, and when the Indians arrived at the fort, the gate opened and a volley of shot met the envoys, killing several. In the fighting that followed, Pamunkey towns along the river were ransacked, forcing the people, including Opechancanough, to flee into the surrounding forest.[13]

Berkeley had returned to the colony in early June 1645 and soon became aware that the settlers were tiring of the costs and inconveniences of continuing the campaigns now that the Indians as a fighting force had been defeated. Giving consideration to "the almost impossibility of a further revenge upon them [Indians]," so much damage had already been done, the governor and General Assembly authorized in the spring of 1646 a large force made up of a ship and a pinnace and sixty horsemen to track down Opechancanough and force him to accept peace on the Englishmen's terms. A letter sent to William Lenthall, Speaker of the House of Commons, in mid-March, reported that "the great salvage king, the bloody contriver of the treacherous massacre of our people, is now either not at all or at least so abandoned by his people, and they so routed, slain, and dispersed that they are no longer a Nation, and what we now suffer under is rather a robbery from a few starved outlaws than a war." Eventually, the whereabouts of Opechancanough was discovered and notice sent to Governor Berkeley who promptly arrived to take the aged chief back to Jamestown in person.[14]

THE GREAT CHIEF's last days were spent in captivity, but he retained his dignity until the end. "Opechancanough," wrote Robert Beverley, "by his great age, and the fatigues of war, . . . was now grown so decrepit, that he was not able to walk alone, but was carried about by his men wherever he had a mind to move. His flesh was all macerated, his sinews slackened, and his eyelids became so heavy, that he could not see, but as they were lifted up by his servants." At Berkeley's insistence, he was treated "with all the respect" that was his right as a high-status prisoner. On one occasion, however, the chief complained of the "great noise of the treading of people about him; upon which he caused his eyelids to be lifted up, and finding that a crowd of people were let in to see him, he called in high indignation for the governor, who being come, Opechancanough scornfully told him, that had it been his fortune to take Sir William Berkeley prisoner, he should not meanly have exposed him as a show to the people." Opechancanough "continued brave to the last moment of his life," Beverley wrote, "and showed not the least dejection at his captivity." But despite the governor's oversight, he could not preserve the great chief's life "above a fortnight. For one of the soldiers, resenting the calamities the colony had suffered by this prince's means, basely shot him through the back, after he was made prisoner; of which wound he died." At nearly one hundred years old, his long fight against European invaders finally ended.[15]

After Opechancanough's murder, Indian resistance quickly collapsed. The new and last paramount chief, Necotowance, about whom next to nothing is known, agreed to a peace treaty in October 1646 that accepted his peoples' subordination to the English. He was forced to acknowledge that henceforth he held his "kingdom" from the king of England, and his successors would be appointed or approved by the colony's governors. Indian peoples were permitted to live north of the Pamunkey River, which for the time being would not be settled by the English, while the entire James-York peninsula from the falls to Kecoughtan was ceded to the colonists. Access to the region was to be strictly controlled, and any Indians entering without permission could be killed. South of the James (Powhatan) River, Indian peoples were similarly excluded from the vast areas inhabited by settlers. In return, the colony's government pledged to protect Necotowance and his heirs from "rebels or other enemies whatsoever," in recognition of which the chief was to present a tribute of twenty beaver skins to the governor annually.

The English honored the treaty for just three years. At the annual tribute ceremony in 1648, William Berkeley informed Necotowance and the five chiefs who accompanied him that the region north of the Pamunkey River would shortly be made available to the English, a decision that led to a massive influx of settlers who quickly took up prime lands as far north as the Potomac. Indian peoples were pushed back to smaller and smaller parcels of their traditional lands, and what was left of the once great Powhatan paramount chiefdom disintegrated. A few years later, John Ferrar wrote that "since the Massacre, the *Savages* have been driven far away, many destroyed of them, their Towns and houses ruinated, [and] their clear grounds possessed by the English to sow Wheat in." The second half of the century would bring hard times to Opechancanough's people.[16]

Epilogue

A Reckoning

HOW TO TAKE THE MEASURE OF THE MAN? OPECHANCA-nough's life spanned a century of massive changes in America and Europe. More than most, his experiences were shaped by the rise of the Spanish and English Atlantic empires, and he learned at an early age that the ocean had another, vastly different, shore. Born into a ruling family in the mid-sixteenth century, his people would have heard of the havoc caused by waves of Spanish invasions to the south of the Chesapeake in the territories of once great Mississippian chiefdoms, which had stretched from modern-day Louisiana to South Carolina. His own initial encounter with the Spanish led to his abduction and long years living in various parts of Spain's rapidly expanding New World possessions. In the royal city of Madrid, the teenager met Philip II, the most powerful monarch of the age, as well as leading churchmen and influential grandees who thronged to the king's newly established court. There, he managed to convince the king and his councilors of his sincere desire to return to his own land to help with the holy work of converting his people to Catholicism. His intelligence, ability to adapt, and powers of persuasion were truly remarkable. Living in Mexico City, New Spain, for several years, he survived a terrible illness, converted to Christianity, and after gaining the trust of first the Dominicans and then the Jesuits eventually succeeded in returning to the Chesapeake.

His life among the Spanish made an enormous impression upon him. He had seen at first hand several of the greatest cities in Spain, innumerable ships plying the Guadalquivir River on their way to Seville, Africans in slave markets, Indians brought from the Americas, and the enormous wealth of the Atlantic trade. In Mexico, he witnessed the destruction of Indian ways of life and beliefs wrought by the invaders and heard about the pitiless slaughter of Mexica (Aztec) peoples forty years before in the conquest of the once beautiful and populous city of Tenochtitlan. In Veracruz, New Spain, and Havana, Cuba, he saw treasure fleets from Peru and Mexico carrying the riches of the New World to the Old. He feared the destruction European invaders would bring in their wake if they established themselves in his lands. His killing of the Jesuits who had attempted to establish a Jesuit mission in the Chesapeake in 1570 was a deadly expression of that fear.

In his prime, as war chief of the Powhatans, he played a leading role in the growth of the paramount chiefdom, ruled initially by his brother, Chief Powhatan. A daring warrior, Opechancanough was a relentless enemy of the English from his earliest meeting with Captain John Smith in the winter of 1607 until his death at Jamestown nearly four decades later. In the massive attacks of 1622 and 1644, he orchestrated the killing of hundreds of settlers and the destruction of plantations and manufactures and inspired widespread panic among the English. He understood the peril posed by European ships and weaponry as well as the vulnerabilities of the English, from their dependence on the Powhatans for food in the early days of settlement to their underestimation of Indian warfare in later years, which was bred of racism and arrogance. Most important, he realized that the fate of his people depended as much on developments taking place across the Atlantic in Madrid or London as on those taking place in his homeland.

I HAVE ARGUED in this book that Opechancanough was the same man as Paquiquineo/Don Luís, which I consider of fundamental importance to an understanding of how he confronted the European threat. Given the theory's importance, a brief summation of the evidence is presented here.

Historians generally agree that Paquiquineo and Opechancanough were born about the same time, in the mid-1540s, and likely in the same general area of the Chesapeake, somewhere on the James or York Rivers, but at that point agreement ends.[1] In regard to tribal affiliation, recent studies have argued that Paquiquineo was either a Paspahegh or Kiskiack, whereas Opechancanough who was from the same family as Chief Powhatan was a Pamunkey. The suggestion that Paquiquineo was either a Paspahegh or Kiskiack is derived from a letter written by the Jesuit fathers shortly after they arrived in the Chesapeake in 1570, in which they described the local people whom they first encountered as "relatives" of the Indian. The fathers, however, gave little clear indication as to where they made landfall, and historians have usually followed a standard authority on the Jesuit mission that speculates they disembarked at College Creek, a couple of miles from Jamestown, and then made their way to a final location near Queen's Creek and the York River. This interpretation is most unlikely, however. Spanish accounts, which provide more detail about the route taken by the Jesuits, are consistent in specifying they sailed at least thirty to forty miles inland from the mouth of the James River. If so, then the Jesuits sailed well past College Creek and Paspahegh territory to the Chickahominy River and headed upriver to a landing place somewhere near Diascund Creek. It was from there, not College Creek, that the Jesuits were guided inland by Paquiquineo/Don Luís to a location upriver between the James and York Rivers, an area close to Pamunkey territory.[2]

Some historians have also claimed that if Opechancanough was the same person as Paquiquineo, he would have known from his experience of the Spanish that it would be imperative to completely wipe out the English in the attacks of 1622 and 1644 or face the possibility of settlers regrouping and launching reprisals. Consequently, he would have been far more diligent in finishing off the settlers rather than allowing his warriors to withdraw after the initial waves of shock attacks.

This line of reasoning is a misinterpretation of what occurred. It was precisely because Opechancanough was well aware of European tactics that he lulled the Spanish and English into a false sense of security and attacked them from within their settlements. In 1622 and 1644, he avoided frontal attacks on fortified positions and the risk of exposing his men to the settlers' lethal musket fire, and in both cases his warriors continued their raids on English settlements for months after the first assaults. In 1622, Opechancanough came very close to driving the English out of his land. "Before the end of two Moons," he told the chief of the Patawomecks, "there should not be an Englishman in all their Countries."

Besides overwhelming force and follow-up raids day and night, his strategy depended on starving the settlers into submission by cutting off food supplies, as he and Chief Powhatan very nearly achieved during the "starving time" of 1609 to 1610. The winter following the 1622 attack was even more devastating for the English than the attack itself in terms of fatalities, and similarly the 1644 uprising could only succeed if the settlers were cut off from English supplies.[3]

Ultimately, however, all efforts by historians to argue that Paquiquineo and Opechancanough were different men must address two, if not three, significant pieces of evidence that indicate the contrary. The first, written by tobacco planter Ralph Hamor in 1614, requires explanation. He wrote that the Chickahominies would "at all times be ready and willing to furnish us [the English] with three or four hundred bowmen to aid us *against the Spaniards*, whose name is odious amongst them, for *Powhatan's* father was driven by them from the *west-Indies*." Hamor's assertion that the Indian driven from the "*west-Indies*" was Chief Powhatan's father makes no sense. Powhatan was born in the 1540s, about the same time or within a few years of Opechancanough. The only Indian known to have been taken from the region in this period was Paquiquineo, abducted in 1561 when still a youth. It would have been impossible for him to have been Powhatan's father. The only other explanation is that an unknown Indian, the father or older kinsman of Powhatan, was taken by the Spanish in the 1530s or early 1540s. But few Spanish ships ventured as far north as the Chesapeake Bay during these years, which is why the discovery of the bay by Captain Antonio Velázquez was so noteworthy and generated such interest at the court of Philip II.[4]

If Paquiquineo/Don Luís was not Powhatan's father, could he have been an older brother? Several Spanish sources from the period, as mentioned above, describe him as "*un indio principal, hermano del cacique,*" a high-ranking Indian and brother of the chief of that country. More intriguing, the contemporary historian Francisco Sacchini states that Paquiquineo was the older brother of the chief (Powhatan) who ruled when he returned to his land in 1570 and whom he nevertheless allowed to continue governing. "An older brother of Luís had died," Sacchini wrote, and "a younger one was ruling, [but] Luís generously returned the rule to him when offered."[5]

Hamor's account is suggestive but taken alone is inconclusive. Only when combined with two other pieces of evidence from later in the seventeenth century does the case for Paquiquineo and Opechancanough being the same person become convincing. In early 1677, following ruinous fighting among Virginia's gentry that came to be known as Bacon's Rebellion, Colonel Francis Moryson, one of the royal commissioners sent to Virginia to investigate the turmoil, sat down to compose a long letter to his superiors in London. To place the fighting in context, and the involvement of Indian peoples, he mentioned that during the great attack of 1644 the governor at the time, Sir William Berkeley (still governor in 1677), had conducted a "War, greater by far than this, for then he had fewer English to lead and more Indians to oppose him, *and those commanded by no less a war captain than he who [had] conquered all along from Mexico thither*" (my italics). The Indian "war captain" Moryson referenced, although left unnamed, was unquestionably Opechancanough, but the pertinent part of the letter is the description of the chief having fought his way "from Mexico thither." Moryson did not elaborate, perhaps because he considered he did not need to. The chief's prowess was adequately highlighted by a mere mention of his having fought the Spanish and English from New Spain to Virginia. Moryson probably picked up the information directly from Berkeley, either in 1677 or when Moryson lived in Virginia in the 1650s and early 1660s. And Berkeley, after all, had had the opportunity to talk to Opechancanough in person in 1646 when the chief was his prisoner at Jamestown.[6]

The last important piece of evidence comes from Robert Beverley's *The History and Present State of Virginia*. Beverley was well versed in the history of the colony and collected stories from local planters and the oral history of Indians for many years. Of Opechancanough, he wrote that he "is called brother to Powhatan, but by the Indians he was not so esteemed. For they say he was a prince of a foreign nation, and came to them a great way from the south west. And by their accounts," he continued, "we suppose him to have come from the Spanish Indians, somewhere near Mexico, or the mines of Saint Barbe." Once again, the connection between Opechancanough and Mexico is explicit.[7]

What appear to be two separate lives and histories—Paquiquineo/ Don Luís recorded by the Spanish and Opechancanough recorded by the English—are therefore actually one and the same. An Indian youth taken from the Chesapeake Bay by Spanish mariners in 1561 and initially named Paquiquineo became Don Luís in Spain. He was born in the mid-to-late 1540s, the same time as Powhatan and Opechancanough, and came from the same area of coastal Virginia. He was styled by Spanish writers as the brother of an important chief in the region, or even *the* chief of the region. For his part, Opechancanough is described in at least two English sources, and possibly a third, as having come from "Mexico" or the West Indies, the latter also being under Spanish rule at this time. It would beggar belief to claim that this evidence, which came from prominent Englishmen and local Indians during Opechancanough's lifetime or within thirty to fifty years of his death, is either unreliable or simply a coincidence. No other Powhatan Indian was as closely connected to the Spanish as Opechancanough.[8]

RECOGNIZING PAQUIQUINEO AND Opechancanough as the same man brings into focus one of the most extraordinary stories of early America. His life reveals an epic that traversed the Spanish and English Atlantics and that pitted his wits and people against multiple waves of European invaders. He outlived them all—kings, queens, church prelates, successive Spanish and English military commanders, Indian chiefs and rivals, all passed on while he lived. King Philip II of Spain, who ruled the greatest global empire the world had seen, died half a century earlier; James I, to whom Opechancanough had sent his trusted councilor, Tomakin, died twenty-five years earlier; Spanish imperial officials such as Pedro Menéndez de Avilés and Virginia leaders such as John Smith, Captain Christopher Newport, Lord De La Warr, Sir Thomas Gates, Sir Thomas Dale, Sir George Yeardley, and Sir Francis Wyatt, together with two generations of English colonists, came and went, yet he remained. During his long life, he survived capture, ocean crossings, European diseases, innumerable battles, and being shot and even poisoned. He was, as he once described himself to Dale, "a great Captain, and did always fight."[9]

No public monuments mark Opechancanough's exploits. In contrast to Powhatan, or his niece Pocahontas, who appear in countless books and movies, he has been largely neglected by the popular media. While numerous books have been written about the great warrior chiefs of the eighteenth and nineteenth centuries and have detailed the shattering conflict in New England of 1675–1678, known by the English as King Philip's War, not a single book-length study considers the Powhatan wars of the first half of the seventeenth century and the achievements of Opechancanough. Yet it was he, under the guise of the pious convert Don Luís, who prevented the expansion of Spanish settlement in North America, and he who resisted English settlement on the mid-Atlantic coast for half a century. He came closer than any other warrior of his time to driving them from American shores.

A charismatic and brilliant leader, toward the end of his long life Opechancanough achieved an almost godlike status. He is honored to this day by his people, the Pamunkeys, who continue to live on the ancient tribal lands he fought to protect.[10]

TIME LINE

1200–1500   Broad environmental, social, and cultural changes sweep
            across eastern North America leading to the gradual
            evolution of larger and more complex chiefdoms.

1480s   European mariners begin appearing off the North Atlantic
            coast of America.

1492–1520   Spanish and Portuguese colonists settle in the West Indies
            and on the mainland.

1519–1521   Hernán Cortes conquers Mexico and Tenochlitlan
            (Mexico City).

1545   Discovery of silver mines in Mexico and Peru.

c. 1545–1549 Birth of Powhatan and Opechancanough/Paquiquineo.

1561   Opechancanough/Paquiquineo and another Indian abducted
            from the Chesapeake by Spanish mariners and taken to
            Madrid to meet the king of Spain, Philip II.

1562   French mariner Jean Ribault establishes a short-lived
            Huguenot (Protestant) settlement at Charlesfort in Spanish
            Florida.

1562   Paquiquineo is named Don Luís de Velasco by the king after
            the Spanish viceroy of New Spain. Philip II permits him to
            return to his homeland, but he is taken to Mexico City.

1562–1566   Paquiquineo/Don Luís lives at the Dominican convent of
            Santo Domingo in Mexico City. He falls dangerously ill and
            converts to Catholicism.

1564   The French move their settlement to Fort Caroline (near present-day Jacksonville, Florida). It is destroyed the following year by the Spanish governor of Florida, Pedro Menéndez de Avilés, who establishes a string of garrisons along the coast.

1565   Menéndez is appointed *adelantado* (military governor) of Florida and soon after destroys Fort Caroline. He founds St. Augustine nearby.

1565–1570   Menéndez establishes a string of garrisons and religious houses along the Florida coast.

1566   Paquiquineo/Don Luís voyages on *La Trinidad* with a couple of Dominicans and a group of soldiers to the Chesapeake Bay, but the pilot fails to find the entrance. The Spanish discover the Outer Banks of North Carolina and then return to Spain. Don Luís makes his way back to Madrid.

1569   Don Luís travels to St. Augustine and then Havana, Cuba, with a group of Jesuit missionaries.

1570–1571   Don Luís leads a small group of Jesuits to a location somewhere between the Powhatan (James) and Pamunkey (York) Rivers where they build a mission house. He returns to his people and subsequently leads a war party to kill the Jesuits.

1572   Menéndez returns with warships to find the Jesuits. He rescues a boy who served them, Alonso de Olmos, and learns about the destruction of the mission by Don Luís. Menéndez takes revenge on Indians, possibly Chickahominies, he captured and then departs. Don Luís disappears.

1570–1600   Powhatan and his brother Opechancanough, a war chief, piece together the great paramount chiefdom of Tsenacommacah.

1584–1590   The English arrive on the Outer Banks of North Carolina and establish a colony on Roanoke Island. An attempt to set up a colony in the Chesapeake Bay fails.

1585–1586   In the winter and spring, a group of English soldiers from Roanoke Island enter the Chesapeake Bay and explore the southern shore of the bay.

1603 An English ship sent by Ralegh arrives in the Rappahannock River.

1606 James I grants the Virginia Company of London permission to found a colony in the mid-Atlantic region centered on the Chesapeake Bay.

1607 An English expedition of 104 men and boys creates a settlement on the lands of the Paspaheghs, which they name Jamestown.

Dec. 1607 Opechancanough and Powhatan meet Captain John Smith for the first time. The English settlement at Jamestown is on the verge of collapse.

1608–1609 Captain Christopher Newport arrives with more supplies and settlers. He meets Powhatan and Opechancanough. The English leaders are unaware that Opechancanough had lived for a decade with the Spanish under the names Paquiquineo and Don Luís.

1609 The Virginia Company undertakes a thorough reform and sends five hundred settlers to the colony. The company urges establishing settlements in North Carolina as well as Virginia. In July, the fleet is dispersed in a hurricane, and the *Sea Venture*, carrying all the colony's new leadership, is wrecked on Bermuda.

1609–1610 A breakdown in relations with the Powhatans leads to the first war in fall 1609. During the starving time that winter, hundreds of English settlers perish and the colony nearly collapses once again. Sir Thomas Gates and Lord De La Warr arrive at Jamestown in May and June of 1610 with scores of veterans from the wars in Europe, along with supplies and arms.

1611 Sir Thomas Dale, high marshal and deputy governor of Virginia, arrives with scores more soldiers and arms. The war begins to turn in favor of the English.

1613 Pocahontas is abducted by Captain Samuel Argall in collusion with Iopassus of the Patawomecks and is taken to Jamestown as a hostage.

1614 Dale's confrontation with the Powhatans at Matchcot on the Pamunkey (York) River results in the ending of the war.

Pocahontas marries John Rolfe on April 5, 1614, at Jamestown and takes the biblical name Rebecca, "mother of two peoples." Her conversion to Protestantism gives the English great hope of eventually converting the entire Powhatan people to Anglicanism.

April 1614   The Chickahominy Indians negotiate their own peace treaty with the English independently of Powhatan and Opechancanough.

1614–1616   Opechancanough becomes de facto ruler of the Powhatans and persuades the Chickahominies to rejoin the chiefdom. Large-scale tobacco production develops along the James River Valley. In 1616, Dale returns to London with Pocahontas and John Rolfe.

1617   Pocahontas/Rebecca dies in the spring and is buried in St. George's Chapel at Gravesend, Essex. Her infant son, Thomas, remains in England while Rolfe returns to Virginia.

1618   Powhatan dies and is succeeded by his brother Opitchapam, who takes Itoyatin as his chiefly name. He is described by the English as ineffectual. Opechancanough broadens his influence and support among the peoples of the chiefdom.

1619–1621   Large numbers of English settlers bringing diseases arrive in the James River Valley and take up lands that once belonged to the Powhatans. Opechancanough bides his time, while the influential settler, George Thorpe, tries to convert him to Christianity.

Fall 1621   Opechancanough tries to launch a large-scale attack against the English using the reburial of Powhatan's remains as a ploy to bring together warriors from throughout the region. The attack is called off when the English discover his plan.

Early 1622   Thorpe believes Opechancanough is ready to convert to Anglicanism. The English learn that Itoyatin and Opechancanough have changed their names to Sasawpen and Mangopeesomon, respectively, but they fail to understand its significance.

Mar. 1622   Opechancanough launches a massive attack along the James River Valley, the beginning of the second Powhatan war.

Three hundred and fifty settlers are killed and plantations and industrial works destroyed. The colony is left devastated.

1622–1623   Sporadic fighting continues throughout the year. The winter brings mass starvation to the English and hundreds perish.

MAY 1623   Opechancanough, Itoyatin, and the chief of the Kiskiacks, together with two hundred "great men," are poisoned and shot by a dozen soldiers led by Captain William Tucker. Opechancanough disappears and is presumed dead by the English.

JUNE 1624   Governor Sir Francis Wyatt leads a force of approximately sixty men in armor to the heartland of the Pamunkey chiefdom where they defeat hundreds of warriors in open field battle.

1625   Charles I becomes king and, after the annulment of the Virginia Company's charter the previous year, designates Virginia a royal colony.

1625–1630   The Indians and English settlers continue to launch sporadic raids on each other's settlements.

1629–1630   Itoyatin dies and Opechancanough becomes the paramount chief, at which time the English population reaches approximately 2,600.

1632   A peace treaty is agreed by Opechancanough and Governor Sir John Harvey, which formally concludes the war.

1634   Against the wishes of Virginia's leaders, Maryland is founded north of the Potomac River.

1634–1640   English immigration increases significantly, and settlements expand along the James and York Rivers. A palisade is constructed by the English from the York River to College Creek on the James River, which creates an enormous area to the east that is available only to colonists.

1642   Civil war breaks out in England, pitching Charles I against Parliamentarian forces.

April 1644   Opechancanough launches another massive attack on the English that focuses on settlements upriver, the south side of the James, and parts of the York River. Four to five hundred settlers are killed. The third Powhatan war begins and continues throughout the summer and fall. Governor Berkeley returns to England in the hope of receiving arms and powder to fight the Powhatans.

1645   Berkeley organizes the construction of several forts at the heads of the major rivers from which to send out expeditions ("marches") against the Indians. The war turns in favor of the English, and Indian captives are transported as slaves to the West Indies.

1646   Berkeley captures Opechancanough and takes him back to Jamestown where one of the soldiers murders him. Powhatan resistance disintegrates, and the last paramount chief, Necotowance, surrenders. By the treaty of 1646, the Indians become tributaries of the English.

Acknowledgments

I wish to express my gratitude to the staffs of the John D. Rockefeller Jr. Library at the Colonial Williamsburg Foundation; the Swem Library of the College of William and Mary; the Library of Virginia; the Nationalbibliothek, Vienna, Austria; the Virginia Museum of History and Culture; the New York Public Library; the John Carter Brown Library; and the National Archives, UK, London, all of whom have been unfailingly helpful. In particular, many thanks to Doug Mayo and Marianne Martin at the Rockefeller Library who assisted me with important documents and gaining permissions for images. I am grateful to my colleagues at Jamestown Rediscovery: Jamie May, who expertly drew the maps, and Michael Lavin, who produced photographic images. Dr. Kirsten Kellogg and Susan V. Webster, the Jane W. Mahoney Emerita of Art History and American Studies at the College of William and Mary, generously provided expert help with translations of Spanish sources, for which I am most appreciative.

I have been fortunate over the years to meet and learn from several chiefs of Virginia Indians and especially privileged to have met Chief Brown of the Pamunkey tribe. In countless conversations, my colleagues at Jamestown Rediscovery, notably Dr. William M. Kelso,

Acknowledgments

David Givens, Michael Lavin, Jamie May, Merry Outlaw, William Balderson, and Mark Summers, have helped me gain a better understanding of the material culture and the complexity of interactions among the Powhatans, English settlers, and enslaved Africans in this period. Many thanks also to the Two Friends of History for great support.

Connor Guy at Basic Books, Hachette, and Brandon Proia have been superb editors, and I thank them for their insightful readings of the manuscript. I owe a debt of thanks also to Lara Heimert of Basic for her encouragement and enthusiasm for this project and to the editorial and production staff, particularly Kelly Lenkevich and Katherine Mueller, for bringing the book to completion.

I thank my family with all my heart for their patience and support throughout the research and writing and dedicate, with much love, the book to them: my wife, Sally, and my children, Liz, Ben, and Alice.

NOTES

Prologue: Two Prophecies

1. William Strachey, *The Historie of Travell into Virginia Britania (1612)*, ed. Louis B. Wright and Virginia Freud (London: Hakluyt Society, 1953), 104–105. The Chesapeakes lived in the area near the Lynnhaven and Elizabeth Rivers on the south side of the Chesapeake Bay. Strachey recorded the prophecies sometime between 1609 and 1612. For other examples of Indian prophecies of this period, see David Beers Quinn, ed., *The Roanoke Voyages, 1584–1590*, 2 vols. (London: Hakluyt Society, 1955), 1:278, 379–380; James Axtell, *Beyond 1492: Encounters in Colonial North America* (New York: Oxford University Press, 1992), 34–36; Jorge Cañizares-Esguerra, *Puritan Conquistadors: Iberianizing the Atlantic, 1550–1700* (Stanford, CA: Stanford University Press, 2006), 54–67.

Chapter 1: Indian Prince, Spanish Don

1. Paul E. Hoffman, *A New Andalucia and a Way to the Orient: The American Southeast During the Sixteenth Century* (Baton Rouge: Louisiana State University Press, 1990), 184; Eugenio Ruidiaz y Caravia, *La Florida: Su Conquista y Colonizacion*, 2 vols. (Madrid: Hijos de J. A. Garcia, 1893), 1:ccii; Henry Kamen, *Philip of Spain* (New Haven, CT: Yale University Press, 1997), 79–95; J. H. Elliott, *Imperial Spain, 1469–1716*, (Harmondsworth, UK: Pelican Books, 1970), 249; Elliott, *Spain and Its World, 1500–1700: Selected Essays* (New Haven, CT: Yale University Press, 1989), 7–24.

2. Herbert Ingram Priestley, ed., *The Luna Papers: Documents Relating to the Expedition of Don Tristán de Luna y Arellano for the Conquest of La Florida in 1559–1561*, 2 vols. (Deland: Florida State Historical Society, 1928), 1:183–194, 2:293–321; John T. McGrath, *The French in Early Florida: In the Eye of the Hurricane* (Gainesville: University Press of Florida, 2000), 25–26; Hoffman, *New Andalucia*, 173–179.

3. Hoffman, *New Andalucia*, 182; Bartolome Barrientos, *Pedro Menéndez de Aviles: Founder of Florida*, trans. Anthony Kerrigan (Gainesville: University of Florida Press, 1965; first published 1567), 24.

4. Clifford M. Lewis and Albert J. Loomie, *The Spanish Jesuit Mission in Virginia, 1570–1572* (Chapel Hill: University of North Carolina Press, 1953), 221; Camilla Townsend, "Mutual Appraisals: The Shifting Paradigms of the English, Spanish, and Powhatans in Tsenacomoco, 1560–1622," in *Early Modern Virginia: Reconsidering the Old Dominion*, ed. Douglas Bradburn and John C. Coombs (Charlottesville: University of Virginia Press, 2011), 58–59.

5. In a later account, Bartolomé Martínez described Paquiquineo/Don Luís as "more than twenty years of age" in the late 1560s, Lewis and Loomie, *Spanish Jesuit Mission*, 156. For another example of the Spanish seizing an Indian youth in the Chesapeake Bay, see the account of Luis Jerónimo de Oré describing a voyage of Vicente González in 1588, in David Beers Quinn, ed., *The Roanoke Voyages, 1584–1590*, 2 vols. (London: Hakluyt Society, 1955), vol. 2, 807. A general account of Native Americans being taken to Europe in the sixteenth century can be found in Alden T. Vaughan, *Transatlantic Encounters: American Indians in Britain, 1500–1776* (New York: Cambridge University Press, 2006), 1–20.

6. Barrientos, *Pedro Menéndez*, 120; Gonzalo Solis de Merás, *Pedro Menéndez de Aviles, Memorial*, trans. Jeannette Thurber Connor (Gainesville: Florida State Historical Society, 1964), 208–209; Félix Zubillaga, *La Florida: La Misión Jesuítica (1566–1572) y la Colonizacion Espanola* (Rome: Institutum Historicum, 1940), 394, n. 9; Hoffman, *New Andalucia*, 183–184; Archivo General de Indias (AGI), Seville, Spain, Contratacíon 5167, Book 2, September 1561, ff. 110, 112.

7. The slave market house (which still stands) was built in the mid-1440s and is evidence of the town's early participation in a trade that by the 1560s had already consigned hundreds of thousands of Africans to perpetual bondage in Europe and the Americas.

8. Elliott, *Spain and Its World*, 7–26; Ruth Pike, *Linajudos and Conversos in Seville: Greed and Prejudice in Sixteenth- and Seventeenth-Century Spain* (New York: International Academic Publishers, 2000), 1–11; Mary Elizabeth Perry, *Crime and Society in Early Modern Seville* (Hanover, NH: University Press of New England, 1980), 12–74.

9. Archivo General de Indias (AGI), Contaduria 286, no. 1, Datas, f. 171v., Seville, Spain. Hoffman discovered the source; see Hoffman, *New Andalucia*, 184.

10. A description of their journey to Madrid has not survived but a route along the Guadalquivir River, possibly by boat to Cordoba or beyond, before heading north overland to Toledo and Madrid is quite plausible. John Lynch, *Spain, 1516–1598: From Nation State to World Empire* (Oxford, UK: Basil Blackwell, 1991), 42–43 (map).

11. Richard L. Kagan, ed., *Spanish Cities of the Golden Age: The Views of Anton van den Wyngaerde* (Berkeley: University of California Press, 1989), 110–118; Kamen, *Philip*, 63–64, 77–78, 181. By 1570, Madrid's population had more than doubled.

12. Alfredo Alvar Ezquerra, *El Nacimiento de Una Capital Europea: Madrid entre 1561 y 1600* (Madrid: Turner Libros, 1989), 208, 212–221; Alvar Ezquerra, *Felipe II, la Corte y Madrid en 1561* (Madrid: Centro de Estudios Históricos, 1985), 63–67; Virgilio Pinto Crespo and Santos Madrazo Madrazo, eds., *Madrid: Atlas Histórico de la Cuidad: Siglos IX–XIX* (Madrid: Centro de Documentacion y Estudios para la Historia de Madrid, 1995), 5, 9, 11, 15, 17, 21, 31–33, 35, 43, 53, 61, 71, 73, 75; José Manuel Barbeito, *Alcázar de Madrid* (Madrid: Comisón de Cultura, 1992), 33–37, 43; Jonathan Brown, "Philip II as Art Collector and Patron," in *Spanish Cities*, 14–39; Henry Kamen, *The Escorial: Art and Power in the Renaissance* (New Haven, CT: Yale University Press, 2010), passim.

13. "Venice: September, 1561," in *Calendar of State Papers Relating To English Affairs in the Archives of Venice, Volume 7, 1558–1580*, ed. Rawdon Brown and G. Cavendish Bentinck (London: Her Majesty's Stationery Office, 1890), 321–336, British History Online, www.british-history.ac.uk/cal-state-papers/venice/vol7/pp321-336 [accessed March 16, 2019]; Elliott, *Imperial Spain*, 230–235; Kamen, *Philip*, 82–84, 92–93, 98–102, 113–120, 123–128, 232–236; Lynch, *Spain*, 342–358, 375–428; Diarmaid MacCulloch, *The Reformation: A History* (New York: Penguin, 2005), 123–131, 213–421, 486 (map 6).

14. Often referred to as the "papal donation," Alexander VI's bulls *Inter caetera* and *Eximiae devotionis* of 1493–1494 became the basis of Spain's legal claim to the Americas; see Anthony Pagden, *Lords of All the World: Ideologies of Empire in Spain, Britain and France, c. 1500–c.1800* (New Haven, CT: Yale University Press, 1995), 29–52; James Muldoon, "Papal Responsibility for the Infidel: Another Look at Alexander VI's *Inter Caetera*," *Catholic Historical Review* 64 (1978): 168–184; Muldoon, *The Americas in the Spanish World Order: The Justification for Conquest in the Seventeenth Century* (Philadelphia: University of Pennsylvania Press, 1994), 15–37; MacCulloch, *Reformation*, 427–431; McGrath, *French in Early Florida*, 12–14; Charles E. Bennett, trans., *Three Voyages, René Laudonnière* (Tuscaloosa: University of Alabama Press, 2001), xv.

15. Eugene Lyon, *The Enterprise of Florida: Pedro Menéndez de Avilés and the Spanish Conquest of 1565–1568* (Gainesville: University Press of Florida, 1976), 10–18; Arthur Percival Newton, *The European Nations in the West Indies, 1493–1688* (London: A. and C. Black, 1933), 51–52, 57–59.

16. McGrath, *French in Early Florida*, 25–26; Paul E. Hoffman, *The Spanish Crown and the Defense of the Caribbean, 1535–1585: Precedent, Patrimonialism, and Royal Parsimony* (Baton Rouge: Louisiana State University, 1980), 63–108; Alejandro de la Fuente, *Havana and the Atlantic in the Sixteenth Century* (Chapel Hill: University of North Carolina Press, 2008); Lyon, *Enterprise of Florida*, passim. "Elizabeth: December 1561, 11–20," in *Calendar of State Papers Foreign: Elizabeth, Volume 4, 1561–1562*, ed. Joseph Stevenson (London: Her Majesty's Stationery Office, 1866), 435–453, British History Online, www.british-history.ac.uk/cal-state-papers/foreign/vol4/pp435-453 [accessed March 16, 2019].

17. Lewis and Loomie, *Spanish Jesuit Mission*, 156, 221; AGI, Seville, Contratacíon 5185, Book 1, March 1562, f. 130 r., v. In March 1562, shortly before his voyage to New

Spain, he was referred to in an official document somewhat dismissively as the "Velasco indio."

18. Bartolomé de las Casas, *An Account, Much Abbreviated, of the Destruction of the Indies*, ed. Franklin W. Knight and trans. Andrew Hurley (Indianapolis, IN: Hackett, 2003); Priestley, *Luna Papers*, 1:37, 42; Kamen, *Philip*, 30, 61.

19. "Carta de Fray Juan Salmerón a Felipe II; México, 1 de enero de 1583," in *Documentos inéditos del siglo XVI para la historia de Mexico*, ed. Mariano Cuevas (Mexico, 1914), 322–323. No evidence exists that confirms Paquiquineo and Las Casas met, but given the proximity of the Dominican and the highly favorable impression the Indian made upon the king and his court, it is highly likely that a meeting took place.

20. Alonso de Aguirre had learned Paquiquineo's language, Algonquian, and could also speak Spanish. Paquiquineo's companion, the *otro indio* who had sailed with him from the Chesapeake, may have been on the voyage, but nothing further is heard of him and possibly he remained in Spain or had died.

21. Elliott, *Spain and Its World*, 14; AGI, Seville, Contratacíon 5185, Book 1, March 1562, f. 130 r.,v.; Hoffman, *New Andalucia*, 185–186; Lewis and Loomie, *Spanish Jesuit Mission*, 156.

Chapter 2: Mexico City to La Florida

1. Paul E. Hoffman, *A New Andalucia and a Way to the Orient: The American Southeast During the Sixteenth Century* (Baton Rouge: Louisiana State University Press, 1990), 186.

2. James Lockhart, *The Nahuas After the Conquest: A Social and Cultural History of the Indians of Central Mexico, Sixteenth Through Eighteenth Centuries* (Stanford, CA: Stanford University Press, 1992), 28–30, 94–127, 176–202; Charles Gibson, *The Aztecs Under Spanish Rule* (Stanford, CA: Stanford University Press, 1964), 32–57, 98–116, 300–325.

3. Francisco Cervantes de Salazar, *Life in the Imperial and Loyal City of Mexico in New Spain . . .*, trans. Minnie Lee Barrett Shepard and intro. Carlos Eduardo Castañeda (Westport, CT: Greenwood Press, 1953; first published 1554), 75; Ross Hassig, *Mexico and the Spanish Conquest* (Norman: University of Oklahoma Press, 2006), 147–193; Bernal Díaz, *The Conquest of New Spain*, trans. J. M. Cohen (Harmondsworth, UK: Penguin, 1963), 405.

4. Lourdes Mondragón Barrios, *Esclavos Africanos En la Ciudad de México: El Servicio Doméstico Durante el Siglo XVI* (Mexico City: Ediciones Euroamericanas, 1999), 43–49; Herman L. Bennett, *Africans in Colonial Mexico: Absolutism, Christianity, and Afro-Creole Consciousness, 1570–1640* (Bloomington: Indiana University Press, 2003), 18, 21–22. "By the mid-sixteenth century," Bennett points out, "people of African descent outnumbered Spaniards in New Spain and comprised the second-largest slave population in the Americas."

5. Fray Toribio de Benavente Motolinia, *Memoriales de Fray Toribio de Benavente Motolinia* (Mexico, 1903), 24; Jonathan Kandell, *La Capital: The Biography*

of Mexico City (New York: Henry Holt, 1990), 129–130; Hernán Cortés, *Hernán Cortés: Letters from Mexico*, trans. and ed. Anthony Pagden (New Haven, CT: Yale University Press, 1986), 270, 321–323; Cervantes, *Life in the Imperial and Loyal City*, 38–62; Mary E. Miller and Barbara E. Mundy, eds., *Painting a Map of Sixteenth-Century Mexico City: Land, Writing, and Native Rule* (New Haven, CT: Yale University Press, 2012), 102; Charlotte M. Gradie, "The Powhatans in the Context of the Spanish Empire," in *Powhatan Foreign Relations, 1500–1722*, ed. Helen C. Rountree (Charlottesville: University Press of Virginia, 1993), 166–168; Jaime Castañeda Iturbide, *Gobernantes de la Nueva España, 1535–1696* (Mexico City: Departamento de Distrito Federal, 1987), 17–24; Barbara E. Mundy, *The Death of Aztec Tenochtitlan, the Life of Mexico City* (Austin: University of Texas Press, 2015), 72–97; Gibson, *Aztecs*, 377–378. The Dominicans were among the first of the mendicant orders to arrive in Mexico City (1526), following the Franciscans who established their first house two years earlier; see Karen Melvin, *Building Colonial Cities of God: Mendicant Orders and Urban Culture in New Spain* (Stanford, CA: Stanford University Press, 2012), 25–31.

6. Archivo General de Indias (AGI), Mexico, 280, 579r–580v, Fray Pedro de Feria a Su Majestad, February 13, 1563. Quotes are from Camilla Townsend, "Mutual Appraisals: The Shifting Paradigms of the English, Spanish, and Powhatans in Tsenacomoco, 1560–1622," in *Early Modern Virginia: Reconsidering the Old Dominion*, ed. Douglas Bradburn and John C. Coombs (Charlottesville: University of Virginia Press, 2011), 60–62; Henry Kamen, *Philip of Spain* (New Haven, CT: Yale University Press, 1997), 98–106.

7. Sarah Lawson, *A Foothold in Florida: The Eye-Witness Account of Four Voyages made by the French to that Region and the Attempt at Colonisation, 1562–1568* (East Grinstead, UK: Antique Atlas, 1992), 5, 94–95, 127; John T. McGrath, *The French in Early Florida: In the Eye of the Hurricane* (Gainesville: University Press of Florida, 2000), 33–49, 120–127. Charlesfort was located on modern-day Parris Island, South Carolina. The River of May is today called St. John's River. During Ribault's 1562 voyage a stone column was erected to mark the formal annexation of Florida by France.

8. Eugenio Ruidiaz y Caravia, *La Florida: Su Conquista y Colonizacion*, 2 vols. (Madrid: Hijos de J. A. Garcia, 1893), 2:320–327; Hoffman, *New Andulucia*, 223–227; Bartolome Barrientos, *Pedro Menéndez de Aviles: Founder of Florida*, trans. Anthony Kerrigan, (Gainesville: University of Florida Press, 1965; first published 1567), 27–28.

9. Woodbury Lowery, *The Spanish Settlements Within the Present Limits of the United States: Florida, 1562–1574* (New York: G. P. Putnam, 1911), 155–207; Eugene Lyon, *The Enterprise of Florida: Pedro Menéndez de Avilés and the Spanish Conquest of 1565–1568* (Gainesville: University Press of Florida, 1976), 100–130; McGrath, *French in Early Florida*, 133–155.

10. L. A. Vigneras, "A Spanish Discovery of North Carolina in 1566," *North Carolina Historical Review* 46 (1969): 398–402.

11. Such ideas about the existence of fabulous wealth lying in the interior or a navigable route through the landmass influenced the French in Florida and subsequently the English at Roanoke and Jamestown; see, in particular, Hoffman, *New*

Andulucia, 3–83, 105–128, 169–202, 232–234, 243–244; Vigneras, "A Spanish Discovery," 403–404; Ruidiaz y Caravia, *La Florida*, 2:92–95, 97–100, 131–132; Clifford M. Lewis and Albert J. Loomie, *The Spanish Jesuit Mission in Virginia, 1570–1572* (Chapel Hill: University of North Carolina Press, 1953), 18–22; and Barrientos, *Pedro Menéndez*, 26.

12. Ruidiaz y Caravia, *La Florida*, 2:92–95, 97–100; Charles Hudson, *Knights of Spain, Warriors of the Sun: Hernando de Soto and the South's Ancient Chiefdoms* (Athens: University of Georgia Press, 1997), 214–216. Coosa lay on the Coosawattee River in a valley of the same name located in northwest Georgia; see Cervantes, *Life in the Imperial and Loyal City*, 79.

13. Caravia, *La Florida*, 2:65, 672.

14. Vigneras, "A Spanish Discovery," 404–407; Charlotte M. Gradie, "Spanish Jesuits in Virginia: The Mission That Failed," *Virginia Magazine of History and Biography* 96 (1988): 136.

Chapter 3: The Spanish Mission

1. L. A. Vigneras, "A Spanish Discovery of North Carolina in 1566," *North Carolina Historical Review* 46 (1969): 407. Las Casas died on July 18, 1566.

2. Woodbury Lowery, *The Spanish Settlements within the Present Limits of the United States: Florida, 1562–1574* (New York: G. P. Putnam, 1911), 240–243; Eugene Lyon, *The Enterprise of Florida: Pedro Menéndez de Avilés and the Spanish Conquest of 1565–1568* (Gainesville: University Press of Florida, 1976), 131–186; Paul E. Hoffman, *A New Andalucia and a Way to the Orient: The American Southeast During the Sixteenth Century* (Baton Rouge: Louisiana State University Press, 1990), 237–249; Gonzalo Solis de Merás, *Pedro Menéndez de Aviles, Memorial*, trans. Jeannette Thurber Connor (Gainesville: Florida State Historical Society, 1964), 209.

3. Lowery, *Spanish Settlements*, 287–288.

4. Hoffman, *New Andalucia*, 250–255; Lyon, *Enterprise of Florida*, 188–197; Félix Zubillaga, *Monumenta Antiquae Floridae* (Rome: Monumenta Historica Societatis Iesu, 1946), 214–218; Ruben Vargas Ugarte, "The First Jesuit Mission in Florida," *Historical Records and Studies* 25 (1935): 72–75, 126–129; Nicholas P. Cushner, *Why Have You Come Here? The Jesuits and the First Evangelization of Native Americans* (New York: Oxford University Press, 2006), 31–46.

5. Solis de Merás, *Menéndez*, 208–209; Zubillaga, *Monumenta*, 214. Whether Don Luís was in Madrid when Menéndez arrived and whether they met to discuss the governor's plans are unknown but offer a plausible scenario. Introducing the Indian to the Jesuits, for example, may have been an additional reason why Menéndez went to Seville in person. Bartolomé Martínez recounted thirty years later that Don Luís stayed in Spain for six or seven years "in a house of the Society, where they instructed him in the matter of our Holy Faith and Christian religion." This is impossible since reliable evidence indicates the Indian lived with the Dominicans in Mexico City from 1562 to 1566, but the mention of "a house of the Society" may

be a reference to a much shorter stay, perhaps six to seven months, in Seville. Father Luis Gerónimo de Oré, writing in 1617–1620, notes that Don Luís lived with the Jesuits in Spain "to be educated." Clifford M. Lewis and Albert J. Loomie, *The Spanish Jesuit Mission in Virginia, 1570–1572* (Chapel Hill: University of North Carolina Press, 1953), 156, 179–180; Francisco Javier Alegre, *Historia de la Compañía de Jesús en Nueva España*, 3 vols. (Mexico City: J. M. Lara, 1841–42), 1:25.

6. Lowry, *Spanish Settlements*, 341–344; Lewis and Loomie, *Spanish Jesuit Mission*, 145; Ugarte, "The First Jesuit Mission," 96–98.

7. Ugarte, "The First Jesuit Mission," 109; Paul E. Hoffman, *Florida's Frontiers* (Bloomington: Indiana University Press, 2002), 54–55. Father Segura wrote from "Guale," the small garrison of San Pedro (fifty men) on the South Carolina coast. Segura believed the Guales together with the peoples of the Santa Elena region were most receptive to the Jesuits' ministries among them.

8. Lewis and Loomie, *Spanish Jesuit Mission*, 118, 131.

9. Ugarte, "The First Jesuit Mission," 131, 140; Lowery, *Spanish Settlements*, 360–361; Lewis and Loomie, *Spanish Jesuit Mission*, 157, 222. Lowery describes Alonso as a small boy from Santa Elena.

10. Lewis and Loomie, *Spanish Jesuit Mission*, 118, 132–133, 221. Timothy was St. Paul's disciple, fellow preacher, and constant companion entrusted with many important assignments.

11. Lewis and Loomie, *Spanish Jesuit Mission*, 133, 185–186. Lewis and Loomie argue that Captain Gonzalez and the Jesuits disembarked at College Creek where they made their way by canoe and overland across the peninsula to a location near Queen's Creek and the York (Pamunkey) River. Lewis and Loomie, *Spanish Jesuit Mission*, 28–38. This interpretation is unlikely. College Creek is too close to the mouth of the Powhatan River (approximately 25 miles) to agree with accounts that suggest the Jesuits sailed at least 30 to 40 miles upriver from their initial landing place near Newport News. I have adopted 3.46 miles to one Spanish league (*legua comun*), which was commonly used in the sixteenth century; see Roland Chardon, "The Elusive Spanish League: A Problem of Measurement in Sixteenth-Century New Spain," *Hispanic American Historical Review* 60 (1980): 294–302.

12. Garcilaso de la Vega, *The Florida of the Inca: A History of the Adelantado, Hernando de Soto . . .*, trans. and ed. John Grier Varner and Jeannette Johnson Varner (Austin: University of Texas Press, 1951), 642; Lewis and Loomie, *Spanish Jesuit Mission*, 90–91, 145, 180–182, 185–186. Given the paucity of detailed information about the precise location of the Jesuit mission this interpretation is suggestive only. That said, the Chickahominy River conforms to the freshwater description of contemporary accounts. Little Creek and reservoir is approximately five miles from the entrance of the Chickahominy River and Diascund Creek and reservoir, near Lanexa, New Kent County, another five miles to the north.

13. Some accounts state that the Jesuits went into the interior alone led by Don Luís without the mariners. I have followed the version of events described by Father Quirós; see Lewis and Loomie, *Spanish Jesuit Mission*, 91.

14. Lewis and Loomie, *Spanish Jesuit Mission,* 89–92, 158, 244, 249; Helen C. Rountree, Wayne E. Clark, and Kent Mountford, *John Smith's Chesapeake Voyages, 1607–1609* (Charlottesville: University of Virginia Press, 2007), 139, 152–153; Carville V. Earle, "Environment, Disease, and Mortality in Early Virginia," in *The Chesapeake in the Seventeenth Century: Essays on Anglo-American Society and Politics,* ed. Thad W. Tate and David L. Ammerman (Chapel Hill: University of North Carolina Press, 1979), 96–115. In his postscript to the letter of September 12, 1570, Father Segura makes the first reference to the place name Axacam to describe the land of Don Luís, which was very likely derived from the Indian himself sometime that year or soon after Don Luís arrived in Havana. In Spanish accounts from the early 1570s onward, the name was variously spelled Ajacán, Ajachán, Jacán, Xacán, and Xacál. Whether it refers generally to Virginia or to a specific area or location is unclear. To avoid confusion, I have chosen to be consistent in using the place names Virginia and Chesapeake.

15. Lewis and Loomie, *Spanish Jesuit Mission,* 109–111, 134–137, 145–146, 159, 181–183. There are significant variations in Spanish accounts describing the martyrdom of the missionaries. For a thorough textual analysis of the differing accounts, see Anna Brickhouse, *The Unsettlement of America: Translation, Interpretation, and the Story of Don Luis de Velasco, 1560–1945* (New York: Oxford University Press, 2015), 75–90.

16. Lewis and Loomie, *Spanish Jesuit Mission,* 110, 120, 159, 183. It is not entirely certain that Alonso was at the mission when the Jesuits were killed. Martinez claims that shortly before the attack, Father Segura sent him to Don Luís's village because he (Alonso) was "very friendly" with the Indian. The boy apparently lost his way, however, and ended up in the village of a powerful chief who subsequently protected him from Don Luís.

17. Lewis and Loomie, *Spanish Jesuit Mission,* 120–121, 134–139, 146, 159, 183–185.

Chapter 4: "King of Pamaunck"

1. Philip L. Barbour, ed., *The Complete Works of Captain John Smith,* 3 vols. (Chapel Hill: University of North Carolina Press, 1986), 1:173–174; William Strachey, *The Historie of Travell into Virginia Britania (1612),* ed. Louis B. Wright and Virginia Freud (London: Hakluyt Society, 1953), 44, 57; Martin D. Gallivan, *Powhatan River Chiefdoms: The Rise of Social Inequality in the Chesapeake* (Lincoln: University of Nebraska Press, 2000), 26–27, 155–181; Martin D. Gallivan, "Reconnecting the Contact Period and Late Prehistory Household and Community Dynamics in the James River Basin," in *Middle and Late Woodland Research in Virginia: A Synthesis,* ed. Theodore D. Reinhart and Mary Ellen Hodges (Richmond: Archeological Society of Virginia, 1992), 43–45; Randolph Turner, "Native American Protohistoric Interactions in the Powhatan Core Area," in *Powhatan Foreign Relations, 1500–1722,* ed. Helen C. Rountree (Charlottesville: University Press of Virginia, 1993), 78; Helen C. Rountree and E. Randolph Turner III, *Before and After Jamestown: Virginia's*

Powhatans and Their Predecessors (Gainesville: University Press of Florida, 2002), 37–59; Stephen R. Potter, *Commoners, Tribute, and Chiefs: The Development of Algonquian Culture in the Potomac Valley* (Charlottesville: University Press of Virginia, 1993), 3–4, 141–147, 154–155; James D. Rice, "'Kings' of the Potomac: Nature, Culture, and the Origins of Algonquian Chiefdoms, 700 A.D.–1608" (unpublished paper, Maryland Early American Seminar, 2001). The Kiskiacks were likely a client population of the Pamunkeys; see Ben C. McCary, "The Kiskiack (Chiskiack) Indians," *Quarterly Bulletin of the Archaeological Society of Virginia* 13 (1958–1959). I follow Robbie Etheridge's description of a paramount chiefdom as "a complex regional chiefdom in which the chief commanded tribute from multiple lesser chiefs across a large area; see Etheridge, *From Chicaza to Chickasaw: The European Invasion and the Transformation of the Mississippian World, 1540–1715* (Chapel Hill: University of North Carolina Press, 2010), 12–41.

2. This line of reasoning raises an intriguing question. Was Paquiquineo a close relative of Powhatan? Gonzalo Solis de Merás, who had been involved with Menéndez's campaigns in Florida and knew Paquiquineo, described him in 1567 as "the brother of *the* cacique [chief] of that country" (my italics), by which he meant the Chesapeake. Other contemporaries who wrote about Menéndez or the martyrdom of the Jesuits also emphasized Paquiquineo's high status. Bartolomé Barrientos, an early biographer of Menéndez, referred to the Chesapeake as "the land governed by Cacique Don Luís." Brother Juan de la Carrera, who voyaged to the region in 1572 with an expedition to search for the Jesuits, described the Indian as "a principal chief," and Francisco Sacchini, an early seventeenth-century historian, called him the "brother of a principal chief." Gonzalo Solis de Merás, *Pedro Menendez de Aviles, Memorial*, trans. Jeannette Thurber Connor (Gainesville: Florida State Historical Society, 1964; first published 1893), 208–209; Bartolome Barrientos, *Pedro Menendez de Aviles, Founder of Florida*, trans. Anthony Kerrigan (Gainesville: University of Florida Press, 1965; first published 1902, written 1567), 26; Clifford M. Lewis and Albert J. Loomie, *The Spanish Jesuit Mission in Virginia, 1570–1572* (Chapel Hill: University of North Carolina Press, 1953), 89–90, 118–119, 131, 133, 221.

3. Joseph Hall, "Between Old World and New: Oconee Valley Residents and the Spanish Southeast, 1540–1621," in *The Atlantic World and Virginia, 1550–1624*, ed. Peter C. Mancall (Chapel Hill: University of North Carolina Press, 2007), 66–96; Charles Hudson, *The Juan Pardo Expeditions: Explorations of the Carolinas and Tennessee, 1566–1568*, 2nd ed. (Tuscaloosa: University of Alabama Press, 2005), 23–168, 319–320; Paul E. Hoffman, *Florida's Frontiers* (Bloomington: Indiana University Press, 2002), 62–86.

4. Strachey, *Virginia Britania*, 43–44, 68–69, 104–105; Barbour, *Complete Works*, 1:174–175; J. Frederick Fausz, "Patterns of Anglo-Indian Aggression and Accommodation along the Mid-Atlantic Coast, 1584–1634," in *Cultures in Contact: The European Impact on Native Cultural Institutions in Eastern North America, A. D. 1000–1800*, ed. William W. Fitzhugh (Washington, DC: Smithsonian Institution,

1985), 235–236; James D. Rice, "Escape from Tsenacommacah: Chesapeake Algonquians and the Powhatan Menace," in *Atlantic World and Virginia*, 97–140; James D. Rice, "War and Politics: Powhatan Expansion and the Problem of Native American Warfare," *William and Mary Quarterly* 77, no. 1 (2020): 22.

5. This estimate does not include Siouan peoples. Strachey, *Virginia Britania*, 56–57; estimates are derived from Christian F. Feest, "Virginia Algonquians," in *Northeast*, ed. Bruce G. Trigger, vol. 15 of *Handbook of North American Indians*, ed. William C. Sturtevant (Washington, DC: Smithsonian Institution, 1978), 15:241–242, 255–256; E. Randolph Turner, "Socio-Political Organization Within the Powhatan Chiefdom and the Effects of European Contact, A.D. 1607–1646," in *Cultures in Contact*, 193; Frederic W. Gleach, *Powhatan's World and Colonial Virginia: A Conflict of Cultures* (Lincoln: University of Nebraska Press, 1997), 34–35; Helen C. Rountree, Wayne E. Clark, and Kent Mountford, *John Smith's Chesapeake Voyages, 1607–1609* (Charlottesville: University of Virginia Press, 2007), 25–52; Gallivan, *Powhatan Landscape*, xxi.

6. Philip L. Barbour, ed., *The Jamestown Voyages Under the First Charter, 1606–1609*, 2 vols. (New York/London: Cambridge University Press, 1969), 1:102; Gallivan, *Powhatan Landscape*, 104–140; Buck Woodard and Danielle Moretti-Langholtz, "'They Will Not Admit of Any Werowance from Him to Govern Them': The Chickahominy Context: A Reassessment of Political Configurations," *Journal of Middle Atlantic Archaeology* 25 (2009): 85–96.

7. News traveled rapidly over large distances by river or along the extensive network of pathways and roads that ran from Canada to Florida; see Rountree, "The Powhatans and Other Woodland Indians as Travelers," in *Powhatan Foreign Relations*, 29–39, 50–51; James Lavin, trans., "Account of Pedro Diaz as Related to Pedro de Araña, March 31, 1589," unpub. ms., Archives of the Indies Seville, AGI 54.I.34, Santo Domingo, 118; David Beers Quinn, ed., *The Roanoke Voyages, 1584–1590*, 2 vols. (London: Hakluyt Society, 1955), 2:791.

8. Quinn, *Roanoke Voyages*, 1:91–116, 275–288, 378–381; Michael Leroy Oberg, *The Head in Edward Nugent's Hand: Roanoke's Forgotten Indians* (Philadelphia: University of Pennsylvania Press, 2007), 31–98; James Horn, *A Kingdom Strange: The Brief and Tragic History of the Lost Colony of Roanoke* (New York: Basic Books, 2010), 39–101.

9. The disastrous four months experienced by the English from July 1607 onward is related in several firsthand accounts by the colonists' leaders; see Philip L. Barbour, ed., *The Jamestown Voyages Under the First Charter, 1606–1609*, 2 vols. (New York/London: Cambridge University Press, 1969), 1:80–98, 143–145, 173–178, 215–226; James Horn, *A Land as God Made It: Jamestown and the Birth of America* (New York: Basic Books, 2005), 56–59. The Indian hunting party was made up of six tribes, the Pamunkeys, Youghtanunds, Mattaponi, Chickahominies, Paspaheghs, and Kiskiacks; see Philip L. Barbour, ed., *The Complete Works of Captain John Smith*, 3 vols. (Chapel Hill: University of North Carolina Press, 1986), 1:91.

10. Opechancanough may have met Smith and several other leaders in late May when the English explored the Powhatan (James) River up to the falls. Captain

Gabriel Archer, who kept a journal of the voyage, recorded they met the "Wyroans Pamaunche," the chief of the Pamunkey, who lived in a "Rich land of Copper and pearl"; see Barbour, *Jamestown Voyages*, 1:93. A few references to the "king" of Pamunkey follow, but Smith was the first Englishman to name him Opechancanough. It is possible that the "Wyroans Pamaunche" was Kekataugh, a brother or kinsman of Opechancanough.

11. This account is based on Captain John Smith's *A True Relation . . .* (London, 1608) and *The Generall Historie* (London, 1632), in Barbour, *Complete Works*, 1:45, 47; 2:146–147. By coincidence, during their expedition along the Chickahominy River, Smith and his companions may have passed close to the location of the Jesuit mission.

12. For the English meaning of the place name Rassawek, see Martin D. Gallivan, *The Powhatan Landscape: An Archaeological History of the Algonquian Chesapeake* (Gainesville: University Press of Florida, 2016), xxii.

13. The phrase is derived from Smith's Algonquian word list in *A Map of Virginia . . .* (Oxford, 1612) in Barbour, *Complete Works* 1:137. I speculate the question was likely to have arisen in conversations with Opechancanough, but there is no definitive proof. The phrase does offer, however, a rare glimpse of Algonquian dialogue (as interpreted by Smith); see Gallivan, *Powhatan Landscape*, 60.

14. Barbour, *Complete Works,* 1:49.

15. Barbour, *Complete Works*, 1:49, 51; Gallivan, *Powhatan Landscape*, xxi.

16. Barbour, *Complete Works*, 1:51, 53; 2:149.

17. Barbour, *Complete Works*, 1:59; 2:149–150; Jorge Cañizares-Esguerra, *Puritan Conquistadors: Iberianizing the Atlantic, 1550–1700* (Stanford, CA: Stanford University Press, 2006), 66.

18. Barbour, *Complete Works*, 1:53, 55, 57; 2:150–151; Gallivan, *Powhatan Landscape*, xxii, 61. Wahunsonacock was the chief's personal name, but the English called him Powhatan, which was his official name in relation to his birthplace and people. Helen C. Rountree discusses his titles, family, and origin in *Pocahontas, Powhatan, and Opechancanough: Three Indian Lives Changed by Jamestown* (Charlottesville: University of Virginia Press, 2005), 25–33. The entirety of the description of Pocahontas's intervention to save Smith's life appears only in Smith's *Generall Historie*; see Barbour, *Complete Works*, 2:151.

19. Barbour, *Complete Works*, 1:49; 2:148; Seth Mallios, *The Deadly Politics of Giving: Exchange and Violence at Ajacan, Roanoke, and Jamestown* (Tuscaloosa: University of Alabama Press, 2006), 26–27.

20. James Horn, "Imperfect Understandings: Rumor, Knowledge, and Uncertainty in Early Virginia," in *The Atlantic World and Virginia, 1550–1624*, ed. Peter C. Mancall (Chapel Hill: University of North Carolina Press, 2007), 513–516.

21. Barbour, *Complete Works*, 1:49–59; 2:149–151; Frederic W. Gleach, *Powhatan's World and Colonial Virginia: A Conflict of Cultures* (Lincoln: University of Nebraska Press, 1997), 112–122; Gallivan, *Powhatan Landscape*, 43–48.

22. Barbour, *Complete Works*, 2:151. For Pocahontas's role see Gleach, *Powhatan's World*, 116–117; Paula Gunn Allen, *Pocahontas: Medicine Woman, Spy, Entrepreneur,*

Diplomat (New York: HarperSanFrancisco, 2003), 31, 39–52; Camilla Townsend, *Pocahontas and the Powhatan Dilemma* (New York: Hill and Wang, 2004), 52–59.

23. Horn, *A Land As God Made It*, 68–71. In addition, access to English trade goods, especially copper, a commodity of great prestige among Indian peoples, would be invaluable in forging alliances within and beyond their territories; see Daniel K. Richter, "Tsenacommacah and the Atlantic World," in *Atlantic World and Virginia*, 32–36.

24. Carl Bridenbaugh, *Early Americans* (New York: Oxford University Press, 1981), 5–49, 239–247, argues at length that Paquiquineo, Don Luís, and Opechancanough was the same person, but recently historians have either been noncommittal or, like Helen C. Rountree, have dismissed the theory. The evidence that forms the basis of my argument is considered in the epilogue.

Chapter 5: Stratagems and Subterfuge

1. My assumption is that given his status as war chief, Paquiquineo/Opechancanough would have played a vital role in the development of the paramount chiefdom. Henceforth, Paquiquineo will be called by the name recorded in English accounts, Opechancanough.

2. William Strachey, *The Historie of Travell into Virginia Britania (1612)*, ed. Louis B. Wright and Virginia Freud (London: Hakluyt Society, 1953), 57, 59–61; Philip L. Barbour, ed., *The Complete Works of Captain John Smith*, 3 vols. (Chapel Hill: University of North Carolina Press, 1986), 1:53; Helen C. Rountree, *Pocahontas, Powhatan, and Opechancanough: Three Indian Lives Changed by Jamestown* (Charlottesville: University of Virginia Press, 2005), 25–33; Gleach, *Powhatan's World*, 33.

3. Such was his reputation in the country at the head of the Pamunkey River that Strachey called the region "Opechancheno." Strachey, *Virginia Britania*, 69. For the quotes regarding Opechancanough's connection to Mexico, see Robert Beverley, *The History and Present State of Virginia*, ed. Louis B. Wright (Chapel Hill: University of North Carolina Press, 1947), 61; and a letter from Col. Francis Moryson to Sir William Jones, King's Attorney General, January 29, 1676–77, National Archives, Kew, England, CO5/1371, 9–10.

4. Robbie Etheridge, *From Chicaza to Chickasaw: The European Invasion and the Transformation of the Mississippian World, 1540–1715* (Chapel Hill: University of North Carolina Press, 2010), 44–47; Gleach, *Powhatan's World*, 34–35; J. Frederick Fausz, "Opechancanough: Indian Resistance Leader," in *Struggle and Survival in Colonial America*, ed. David G. Sweet and Gary B. Nash (Berkeley/Los Angeles: University of California Press, 1981), 23.

5. Strachey, *Virginia Britania*, 64.

6. Created by royal charter in April 10, 1606, under the seal of James I, the Virginia Company was one of many trading ventures that blossomed during the previous half century, evidence of the growing wealth of English, especially London, merchants. Two colonies were created by the charter. One in the mid-Atlantic, corresponding to an area that stretched from Cape Fear in North Carolina to New

York, was named the first colony of Virginia. The other, which included New England but reached as far south as the Chesapeake Bay, was called the second colony of Virginia. Together, they represented the twin centers of English activity of the previous twenty years and were sponsored by London and West Country political and mercantile interests, respectively; see Samuel M. Bemiss, *The Three Charters of the Virginia Company of London, with Seven Related Documents; 1606–1621* (Williamsburg: Virginia 350th Anniversary Celebration, 1957), 1–12; and Andrew Fitzmaurice, "The Company Commonwealth," in *Virginia 1619: Slavery, Freedom, and the Construction of English America*, ed. Paul Musselwhite, James Horn, and Peter C. Mancall (Chapel Hill: University of North Carolina, 2019), 193–214. For promoters of American ventures in the 1570s and 1580s who emphasized commercial benefits, see David B. Quinn, ed., *New American World: A Documentary History of North America to 1612*, 5 vols. (New York: Arno Press and Hector Bye, 1979), 3:27–34 (Christopher Carleill), 49–53 (Sir George Peckham), and 61–123 (the two Richard Hakluyts); Karen Ordahl Kupperman, *The Jamestown Project* (Cambridge, MA: Harvard University Press, 2007), 12–42, 183–217; and James Horn, *A Land As God Made It: Jamestown and the Birth of America* (New York: Basic Books, 2005), 33–37, 46–51. Regarding European attitudes toward American Indian peoples and their right to the territories they occupied, see Philip L. Barbour, ed., *The Jamestown Voyages Under the First Charter, 1606–1609*, 2 vols. (New York/London: Cambridge University Press, 1969), 1:24; Ken MacMillan, *Sovereignty and Possession in the English New World: The Legal Foundations of Empire, 1576–1640* (Cambridge, UK: Cambridge University Press, 2006), 29–41; John T. Juricek, "English Territorial Claims in North America Under Elizabeth and the Early Stuarts," *Terrae Firma* 7 (1976): 7–22. Stuart Banner considers the complexity of the issue and contrasting opinions in *How the Indians Lost Their Land: Law and Power on the Frontier* (Cambridge, MA: Harvard University Press, 2005), 10–48.

7. Barbour, *Complete Works*, 1:61, 206–215; Barbour, *Jamestown Voyages*, 1:80–95, 98–102; Strachey, *Virginia Britania*, 58. One of the first Englishmen killed in the attack was recently discovered at the site of James Fort. A youth of fifteen years, either Richard Mutton or James Brumfield, died from an arrow wound in his left leg just above the knee; see William M. Kelso, *Jamestown: The Buried Truth* (Charlottesville: University of Virginia Press, 2007), 162–163, and the archaeologists of Jamestown Rediscovery (Preservation Virginia), which has been in progress since 1994.

8. Barbour, *Complete Works*, 1:61; 2:157. For the extraordinarily cold weather of this period, see Sam White, *A Cold Welcome: The Little Ice Age and Europe's Encounter with North America* (Cambridge, MA: Harvard University Press, 2017), 119.

9. Barbour, *Complete Works*, 1:63–67.

10. J. H. Elliott writes, "If, as has been suggested, [Don Luís] Velasco was none other than Opechancanough, the brother of the local 'emperor' Powhatan, Newport and his men had fixed their sights on a land where the ways of Europeans were already known and not admired." See Elliott, *Empires of the Atlantic World: Britain and Spain in America, 1492–1830* (New Haven, CT: Yale University Press, 2006), 10.

11. Barbour, *Complete Works*, 1:69–71; 2:156. See also Karen Ordahl Kupperman, *Pocahontas and the English Boys: Caught Between Cultures in Early Virginia* (New York: New York University Press, 2019); and Alden T. Vaughan, "Powhatans Abroad: Virginia Indians in England," in *Envisioning an English Empire: Jamestown and the Making of the North Atlantic World*, ed. Robert Appelbaum and John Wood Sweet (Philadelphia: University of Pennsylvania Press, 2007), 51–55.

12. Barbour, *Complete Works*, 1:77, 217; Helen C. Rountree, *The Powhatan Indians of Virginia: Their Traditional Culture* (Norman: University of Oklahoma Press, 1989), 109–111; Daniel K. Richter, "Tsenacommacah and the Atlantic World," in *The Atlantic World and Virginia, 1550–1624*, ed. Peter C. Mancall (Chapel Hill: University of North Carolina Press, 2007), 29–36.

13. Barbour, *Complete Works*, 1:81–93, 219–233; 2:158–180.

14. Bemiss, *The Three Charters of the Virginia Company of London*, 1–12; Barbour, *Jamestown Voyages*, 1:98–112, 234–235; Horn, *A Land As God Made It*, 33–37, 46–51. See also note 6 above.

15. Barbour, *Complete Works*, 1:49, 55, 63, 79, 219; Barbour, *Jamestown Voyages*, 1:236–240.

16. James Horn, *A Kingdom Strange: The Brief and Tragic History of the Lost Colony of Roanoke* (New York: Basic Books, 2010), 211–215; Edward Wright Haile, ed., *Jamestown Narratives. Eyewitness Accounts of the Virginia Colony, The First Decade: 1607–1617* (Champlain, VA: Round House, 1998), 367.

17. Barbour, *Complete Works*, 1:234–236; 2:181–184. Following his second voyage around the Chesapeake Bay, Smith had reluctantly arrived at the conclusion that neither the Powhatan River nor any of the region's major rivers led to the Pacific Ocean. It is possible, therefore, he put these words in Powhatan's mouth to make Newport appear a fool.

18. John White reported "our Savage Manteo, by the command of Sir Walter Ralegh, was christened in Roanoak, and called Lord thereof, and of Dasamongueponke, in reward of his faithful service"; see David Beers Quinn, ed., *The Roanoke Voyages, 1584–1590*, 2 vols. (London: Hakluyt Society, 1955), 1:279; 2:531. Evidently, conversion to Christianity was not considered a necessary precondition for Powhatan's coronation; see Barbour, *Complete Works*, 1:236–237; 2:183–184.

19. Henry Spelman, *Relation of Virginia: A Boy's Memoir of Life with the Powhatans and Patawomecks*, ed. Karen Ordahl Kupperman (New York: New York University Press, 2019), 58, 72; Horn, *A Land As God Made It*, 104–108; Richter, "Tsenacommacah and the Atlantic World," 52–54.

20. Barbour, *Complete Works*, 1:239–245.

21. Barbour, *Complete Works*, 1:245–248, 264–265; 2:194–196; Strachey, *Virginia Britania*, 104–105.

22. Barbour, *Complete Works*, 1:248–250; 2:197–200. A severe drought in these years made the competition for food especially desperate; see David Stahle et al., "The Lost Colony and Jamestown Droughts," *Science* 280 (1998): 564–567; and Dennis B. Blanton, "The Climate Factor in Late Prehistoric and Post-Contact Human

Affairs," in *Indians and European Contact in Context*, ed. Blanton and Julia A. King (Gainesville: University Press of Florida, 2004), 12–17.

23. Barbour, *Complete Works*, 1:248–250; 2:197–200.

24. Barbour, *Complete Works*, 1:250–256; 2:200–205.

25. Strachey, *Virginia Britania*, 57; Horn, *A Land As God Made It*, 128–130. For the significance of Werowocomoco, see Martin D. Gallivan's superb analysis in *The Powhatan Landscape: An Archaeological History of the Algonquian Chesapeake* (Gainesville: University Press of Florida, 2016), 141–178; and Virginia Company, *A True and Sincere Declaration of the Purpose and Ends of the Plantation in Virginia* (London, 1610), 11.

Chapter 6: Starving Times

1. Samuel M. Bemiss, *The Three Charters of the Virginia Company of London, with Seven Related Documents; 1606–1621* (Williamsburg: Virginia 350th Anniversary Celebration, 1957), 42, 47–48; James Horn, *A Land As God Made It: Jamestown and the Birth of America* (New York: Basic Books, 2005), 132–138; Karen Ordahl Kupperman, *The Jamestown Project* (Cambridge, MA: Harvard University Press, 2007), 241–247.

2. Richard Johnson, *Nova Britannia: Offering Most Excellent Fruits by Planting in Virginia . . .* (London, 1609), 5–6, 9–13; E. G. R. Taylor, ed., *The Original Writings and Correspondence of the Two Richard Hakluyts*, 2 vols. (London: Hakluyt Society, 1935), 2:233–234, 315.

3. Alexander Brown, *The Genesis of the United States*, 2 vols. (New York, 1890), 1:256, 298–299, 314, 369, 374–375; Robert Gray, *A Good Speed to Virginia* (London, 1609), C4v.

4. John Parker, "Religion and the Virginia Colony, 1609–10," in *The Westward Enterprise: English Activities in Ireland, the Atlantic and America, 1480–1650*, ed. K. R. Andrews, N. P. Canny, and P. E. H. Hair (Liverpool, UK: Liverpool University Press, 1978), 247–260; Edward L. Bond, *Damned Souls in a Tobacco Colony: Religion in Seventeenth-Century Virginia* (Macon, GA: Mercer University Press, 2000), 1–29; Douglas Bradburn, "The Eschatological Origins of the English Empire," in *Early Modern Virginia: Reconsidering the Old Dominion*, ed. Douglas Bradburn and John C. Coombs (Charlottesville: University of Virginia Press, 2011), 17–36; Lauren Working, "'The Savages of Virginia Our Project': The Powhatans in Jacobean Political Thought," in *Virginia 1619: Slavery and Freedom in the Making of the English America*, ed. Paul Musselwhite, Peter C. Mancall, and James Horn (Chapel Hill: University of North Carolina Press, 2019), 42–43.

5. William Strachey, *The Historie of Travell into Virginia Britania (1612)*, ed. Louis B. Wright and Virginia Freud (London: Hakluyt Society, 1953), 34–36, 91, 106.

6. Strachey, *Virginia Britania*, 106–107.

7. This argument is presented in more detail in James Horn, *A Kingdom Strange: The Brief and Tragic History of the Lost Colony of Roanoke* (New York: Basic Books, 2010), 224–234.

8. Strachey, *Virginia Britania*, 56, 104, 106; Samuel Purchas, *Hakluytus Posthumus or Purchas His Pilgrimes . . .* , 20 vols. (Glasgow, 1906–1908), 18:527; 19:228; Clarence Walworth Alvord and Lee Bidgood, *The First Explorations of the Trans-Allegheny Region by the Virginians, 1650–1674* (Cleveland, OH: Arthur H. Clark, 1912), 122–123, 125, 128; Alan Vance Briceland, *Westward from Virginia: The Exploration of the Virginia-Carolina Frontier, 1650–1710* (Charlottesville: University Press of Virginia, 1987), 28–91.

9. Strachey, *Virginia Britania*, 89, 91; Gray, *Good Speed*, C2r.

10. Brown, *Genesis*, 1:238–240, 248–253; Kent History and Library Center, Maidstone, Kent, England, Sandwich Borough Records, Sa/ZB2/64–68; Bemiss, *Three Charters*, 58–67; Richard Crakanthorpe, *A Sermon at the Solemnizing of the Happie Inauguration of . . . King James* (London, 1609), D2v; Johnson, *Nova Britannia*, 5.

11. Barbour, *Complete Works*, 2:208–220.

12. Smith has the number of men sent to Nansemond with Captain Martin as "near as many" as went to the falls (120), whereas George Percy states West went to the falls with 140 men, and he and Martin went with 60 to Nansemond; see Barbour, *Complete Works*, 1:269; 2:220; and Mark Nicholls, "George Percy's "Trewe Relacyon": A Primary Source for the Jamestown Settlement," *Virginia Magazine of History and Biography* (hereafter *VMHB*) 113 (2005): 244–245. William Strachey wrote a long description about the devastation caused by the hurricane in "A True Reportory of the wrack [*sic*] and redemption of Sir Thomas Gates, knight, upon and from the Islands of the Bermudas . . . ," which was likely the origin story for Shakespeare's *The Tempest*; see Lori Glover and Daniel Blake Smith, *The Shipwreck That Saved Jamestown: The Sea Venture Castaways and the Fate of America* (New York: John MacRae Books, 2008).

13. J. Frederick Fausz, "An 'Abundance of Blood Shed on Both Sides': England's First Indian War, 1609–1614," *VMHB* 98 (1990): 22–24; Percy, "Trewe Relacyon," 244–245; Strachey, *Virginia Britania*, 66; Henry Spelman, *Relation of Virginia: A Boy's Memoir of Life with the Powhatans and Patawomecks*, ed. Karen Ordahl Kupperman (New York: New York University Press, 2019), 16.

14. Smith was accused of a broad range of misconduct, including attempting to starve his men, establishing himself as the sole ruler of the colony, and marrying Pocahontas and becoming an Indian "king"; see Barbour, *Complete Works*, 1:274; and Edward Wright Haile, ed., *Jamestown Narratives: Eyewitness Accounts of the Virginia Colony, The First Decade: 1607–1617* (Champlain, VA: Round House, 1998), 354–355.

15. Strachey, *Virginia Britania*, 104. For an example of a war council, described by Ralph Lane, governor of the first Roanoke colony, as a "general Assembly," see David Beers Quinn, ed., *The Roanoke Voyages, 1584–1590*, 2 vols. (London: Hakluyt Society, 1955), 1:265–266.

16. Percy, "Trewe Relacyon," 246–247; Barbour, *Complete Works*, 1:275.

17. Percy, "Trewe Relacyon," 247–248; Spelman, *Relation of Virginia*, 19–20.

18. Percy "Trewe Relacyon," 248; *A True Declaration of the estate of the Colonie in Virginia . . .* , (London: Councell of Virginia, 1610), 12; William Strachey, "A True

Reportory of the wrack and redemption of Sir Thomas Gates . . . ," in *Jamestown Narratives*, 440.

19. Percy, "Trewe Relacyon," 248–249; Barbour, *Complete Works*, 2:232–233. Examples of cannibalism practiced by Europeans in this period are rare, but see Percy, "Trewe Relacyon," 242–243. Recent archaeological evidence from fieldwork undertaken by Jamestown Rediscovery supports Percy's descriptions of settlers eating fish, turtles, horses, dogs, cats, snakes, and rats, as well as providing conclusive proof of cannibalism; see James Horn, William M. Kelso, Douglas Owsley, and Beverley Straube, *Jane: Starvation, Cannibalism, and Endurance at Jamestown* (Richmond, VA, 2013); Haile, *Jamestown Narratives*, 456–457, 473–474, 895–896; Brown, *Genesis*, 1:392; and Purchas, *Hakluytus Posthumus*, 19:70.

20. My estimates of English casualties during this period are considerably higher than those of Fausz because I assume 350 settlers arrived at Jamestown in August 1609 rather than his 250; see Fausz, "An 'Abundance of Blood,'" 27, 55.

21. Percy, "Trewe Relacyon," 249–250. Captain James Davis had arrived in October 1609 with sixteen men on the pinnace *Virginia* and was placed in charge of Fort Algernon following Ratcliffe's death.

22. Percy, "Trewe Relacyon," 250–251; Purchas, *Hakluytus Posthumus*, 19:44–45; *A True Declaration*, 12; Haile, *Jamestown Narratives*, 456–457.

23. Percy, "Trewe Relacyon," 251; Purchas, *Hakluytus Posthumus*, 19:44–46, 52–54; Brown, *Genesis*, 1:363; Haile, *Jamestown Narratives*, 702. Gates intended to wait at Point Comfort for ten days before setting off for Newfoundland in case De La Warr's fleet arrived.

Chapter 7: *"An Abundance of Blood"*

1. Philip L. Barbour, ed., *The Complete Works of Captain John Smith*, 3 vols. (Chapel Hill: University of North Carolina Press, 1986), 2:234; Samuel Purchas, *Hakluytus Posthumus or Purchas His Pilgrimes . . .* , 20 vols. (Glasgow, 1906–1908), 19:54, 59–61; Edward Wright Haile, ed., *Jamestown Narratives: Eyewitness Accounts of the Virginia Colony, The First Decade: 1607–1617* (Champlain, VA: Round House, 1998), 466–467.

2. David H. Flaherty, ed., *Lawes Divine, Morall and Martiall, etc.* (Charlottesville: University Press of Virginia, 1969), x–xxxv, 10–17; David Thomas Konig, "'Dale's Laws' and the Non-Common Law Origins of Criminal Justice in Virginia," *American Journal of Legal History* 26 (1982): 354–375; Edward L. Bond, *Damned Souls in a Tobacco Economy: Religion in Seventeenth-Century Virginia* (Macon, GA: Mercer University Press, 2000), 90, 83; Darrett B. Rutman, "The Virginia Company and Its Military Regime," in *The Old Dominion: Essays for Thomas Perkins Abernethy*, ed. Rutman (Charlottesville: University Press of Virginia, 1964), 10–11.

3. Samuel M. Bemiss, *The Three Charters of the Virginia Company of London, with Seven Related Documents; 1606–1621* (Williamsburg: Virginia 350th Anniversary Celebration, 1957), 73; Purchas, *Hakluytus Posthumus*, 19:63–65; Alexander Brown, *The Genesis of the United States*, 2 vols. (New York, 1890), 1:362.

4. William Strachey, "A True Reportory of the wrack and redemption of Sir Thomas Gates . . . ," in *Jamestown Narratives*, 435–437.

5. Mark Nicholls, "George Percy's 'Trewe Relacyon': A Primary Source for the Jamestown Settlement," *Virginia Magazine of History and Biography* (hereafter *VMHB*) 113 (2005): 253; Haile, *Jamestown Narratives*, 897.

6. E. G. R. Taylor, ed., *The Original Writings and Correspondence of the Two Richard Hakluyts*, 2 vols. (London: Hakluyts Society, 1935), 2:503; Strachey, "A True Reportory," 437.

7. David Beers Quinn, ed., *The Roanoke Voyages, 1584–1590*, 2 vols. (London: Hakluyt Society, 1955), 1:130; 2:552; Philip L. Barbour, ed., *The Jamestown Voyages Under the First Charter, 1606–1609*, 2 vols. (New York/London: Cambridge University Press, 1969), 1:103; Barbour, *Complete Works*, 2:236; Henry Spelman, *Relation of Virginia: A Boy's Memoir of Life with the Powhatans and Patawomecks*, ed. Karen Ordahl Kupperman (New York: New York University Press, 2019), 44.

8. Percy, "Trewe Relacyon," 252; Strachey, *Virginia Britania*, 67–68; Haile, *Jamestown Narratives*, 434–435, 897–898. The emphasis on promoting Mediterranean products is found in the writings of Robert Johnson, the two Richard Hakluyts, younger and elder, Thomas Hariot, and William Strachey among others. English promoters would have been well aware of similar Spanish and French ambitions.

9. Percy, "Trewe Relacyon," 253–254; Barbour, *Complete Works*, 2:209–210.

10. Purchas, *Hakluytus Posthumus*, 19:66–67; Strachey, *Virginia Britania*, 65–66; Percy, "Trewe Relacyon," 254–255.

11. Strachey, *Virginia Britania*, 64; Percy, "Trewe Relacyon," 255–256; Haile, *Jamestown Narratives*, 898. Opossunoquonuske was the female chief of the Appomattocs who had been present when John Smith first met Powhatan.

12. Strachey, *Virginia Britania*, 85–86, 89; Percy, "Trewe Relacyon," 256–258.

13. Percy, "Trewe Relacyon," 256–257; *The Relation of the Right Honourable the Lord De La Warre* (London, 1611), 1–3; Haile, *Jamestown Narratives*, 530–532.

14. Barbour, *Complete Works*, 2:234–235; *A True Declaration of the estate of the Colonie in Virginia . . .* (London: Councell of Virginia, 1610), n.p. See also Richard (or Robert) Rich, "News from Virginia," in *Jamestown Narratives*, 372–379.

15. Geoffrey Parker, *The Military Revolution: Military Innovation and the Rise of the West, 1500–1800*, 2nd ed. (Cambridge, UK: Cambridge University Press, 1996), 6–44; Susan Myra Kingsbury, ed., *The Records of the Virginia Company of London*, 4 vols. (Washington, DC, 1906–1935), 3:665, 676, 678–679; D. A. Tisdale, *Soldiers of the Virginia Colony, 1607–1699: A Study of Virginia's Military, Its Origins, Tactics, Equipment, and Development* (Petersburg, VA: Dietz PR, 2000); William L. Shea, *The Virginia Militia in the Seventeenth Century* (Baton Rouge: Louisiana State University Press, 1983), 1–22. A large amount of military equipment as well as innumerable Indian arrow points have been unearthed by archaeologists of the Jamestown Rediscovery project at the original site of the fort at Jamestown; see William M. Kelso, *Jamestown, The Buried Truth* (Charlottesville: University of Virginia Press, 2006), passim. For broader perspectives, see John McGurk, *The Elizabethan Conquest of Ireland: The 1590s Crisis* (New York: St. Martin's Press, 1997), 227–235; and Guy Chet, *Conquering*

the American Wilderness: The Triumph of European Warfare in the Colonial Northeast (Boston: University of Masschusetts Press, 2003).

16. Brown, *Genesis*, 1:442–443; Dale to the Earl of Salisbury, August 17, 1611, in *Jamestown Narratives*, 554; Chet, *Conquering the American Wilderness*, 11–12.

17. Strachey, *Virginia Britania*, 66; Percy, "Trewe Relacyon," 258–259; J. Frederick Fausz, "An 'Abundance of Blood Shed on Both Sides': England's First Indian War, 1609-1614," *VMHB* 98 (1990): 40–41.

18. Alexander Whitaker to the Reverend William Crashaw, August 9, 1611, in *Jamestown Narratives*, 548–550; [Robert Johnson], *The New Life of Virginea . . . Being the Second part of Nova Britannia* (London, 1612), 9, 18; Jorge Cañizares-Esguerra, *Puritan Conquistadors: Iberianizing the Atlantic, 1550–1700* (Stanford, CA: Stanford University Press, 2006), 12, 14.

19. Ralph Hamor, *A True Discourse of the Present State of Virginia* (London, 1615), 27–29; Percy, "Trewe Relacyon," 259–262; Berkshire Record Office, Trumbull MS., Sir Francis Cottington to William Trumbull, January 10, 1610/11, in Virginia Colonial Records Project, R.7, John D. Rockefeller, Jr., Library; Brown, *Genesis*, 1:511–515; Lyon Gardiner Tyler, ed., *Narratives of Early Virginia, 1606–1625* (New York: Barnes and Noble, 1966; first published 1907), 221.

20. Barbour, *Complete Works*, 2:241–243; Hamor, *True Discourse*, 31–32; Charles E. Hatch, *The First Seventeen Years: Virginia, 1607–1624* (Charlottesville: University Press of Virginia, 1957), 12–16, 47–53, 60–65; Paul Musselwhite, *Urban Dreams, Rural Commonwealth: The Rise of Plantation Society in the Chesapeake* (Chicago: University of Chicago Press, 2019), 29–33.

21. Fausz, "An 'Abundance of Blood,'" 41–42.

Chapter 8: Betrayal

1. A highly evocative description of the Patawomeck landscape is given by James D. Rice, *Nature and History in the Potomac Country: From Hunter-Gatherers to the Age of Jefferson* (Baltimore, MD: Johns Hopkins University Press, 2009), 53, 61–69; and Philip L. Barbour, ed., *The Complete Works of Captain John Smith*, 3 vols. (Chapel Hill: University of North Carolina Press, 1986), 2:119, 175–176.

2. Rice, *Nature and History*, 83; Edward Wright Haile, ed., *Jamestown Narratives: Eyewitness Accounts of the Virginia Colony, The First Decade: 1607–1617* (Champlain, VA: Round House, 1998), 753.

3. Ralph Hamor, *A True Discourse of the Present State of Virginia* (London, 1615), 4–7; Samuel Purchas, *Hakluytus Posthumus or Purchas His Pilgrimes . . .* , 20 vols. (Glasgow, 1906–1908), 19:90–93.

4. J. Frederick Fausz, "An 'Abundance of Blood Shed on Both Sides': England's First Indian War, 1609–1614," *Virginia Magazine of History and Biography* (hereafter *VMHB*) 98 (1990): 44–45; April Lee Hatfield, "Spanish Colonization Literature, Powhatan Geographies, and English Perceptions of Tsenacommacah/Virginia," *Journal of Southern History* 69 (2003): 272–273; Alexander Brown, *The Genesis of the United States*, 2 vols. (New York, 1890), 2:569–570, 572–573, 575,

588–590, 592–594, 646–654, 656–657; "Letters and papers of Sir Ralph Winwood, 1564–1638," calendared by R. E. G. Kirk, *Historical Manuscripts Commission*, No. 45 (London, 1899), 148.

5. Hamor, *True Discourse*, 7; Irene A. Hecht, "The Virginia Colony, 1607–1640: A Study in Frontier Growth" (PhD diss., University of Washington, 1969), 68–71.

6. Hamor, *True Discourse*, 7–11, 52–55. In terms of succession, Opitchapam (?–1630) was the next in line to Powhatan, but Opechancanough was generally accepted as the de facto leader.

7. Hamor, *True Discourse*, 61–68. For example, Karen Ordahl Kupperman, *Pocahontas and the English Boys: Caught Between Cultures in Early Virginia* (New York: New York University Press, 2019), 92–112. Linwood "Little Bear" Custalow and Angela L. Daniel "Silver Star," in their book *The True Story of Pocahontas: The Other Side of History* (Golden, CO: Fulcrum, 2007), offer an alternative interpretation of her abduction and English behavior generally based on Mattaponi oral history, which emphasizes the colonists' repeated use of force and threats to achieve their aims. See also Helen C. Rountree, *Pocahontas, Powhatan, and Opechancanough: Three Indian Lives Changed by Jamestown* (Charlottesville: University of Virginia Press, 2005); Frances Mossiker, *Pocahontas: The Life and the Legend* (New York: Da Capo Press, 1996); Camilla Townsend, *Pocahontas and the Powhatan Dilemma* (New York: Hill and Wang, 2004); Robert S. Tilton, *Pocahontas: The Evolution of an American Narrative* (Cambridge, UK: Cambridge University Press, 1994); Ann Uhry Abrams, *The Pilgrims and Pocahontas: Rival Myths of American Origins* (Boulder, CO: Westview Press, 1999); and James Horn, *A Land As God Made It: Jamestown and the Birth of America* (New York: Basic Books, 2005), 228–232. Pocahontas had already been married for three years to a warrior named Kocoum when she was kidnapped. Rebecca's story is told in Genesis 24:10–67; 25:20–26, 28; 26:6–11; 27:5–11. The Lord told Rebecca: "Two nations are in your womb. Two peoples shall be separated from your body. One people shall be stronger than the other," Gen. 25:23.

8. Haile, *Jamestown Narratives*, 761.

9. Hamor, *True Discourse*, 11–16.

10. Dale was already married to Elizabeth Throckmorton in England.

11. Hamor, *True Discourse*, 37–46.

12. Haile, *Jamestown Narratives*, 875–876; Hamor, *True Discourse*, 68–69.

Chapter 9: Locust Years

1. Ralph Hamor, *A True Discourse of the Present State of Virginia* (London, 1615), 42, 53.

2. Helen C. Rountree, *Pocahontas, Powhatan, and Opechancanough: Three Indian Lives Changed by Jamestown* (Charlottesville: University of Virginia Press, 2005), 191–193. The apparent lack of active engagement in the war, 1610–1613, by Powhatan and Opechancanough may have been more a reflection of lack of evidence than deliberate policy by the chiefs. Both were likely very much involved in war councils, which would have been unknown and unrecorded by the English. Yet, had the

chiefs been in contact with Gates, De La Warr, or Dale in these years, there can be little doubt the English would have noted their discussions. The flurry of meetings between Powhatan and Opechancanough and Smith and Newport, 1607–1609, were not mirrored by meetings with later English commanders, none of whom met the two chiefs in person.

3. Strikingly, too, apart from the killing of John Ratcliffe and his men in the fall of 1609, the war was fought entirely along the Powhatan River. Only when Dale and Argall sailed up the Pamunkey River in early April 1614, in a blatant act of provocation, were the Pamunkey and other peoples of the region directly impacted by the war.

4. Elizabeth McClure Thomson, *The Chamberlain Letters* (New York: Putnam, 1965), 214; Samuel Purchas, *Purchas his Pilgrimage, or Relations of the world and the religions observed in all ages and places discovered, from Creation unto the present . . .* , 4 vols. (London, 1625), 4:1774.

5. Philip L. Barbour, ed., *The Complete Works of Captain John Smith*, 3 vols. (Chapel Hill: University of North Carolina Press, 1986), 2:256–257; Susan Myra Kingsbury, ed., *The Records of the Virginia Company of London* (hereafter *RVC*), 4 vols. (Washington, DC, 1906–1935), 4:117–118. Diascund Creek is near the location where the Jesuits built their mission and where they were killed by a war party led by Paquiquineo/Opechancanough.

6. Kingsbury, *RVC*, 3:73–74.

7. Camilla Townsend, *Pocahontas and the Powhatan Dilemma* (New York: Hill and Wang, 2004), 139–158; Karen Ordahl Kupperman, *Pocahontas and the English Boys: Caught Between Cultures in Early Virginia* (New York: New York University Press, 2019), 113–140; Frances Mossiker, *Pocahontas: The Life and the Legend* (New York, 1996), 219–283; Robert Beverley, *The History and Present State of Virginia*, ed. Louis B. Wright (Chapel Hill: University of North Carolina Press, 1947), 43–44; Purchas, *Purchas his Pilgrimage . . .* , 4:1774; Barbour, *Complete Works*, 2:258–262; Alexander Brown, *The Genesis of the United States*, 2 vols. (New York, 1890), 2:775. Pocahontas's infant son, Thomas Rolfe, was also sickly at the beginning of the voyage and was left at Plymouth. Three Indians died while staying at Sir Thomas Smythe's residence in Philpot Lane, and a maid who lived with Mr. Gough (probably the Reverend William, cousin of Alexander Whitaker) at Blackfriars, London, was reported very weak of "consumption" (tuberculosis) in May 1620. Two other "maids" were shipped to Bermuda as wives for planters a year later, one of whom died during the voyage, Kingsbury, *RVC*, 1:338, 496.

8. *A Briefe Declaration of the present state of things in Virginia, and of a Division to be now made, of some part of those Lands in our actuall possession,* . . . (London, 1616), 5–6; John Rolfe, *A True Relation of the State of Virginia lefte by Sir Thomas Dale Knight in May Last 1616* (Charlottesville: University Press of Virginia, 1971), 3, 9–11; Don Diego Sarmiento de Acuña, Count of Gondomar, Spanish ambassador in London to Philip III, King of Spain, December 7, 1616, Alexander Brown Papers II, Box VII, Folder 128, College of William and Mary Special Collections; Brown, *Genesis*, 2:776–779; Edward Wright Haile, ed., *Jamestown Narratives: Eyewitness*

Accounts of the Virginia Colony. The First Decade: 1607–1617 (Champlain, VA: Round House, 1988), 757; Thomson, *Chamberlain Letters*, 214.

9. Samuel M. Bemiss, *The Three Charters of the Virginia Company of London, with Seven Related Documents; 1606–1621* (Williamsburg: Virginia 350th Anniversary Celebration, 1957); Philip L. Barbour, ed., *The Jamestown Voyages Under the First Charter, 1606–1609*, 2 vols. (New York/London: Cambridge University Press, 1969), 1:13–21, 24–34. John T. Juricek, "English Territorial Claims in North America Under Elizabeth and the Early Stuarts," *Terrae Firma* 7 (1976): 7–22; Ken MacMillan, *Sovereignty and Possession in the English New World: The Legal Foundations of Empire, 1576–1640* (Cambridge, UK: Cambridge University Press, 2006), 29–41, 89–96; Stuart Banner, *How the Indians Lost Their Land: Law and Power on the Frontier* (Cambridge, MA: Harvard University Press, 2005), 10–48; Jorge Cañizares-Esguerra, *Puritan Conquistadors: Iberianizing the Atlantic, 1550–1700* (Stanford, CA: Stanford University Press, 2006), 3–14, 35–54, 71–76.

10. Charles E. Hatch, *The First Seventeen Years: Virginia, 1607–1624* (Charlottesville: University Press of Virginia, 1957), 18, 35–39, 104–105; Kingsbury, *RVC*, 3:68, 103; Lorena S. Walsh, *Motives of Honor, Pleasure, and Profit: Plantation Management in the Colonial Chesapeake, 1607–1763* (Chapel Hill: University of North Carolina Press, 2010), 38–46.

11. Hamor, *True Discourse*, 24; Barbour, *Complete Works*, 2:262–263; Kingsbury, *RVC*, 1:423; 3:307; Jeffrey Knapp, "Elizabethan Tobacco," in *New World Encounters*, ed. Stephen Greenblatt (Berkeley: University of California Press, 1993), 272–312; Wesley Frank Craven, *The Southern Colonies in the Seventeenth Century, 1607–1689* (Baton Rouge: Louisiana State University Press, 1970), 116–124; Walsh, *Motives of Honor, Pleasure, and Profit*, 38–46. In England, cultivating tobacco on small holdings and marginal lands became popular during this period also.

12. Kingsbury, *RVC*, 3:245–248; J. Frederick Fausz, "The Powhatan Uprising of 1622: A Historical Study of Ethnocentrism and Cultural Conflict" (PhD diss., College of William and Mary, 1977), 310–311; Rountree, *Pocahontas, Powhatan, and Opechancanough*, 199–201.

13. Irene A. Hecht, "The Virginia Colony, 1607–1640: A Study in Frontier Growth" (PhD diss., University of Washington, 1969), 79–80; Engel Sluiter, "New Light on the '20. and Odd Negroes' Arriving in Virginia, August 1619," *William and Mary Quarterly* (hereafter *WMQ*) 54, no. 2 (1997): 395–398; Mark G. Hanna, *Pirate Nests and the Rise of the British Empire, 1570–1740* (Chapel Hill: University of North Carolina Press, 2015), 70–77; James Horn, *1619: Jamestown and the Forging of American Democracy* (New York: Basic Books, 2018), 85–103. Population figures are derived from John Rolfe, *A True Relation of the State of Virginia lefte by Sir Thomas Dale Knight in May Last 1616* (Charlottesville: University Press of Virginia, 1971), 11; and Martha W. McCartney, "An Early Virginia Census Refined," [1620] *Quarterly Bulletin of the Archaeological Society of Virginia* 54 (1999): 179.

14. Kingsbury, *RVC*, 1:320; 3:92, 220, 245–248, 275; Fausz, "Powhatan Uprising," 314; David Beers Quinn, ed., *The Roanoke Voyages, 1584–1590*, 2 vols. (London: Hakluyt Society, 1955), 1:380; Purchas, *Purchas his Pilgrimage*, 4:1775; Paul Kelton,

Epidemics and Enslavement: Biological Catastrophe in the Native Southeast, 1492–1715 (Lincoln: University of Nebraska Press, 2007), 47–99. The severity of Virginia's 1619 epidemic can be gauged by the report of three hundred deaths among the colonists alone, which represented between a fifth and quarter of the English population. A broadside of May 17, 1620, mentioned "the mortality, which this last year has there wrought upon the People, to the consumption of divers [many] hundreds, and almost the utter destruction of some particular *Plantations*."

15. Kingsbury, *RVC*, 3:92; Purchas, *Purchas his Pilgrimage*, 4:1775; Hamor, *True Discourse*, 10.

16. Barbour, *Complete Works*, 2:264–265; Kingsbury, *RVC*, 3:147, 157; 4:515; James D. Rice, "'These Doubtfull Times, between Us and the Indians': Indigenous Politics and the Jamestown Colony in 1619," in *Virginia 1619: Slavery and Freedom in the Making of English America*, ed. Paul Musselwhite, Peter C. Mancall, and James Horn (Chapel Hill: University of North Carolina Press, 2019), 217–222.

17. Kingsbury, *RVC*, 3:93, 170–171, 174–175, 228, 242, 151; Ferrar Papers, FP 113, Robert Poole, July 13, 1619, *Virginia Company Archives*, Adam Mathew Digital (2007); Rice, "These Doubtfull Times," 223–229; Kupperman, *Pocahontas*, 145–151.

18. Kingsbury, *RVC*, 1:423; 3:307–316; Hecht, "Virginia Colony," 79.

19. Kingsbury, *RVC*, 1:220–221, 537, 539; 3:102, 128–129, 147, 165–166.

20. Kingsbury, *RVC*, 1:379; 3:123–124, 446–448.

21. Kingsbury, *RVC*, 3:556; 4:10.

22. Kingsbury, *RVC*, 3:447, 469–470.

23. Kingsbury, *RVC*, 3:447; 4:11; Barbour, *Complete Works*, 2:293; Fausz, "Powhatan Uprising," 330–357; Helen C. Rountree, *Pocahontas's People: The Powhatan Indians of Virginia Through Four Centuries* (Norman: University of Oklahoma Press, 1990), 73. The meaning and precise significance of the name are unknown, but may signify Opechancanough had taken on a different role (persona) in organizing his peoples and allies for war with the English, temporarily ruling over them as battle leader. His name was likely changed after lengthy consultation with his priests and leading councilors. Itoyatin took the name Sasawpen, confirming his support for the attack.

Chapter 10: World's End

1. Susan Myra Kingsbury, ed., *The Records of the Virginia Company of London* (hereafter *RVC*), 4 vols. (Washington, DC, 1906–1935), 1:257, 313, 317–318; 2:374–375; 3:92, 93, 581–588; 4:259–262; Edward Wright Haile, ed., *Jamestown Narratives: Eyewitness Accounts of the Virginia Colony. The First Decade: 1607–1617* (Champlain, VA: Round House, 1988), 749, 751; Nicholas M. Luccketti, "Nansemond Pallizado and Virginia Palisade Fortifications," in *First Forts: Essays on the Archaeology of Proto-colonial Fortifications*, ed. Eric Klingelhofer (Boston: Brill, 2010), 97–102; Charles Thomas Hodges, *Forts of the Chieftains: A Study of Vernacular, Classical, and Renaissance Influence on Defensible Town and Villa Plans in 17th-Century Virginia*, vol. 47 of *Volumes in Historical Archaeology*, ed. Stanley South (Columbia: University of South Carolina, 2009), 96–97.

2. Kingsbury, *RVC*, 3:584; Samuel Purchas, *Purchas his Pilgrimage, or Relations of the world and the religions observed in all ages and places discovered, from Creation unto the present . . .* , 4 vols. (London, 1625), 4:1787. For the sake of clarity, I have retained his name as Opechancanough throughout this chapter.

3. Kingsbury, *RVC*, 1:613, 628–629; Patrick Copland, *Virginia's God be Thanked, or a Sermon of Thanksgiving for the Happie Successe of the Affayres in Virginia this Last Yeare* (London, 1622), 9–10, 28–29.

4. Estimates are tentative and derived from warrior numbers made by Captain John Smith and William Strachey before 1612; see Philip L. Barbour, ed., *The Complete Works of Captain John Smith*, 3 vols. (Chapel Hill: University of North Carolina Press, 1986), 1:146–150; William Strachey, *The Historie of Travell into Virginia Britania* (1612), ed. Louis B. Wright and Virginia Freud (London, 1953), 63–69. George Sandys, treasurer of the company in Virginia, mentioned, in late March 1623, an enemy force of one thousand, which was clearly a very rough estimate; see Kingsbury, *RVC*, 3:707, 4:67; Christian F. Feest, "Virginia Algonquians," in *Northeast*, ed. Bruce G. Trigger, vol. 15 in *Handbook of North American Indians*, ed. William C. Sturtevant (Washington, DC: Smithsonian Institution, 1978), 15:241–242, 255–256; and E. Randolph Turner, "A Re-examination of Powhatan Territorial Expansion and Population, ca. A.D. 1607," *Quarterly Bulletin of the Archaeological Society of Virginia* 37 (1982): 45–57.

5. Kingsbury, *RVC*, 3:551. I am indebted to J. Frederick Fausz, "The Powhatan Uprising of 1622: A Historical Study of Ethnocentrism and Cultural Conflict" (PhD diss., College of William and Mary, 1977), who provides a detailed account of the attack. Estimates of the number of English killed vary from three hundred to four hundred, the latter being nearer the mark in my view. No figures of Powhatan casualties were recorded.

6. Kingsbury, *RVC*, 3:565–566; Robert Beverley, *The History and Present State of Virginia*, ed. Louis B. Wright (Chapel Hill: University of North Carolina Press, 1947), 55; Fausz, "Powhatan Uprising," 370–374; Charles E. Hatch, "The First American Blast Furnace: The Birth of a Mighty Industry on Falling Creek in Virginia," *Virginia Magazine of History and Biography* (hereafter *VMHB*) 70 (1962): 259–296.

7. Kingsbury, *RVC*, 3:552, 565–567; Charles E. Hatch, *The First Seventeen Years: Virginia, 1607–1624* (Charlottesville, VA, 1957), 66; Fausz, "Powhatan Uprising," 375–378.

8. Kingsbury, *RVC*, 3:552–553, 566–569. The state of fortifications at Flowerdew in 1622 is a matter of conjecture; see James Deetz, *Flowerdew Hundred: The Archaeology of a Virginia Plantation, 1619–1864* (Charlottesville, VA, 1993), 46–51; and Hodges, "Forts of the Chieftains," 58–92. For speculation about Africans and the attack, see Tim Hashaw, *The Birth of Black America: The First African Americans and the Pursuit of Freedom at Jamestown* (New York, 2007), 159–160.

9. Kingsbury, *RVC*, 3:555, 567; Anonymous, "Two Tragical Events . . . ," *William and Mary Quarterly* (hereafter *WMQ)* 9, no. 4 (1901): 212–213; Fausz, "Powhatan Uprising," 381–388, 392–393; Helen C. Rountree, *Pocahontas, Powhatan, and*

Opechancanough: Three Indian Lives Changed by Jamestown (Charlottesville: University of Virginia Press, 2005), 213–214. War canoes could be up to forty-five feet long; see William Strachey, *Virginia Britania*, 82.

10. Kingsbury, *RVC*, 3:569–571; 4:41; Barbour, *Complete Works*, 2:295–296; Martha W. McCartney, *Virginia Immigrants and Adventurers, 1607–1635: A Biographical Dictionary* (Baltimore, MD, 2007), 104, 358–360, 370; Ivor Noel Hume, *Martin's Hundred: The Discovery of a Lost Colonial Virginia Settlement* (New York, 1982), 217–224.

11. Kingsbury, *RVC*, 3:556, 612; Barbour, *Complete Works*, 2:308; Frederic W. Gleach, *Powhatan's World and Colonial Virginia: A Conflict of Cultures* (Lincoln: University of Nebraska Press, 1997), 158; James D. Rice, "Second Anglo-Powhatan War (1622–1632)," Encyclopedia Virginia, www.EncyclopediaVirginia.org/Anglo-Powhatan_War_Second_1622-1632.

12. Kingsbury, *RVC*, 2:395; J. Frederick Fausz and Jon Kukla, "A Letter of Advice to the Governor of Virginia, 1624," *WMQ* 34, no. 1 (1977): 113, 116–118; H. R. McIlwaine, ed., *Journals of the House of Burgesses of Virginia, 1619–1658/59* (Richmond, VA, 1915), 36; Beverley, *History and Present State of Virginia*, 50. A pawn mate is an unexpected checkmate by the pawn. In fact, George Wyatt expresses considerable admiration for the planning and execution of Opechancanough's attack.

13. Barbour, *Complete Works*, 2:302; Kingsbury, *RVC*, 2:520; 3:612–613, 652; 4:38, 41, 58.

14. Kingsbury, *RVC*, 2:520; 3:613–615, 656–657; William S. Powell, "Aftermath of the Massacre: The First Indian War, 1622–1632," *VMHB* 66 (1958): 53–54; Barbour, *Complete Works*, 2:308, 312.

Chapter 11: *"War Without Peace or Truce"*

1. Susan Myra Kingsbury, ed., *The Records of the Virginia Company of London* (hereafter *RVC*), 4 vols. (Washington, DC, 1906–1935), 3:544–545, 665, 669–670, 676, 683; 4:147.

2. Kingsbury, *RVC*, 3:665, 671–673, 676, 678–679, 683; 4:9, 147, 451; Philip L. Barbour, ed., *The Complete Works of Captain John Smith*, 3 vols. (Chapel Hill: University of North Carolina Press, 1986), 2:315; "Letter of Sir Francis Wyatt, Governor of Virginia, 1621–1626," *William and Mary Quarterly* (hereafter *WMQ*) 6, no. 2 (1926): 118–119; J. Frederick Fausz and Jon Kukla, "A Letter of Advice to the Governor of Virginia, 1624," *WMQ* 34, no. 1 (1977): 117; J. Frederick Fausz, "The Powhatan Uprising of 1622: A Historical Study of Ethnocentrism and Cultural Conflict" (PhD diss., College of William and Mary, 1977), 454–463; Alden T. Vaughan, *Roots of American Racism: Essays on the Colonial Experience* (New York: Oxford University Press, 1995), 125–126.

3. Kingsbury, *RVC*, 2:375; 4:25, 65–68, 89, 94, 109, 147, 151, 160–161, 216, 231–235; Martha W. McCartney, *Virginia Immigrants and Adventurers, 1607–1635: A Biographical Dictionary* (Baltimore, MD: Genealogical Publishing, 2007), 91–92, 314, 387.

4. Kingsbury, *RVC,* 4:41, 58–59, 59–62, 175, 230–235; Emily Rose, "The Politics of Pathos: Richard Frethorne's Letters Home," in *Envisioning an English Atlantic: Jamestown and the Making of the North Atlantic World,* ed. Robert Appelbaum and John Wood Sweet (Philadelphia: University of Pennyslvania Press, 2005), 92–108.

5. Kingsbury, *RVC* 4:108–109, 234; Barbour, *Complete Works,* 2:320–321; James D. Rice, *Nature and History in the Potomac Country: From Hunter-Gatherers to the Age of Jefferson* (Baltimore, MD, 2009), 88–89.

6. Kingsbury, *RVC,* 2:483; 4:98.

7. Kingsbury, *RVC,* 2:482, 486; 3:228; 4:11, 221–222, 451; Rice, *Nature and History in the Potomac Country,* 89–90.

8. Kingsbury, *RVC,* 2:482; 4:209, 451, 507–508; Fausz, "Powhatan Uprising," 495–511; Frederic W. Gleach, *Powhatan's World and Colonial Virginia: A Conflict of Cultures* (Lincoln: University of Nebraska Press, 1997), 164–165.

9. William Waller Hening, ed., *The Statutes at Large, Being a Collection of All the Laws of Virginia . . . ,* 13 vols. (Richmond, VA, 1809–23), 1:127; Robert C. Johnson, "A Poem on the Late Massacre in Virginia," *Virginia Magazine of History and Biography* (hereafter *VMHB*) 72, (1964): 262; Kingsbury, *RVC,* 3:542, 553, 557–559, 561–562; Samuel Purchas, *Purchas his Pilgrimage, or Relations of the world and the religions observed in all ages and places discovered, from Creation unto the present . . . ,* 4 vols. (London, 1625), 4:1811, 1814.

10. Purchas, *Purchas his Pilgrimage,* 4:1811–1818. A verger is a church official who maintains order during services and takes care of the church interior.

11. Kingsbury, *RVC,* 3:558–559, 672–673, 705–707; H. R. McIlwaine, ed., *Minutes of the Council and General Court of Colonial Virginia,* 2nd ed. (Richmond: Virginia State Library, 1979), 111; C. S. Everett, "'They shalbe slaves for their lives': Indian Slavery in Colonial Virginia," in *Indian Slavery in Colonial America,* ed. Alan Gallay (Lincoln: University of Nebraska Press, 2009), 69; Kristalyn Marie Shefveland, *Anglo-Native Virginia: Trade, Conversion, and Indian Slavery in the Old Dominion, 1646–1722* (Athens: University of Georgia Press, 2016), 6–79; Alden T. Vaughan, *Roots of American Racism: Essays on the Colonial Experience* (New York: Oxford University Press, 1995), 122–125.

12. Kingsbury, *RVC,* 2:374–376, 381–387; 4:80–88, 93–94, 116–118, 123–126, 130–156, 170–187, 198–200, 211–218, 228–239, 241–242, 251, 253–256, 261–262, 290–291, 295–398, 464–465, 476, 484–486. 490–504, 519–551, 559–580. Proceedings were held in the Court of King's Bench under a writ of *Quo Warranto.* The Virginia Company was the only significant mercantile company of the period to have its charter rescinded by authority of the king's prerogative powers.

13. Helen C. Rountree, *Pocahontas, Powhatan, and Opechancanough: Three Indian Lives Changed by Jamestown* (Charlottesville: University of Virginia Press, 2005), 220; Frederic W. Gleach, *Powhatan's World and Colonial Virginia: A Conflict of Cultures* (Lincoln: University of Nebraska Press, 1997), 162.

14. Kingsbury, *RVC,* 4:568–569; McIlwaine, *Minutes,* 141, 147, 151, 155, 172, 184–185, 189, 190–191, 198; Conway Robinson, "Notes from the Council and General Court Records, 1641–1659," *VMHB* 13 (1905–1906): 399–400; James D. Rice, *Nature and*

Notes to Chapter 12

History in the Potomac Country: From Hunter-Gatherers to the Age of Jefferson (Baltimore, MD: Johns Hopkins University, 2009), 90–91.

15. Kingsbury, RVC, 4:102–103; "Letter of Sir Francis Wyatt, Governor of Virginia, 1621–1626," WMQ 6, no. 2 (1926): 118; Philip L. Barbour, ed., The Complete Works of Captain John Smith, 3 vols. (Chapel Hill: University of North Carolina Press, 1986), 2:303; "Governor and Council of Virginia to Privy Council, May 17, 1626," National Archives, UK, CO/1/4, f.21. Captain John West (brother of Francis) and Captain John Utie (Uty) were granted six hundred acres each at Kiskiack in 1630; see Conway, "Notes," 389, 390, 393, 401; "Sir John Harvey, May 29, 1630," in Calendar of State Papers, Colonial Series, 1574–1660, ed. W. Noel Sainsbury (London, 1860), 116; Irene W. D. Hecht, "The Virginia Muster of 1624/25 as a Source for Demographic History," WMQ 30, no. 1 (1973): 70–77; William Pierce, "A relation in general of the present state of his Majesty's Colony of Virginia," National Archives, UK, CO/1/5, f.23; and Rountree, Pocahontas, Powhatan, and Opechancanough, 224–225.

Chapter 12: The Last Stand

1. "Sir John Harvey and the Council of Virginia to the Lords Commissioners, December 22, 1631," Kent History and Library Center, Maidstone, Kent, UK, U269/1 Ov20; and Robert C. Johnson, "Virginia in 1632," Virginia Magazine of History and Biography (hereafter VMHB) 65 (1957): 458–466. He addressed his letter to the Lords Commissioners, headed by Sir Edward Sackville, earl of Dorset, who hoped to persuade Charles I to agree to reforms that would secure the council and General Assembly in Virginia as well as the colony's original bounds; see Alexander B. Haskell, For God, King, and People: Forging Commonwealth Bonds in Renaissance Virginia (Chapel Hill: University of North Carolina Press, 2017), 259; "Virginia in 1631," VMHB 8 (1900): 38–40; William Waller Hening, ed., The Statutes at Large, Being a Collection of All the Laws of Virginia . . . , 13 vols. (Richmond, VA, 1809–23), 1:126, 150, 163; and National Park Service, Jamestown Archaeological Assessment (Washington, DC, n.d.), 65–87.

2. Edmund S. Morgan, American Slavery, American Freedom: The Ordeal of Colonial Virginia (New York: W. W. Norton, 1975), 404; Warren M. Billings, Sir William Berkeley and the Forging of Colonial Virginia (Baton Rouge: Louisiana State University Press, 2004), 55. The 1630s and 1640s are often associated with the large-scale movement of people to New England, particularly Massachusetts, but a much larger number of people moved in this period to the plantation colonies of the Chesapeake and British West Indies; see Alison Games, "Migration," in The British Atlantic World, 1500–1800, ed. David Armitage and Michael J. Braddick (London: Palgrave, 2002), 31–50; Russell R. Menard, "British Migration to the Chesapeake Colonies in the Seventeenth Century," in Colonial Chesapeake Society, ed. Lois Green Carr, Philip D. Morgan, and Jean B. Russo (Chapel Hill: University of North Carolina Press, 1988), 100–106; Alison Games, Migration and the Origins of the English Atlantic World (Cambridge, MA: Harvard University Press, 1999), 102–114; Frederic

W. Gleach, *Powhatan's World and Colonial Virginia: A Conflict of Cultures* (Lincoln: University of Nebraska Press, 1997), 169–170; and Helen C. Rountree, *Pocahontas, Powhatan, and Opechancanough: Three Indian Lives Changed by Jamestown* (Charlottesville: University of Virginia Press, 2005), 217–229.

3. Susan Myra Kingsbury, ed., *The Records of the Virginia Company of London* (hereafter *RVC*), 4 vols. (Washington, DC, 1906–1935), 4:24; Timothy H. Breen, "George Donne's 'Virginia Reviewed': A 1638 Plan to Reform Colonial Society," *WMQ* 30, no. 3 (1973): 466; Hening, *Statutes*, 1:123, 202; Haskell, *For God, King and People*, 258–269; Warren M. Billings, *A Little Parliament: The Virginia General Assembly in the Seventeenth Century* (Richmond: Library of Virginia, 2004), 20–21; Billings, *Sir William Berkeley*, 49.

4. David Cressy, *England on the Edge: Crises and Revolution, 1640–1642* (Oxford, UK: Oxford University Press, 2006); Austin Woolrych, *Britain in Revolution, 1625–1660* (Oxford, UK: Oxford University Press, 2002), 47–295.

5. John Ferrar, *A Perfect Description of VIRGINIA* (London, 1649), 10–11. I am indebted to David Ransome who made the attribution of the tract *A Perfect Description* to John Ferrar (private communication from Peter Thompson).

6. Joseph Frank, ed., "News From Virginny, 1644," *VMHB* 65 (1957): 84–87; Robert Beverley, *The History and Present State of Virginia*, ed. Louis B. Wright (Chapel Hill: University of North Carolina Press, 1947), 60–61; Lars C. Adams, *Breaking the House of Pamunkey: The Final Powhatan War and the Fall of an American Indian Empire* (Crofton, KY: Backintyme, 2017), 71–77; William L. Shea, *The Virginia Militia in the Seventeenth Century* (Baton Rouge: Louisiana State University Press, 1983), 58–61.

7. Beauchamp Plantagenet, *A Description of the Province of New Albion* (London, 1648), 2–3; Peter Wilson Coldham, *The Complete Book of Emigrants, 1607–1660* (Baltimore, MD: Genealogical, 1992), 181.

8. John Winthrop, *The History of New England from 1630–1649*, ed. James Kendall Hosmer, 2 vols. (New York, 1908), 168; Bernard Bailyn, *The Barbarous Years, The Peopling of British North America: The Conflict of Civilizations, 1600–1675* (New York: Vintage, 2012), 154–157, 218–223, 286–287. I am grateful to Lars Adams for his emphasis on the regional (mid-Atlantic) dimension of Indian resistance; see Adams, *Breaking the House of Pamunkey*, 53–63. Major Indian peoples of the region involved in conflicts with Europeans in the early to mid-1640s included the Chowanoacs, Powhatans, Susquehannocks, Lenapes, and Raritans.

9. David Peterson De Vries, *Voyages from Holland to America, 1632–1644*, trans. Henry C. Murphy (New York, 1853), 185–187; Winthrop, *History of New England*, 167–168; Frank, "News From Virginny," 85–86; Beverley, *History and Present State of Virginia*, 63; John Nutkin from Wokingham, Berkshire, England, wrote to Captain William Julian, on the Elizabeth River, on October 1, 1642: "Here is but little news that is good in England all in Combustion, which I doubt not but you are fully acquainted with"; see Lower Norfolk County, Wills and Deeds B, f.4, John D. Rockefeller Jr. Library, the Colonial Williamsburg Foundation, microfilm M 1365-17.

10. Exposed on the frontier, settlements along the York River appear to have been especially unstable in these years. In the late summer 1644, probably when Captain Wormeley was away from his plantation taking part in one of the "marches" against the Pamunkeys, the General Court adjudicated a case involving the "riotous and rebellious conduct of Mrs. Wormeley's negroes." No details are given of what may have been the first attempt by a group of enslaved Africans in Virginia to escape from bondage, possibly by joining forces with the Indians. "The Wormeley Family (continued)," *VMHB* 36 (1928): 98–101. Wormeley was a wealthy and well-connected gentleman-planter who had established a large plantation on the Pamunkey (York) River in 1639.

11. "Acts, Orders, and Resolutions of the General Assembly of Virginia, at Sessions of 1643–1646," *VMHB* 23 (1915): 229–238; McIlwaine, *Minutes*, 501–502; Adams, *Breaking the House of Pamunkey*, 237–241; Shea, *Virginia Militia*, 62–64; Warren M. Billings, ed., *The Papers of Sir William Berkeley, 1605–1677* (Richmond: Library of Virginia, 2007), 65.

12. Billings, *Papers of Sir William Berkeley*, 62–65; McIlwaine, *Minutes*, 501–502; Hening, *Statutes*, 1:282–200; Adams, *Breaking the House of Pamunkey*, 113–125; Timothy Riordan, *The Plundering Time: Maryland and the English Civil War, 1645–1646* (Baltimore: Maryland Historical Society, 2004), 157–160.

13. C. S. Everett, "'They shalbe slaves for their lives': Indian Slavery in Colonial Virginia," in *Indian Slavery in Colonial America*, ed. Alan Gallay (Lincoln: University of Nebraska Press, 2009), 70–72; Adams, *Breaking the House of Pamunkey*, 203–204, 211–212.

14. McIlwaine, *Minutes*, 564–565; Shea, *Virginia Militia*, 66–67; Adams, *Breaking the House of Pamunkey*, 144–189; House of Lords Archives, UK, Main Papers, HL /Po/Jo/10/1/225, March 17, 1615/6.

15. Beverley, *History and Present State of Virginia*, 61–62.

16. Helen C. Rountree, *Pocahontas's People: The Powhatan Indians of Virginia Through Four Centuries* (Norman: University of Oklahoma Press, 1990), 86–91; Rountree, *Pocahontas, Powhatan, and Opechancanough*, 232–235; Frederic W. Gleach, *Powhatan's World and Colonial Virginia: A Conflict of Cultures* (Lincoln: University of Nebraska Press, 1997), 176–183; John Ferrar, *A Perfect Description of Virginia* (London, 1649), 13; and William Waller Hening, ed., *The Statutes at Large, Being a Collection of All the Laws of Virginia* . . . , 13 vols. (Richmond, VA, 1809–23), 1:292–294, 296, 311, 315, 317–319, 323–329.

Epilogue: A Reckoning

1. [John Ferrar], *A Perfect Description of Virginia* (London, 1649), 7; Robert Beverley, *The History and Present State of Virginia*, ed. Louis B. Wright (Chapel Hill: University of North Carolina Press, 1947), 61. For contemporary accounts of Paquiquineo/Don Luis, see Clifford M. Lewis and Albert J. Loomie, *The Spanish Jesuit Mission in Virginia, 1570–1572* (Chapel Hill: University of North Carolina

Notes to Epilogue

Press, 1953), 16–17, 118, 156, 179, 221. The majority of accounts indicate he was a youth or young man; only Francisco Sacchini describes him as an older man "of fifty years."

2. Helen C. Rountree, *Pocahontas, Powhatan, and Opechancanough: Three Indian Lives Changed by Jamestown* (Charlottesville: University of Virginia Press, 2005), 26–29; Camilla Townsend, "Mutual Appraisals: The Shifting Paradigms of the English, Spanish, and Powhatans in Tsenacomoco, 1560–1622," in *Early Modern Virginia: Reconsidering the Old Dominion*, ed. Douglas Bradburn and John C. Coombs (Charlottesville: University of Virginia Press, 2011), 59, 89 n. 53; Lewis and Loomie, *Spanish Jesuit Mission*, 28–38. This interpretation is unlikely: College Creek is too close to the mouth of the James River (approximately twenty-five miles) to agree with accounts that suggest the Jesuits sailed at least thirty to forty miles inland from their initial landing place near Newport News. See Roland Chardon, "The Elusive Spanish League: A Problem of Measurement in Sixteenth-Century New Spain," *Hispanic American Historical Review* 60 (1980): 294–302.

3. See Helen C. Rountree and E. Randolph Turner III, *Before and After Jamestown: Virginia's Powhatans and Their Predecessors* (Gainesville: University Press of Florida, 2002), 52–53; and Helen C. Rountree, "Opechancanough (d. 1646)," *Encyclopedia Virginia*, https://encyclopediavirginia.org/entries/opechancanough-d-1646/#start_entry. Other theories suggest that Paquiquineo was an older relative, possibly an uncle of Opechancanough; see Daniel K. Richter "Tsenacommacah and the Atlantic World," in *The Atlantic World and Virginia, 1550–1624*, ed. Peter C. Mancall (Chapel Hill: University of North Carolina Press, 2007), 36–37; and also Frederic W. Gleach, *Powhatan's World and Colonial Virginia: A Conflict of Cultures* (Lincoln: University of Nebraska Press, 1997), 142–143. Rountree argues that whereas Spanish sources mention only one brother of Paquiquineo's, Opechancanough had at least two and possibly three. It is quite possible, however, the Spanish simply did not record all of his relatives; see Helen C. Rountree, *Pocahontas's People: The Powhatan Indians of Virginia Through Four Centuries* (Norman: University of Oklahoma Press, 1990), 19–20; and Philip L. Barbour, ed., *The Complete Works of Captain John Smith*, 3 vols. (Chapel Hill: University of North Carolina Press, 1986), 2:308. For the challenges of reconstructing Virginia Indian histories and individual lives in this period, see, for example, Helen C. Rountree, *The Powhatan Indians of Virginia: Their Traditional Culture* (Norman: University of Oklahoma Press, 1989), 3–16; Gleach, *Powhatan's World*, 1–21; Camilla Townsend, *Pocahontas and the Powhatan Dilemma* (New York: Hill and Wang, 2004), 211–212; Helen C. Rountree, *Pocahontas, Powhatan, Opechancanough: Three Indian Lives Changed by Jamestown* (Charlottesville: University of Virginia Press, 2005), 1–4; and Martin D. Gallivan, *The Powhatan Landscape: An Archaeological History of the Algonquian Chesapeake* (Gainesville: University Press of Florida, 2016), 8–13. More generally, see Robbie Ethridge, *From Chicaza to Chickasaw: The European Invasion and the Transformation of the Mississippian World, 1540–1715* (Chapel Hill: University of North Carolina Press, 2010), 5–8.

4. Hamor, Hoffman, and Gleach speculate that Don Luis and Opechancanough were brothers; see Ralph Hamor, *A True Discourse of the Present State of Virginia*

Notes to Epilogue

K. Steele, *Warpaths: Invasions of North America* (Oxford: Oxford University Press, 1994), 37.

5. Bartolome Barrientos, *Pedro Menendez de Aviles, Founder of Florida*, trans. Anthony Kerrigan (Gainesville: University of Florida Press, 1965; first published 1902), 120; Gonzalo Solis de Meras, *Pedro Menendez de Aviles, Memorial*, trans. Jeannette Thurber Connor (Gainesville: Florida State Historical Society, 1964; first published 1893), 208–209; Eugenio Ruidiaz y Caravia, *La Florida: Su conquista y colonizacion*, 2 vols. (Madrid: Hijos de J. A. Garcia, 1893), 1:ccii; Francisco Sacchini, "Borgia, the Third Part of the History of the Society of Jesus," in *The Spanish Jesuit Mission in Virginia, 1570–1572* by Francisco Sacchini, Clifford M. Lewis, and Albert J. Loomie (Chapel Hill: University of North Carolina Press, 1953), 221.

6. Col. Francis Moryson to Sir William Jones, January 29, 1677, National Archives, England (hereafter TNA), CO5/1371, 10. Moryson was a royalist who left England for Virginia after the execution of King Charles I in January 1649. He was briefly a member of the House of Burgesses and knew Governor Berkeley well. He returned to England in 1663 to live.

7. Robert Beverley, *The History and Present State of Virginia*, ed. Louis B. Wright (Chapel Hill: University of North Carolina Press, 1947; first published 1705), 61.

8. See also the consideration of the similarity in the names Paquiquineo and St. Barbara, a third-century Christian martyr, was the patron saint of miners. Opechancanough, allowing for differing Spanish and English translations, in Brendan Wolfe, "Don Luis de Velasco/Paquiquineo (fl. 1561–1571)," Encyclopedia Virginia, https://encyclopediavirginia.org/entries/don-luis-de-velasco-paquiquineo-fl-1561-1571/.

9. Hamor, *A True Discourse*, 54. The only modern historian who has argued in favor of them being the same man is Carl Bridenbaugh in *Early Americans* (New York: Oxford University Press, 1981), 5–49, 239–247.

10. Statues of Powhatan (Wahunsonacock) can be found at Jamestown Settlement, Living History Museum, near Jamestown, Virginia, and somewhat incongruously at the Short Pump Shopping Center a few miles outside Richmond. Statues of Pocahontas are located at Historic Jamestowne (the original site of the first English settlement) and St. George's Church, Gravesend, Kent, England, where she is buried. A highway marker, "Headquarters of Opechancanough," erected in 2005 by the Department of Historic Resources, describes his principal residence. It is located on the Richmond-Tappahannock Highway, Route 360, King William County, Virginia, near the Pamunkey Indian reservation.

INDEX

© *Michael Lavin*

James Horn is the president of Jamestown
Rediscovery. He is author and editor of eight
books on colonial America, including *1619*
and *A Land As God Made It*. He lives in
Richmond, Virginia.